The Work of Edgar Cayce
as Seen Through His Letters

The Work of Edgar Cayce as Seen Through His Letters

Charles Thomas Cayce
Jeanette M. Thomas

ASSOCIATION FOR
RESEARCH AND
ENLIGHTENMENT

A.R.E. Press • Virginia Beach • Virginia

A.R.E. Press
215 67th Street
Virginia Beach, VA 23451-2061

Cayce, Edgar, 1877-1945.
    The work of Edgar Cayce as seen through his letters / [edited by] Charles Thomas Cayce, Jeanette Thomas.
        p.   cm.
    Includes bibliographical references.
    ISBN 0-87604-407-0 (hc.)
    1. Cayce, Edgar, 1877-1945—Correspondence. I. Cayce, Charles Thomas. II. Thomas, Jeanette M. III. Title
BF1027.C3C27   2000
133.8'092—dc21
[B]   99-41418

Cover design by Lightbourne

This book combines materials from many of the letters written by Edgar Cayce, as well as other private and published sources, to illustrate the development over time of what he called "the Work," the information in the Edgar Cayce readings, and the effect the Work had on his life, the lives of those around him, and all whose lives he touched.

Much has been written on the life of Edgar Cayce. This book is the first account published from his own letters and the letters of people associated with him. His unique spelling of some words, such as "wrather" for "rather," has been preserved, as has the use of dashes for expression, spellings, and hyphenated words that were editorially correct at the time. Other than the correction of obvious typographical errors or misspellings and the omission of unrelated passages, there has been no editing of any of the correspondence.

Brief timelines appear at the beginning of each chapter to give the reader a context for the events described in the letters and articles.

Where quotes are used from the Edgar Cayce readings, reading citations are given in the format of 000-0, where the numerals before the hyphen represent the number assigned to the person for whom the reading was given, and the numerals following the hyphen represent the number of the reading for that person. Some additional citations will include a designation such as R5, which indicates correspondence that is dated *after* the date of the reading.

Contents

Foreword

TWICE A DAY, for nearly forty-two years, Edgar Cayce would lie on a couch, turn his attention inward, and respond to questions, eventually producing more than 14,000 "readings" or "discourses," sixty-five percent of which dealt with the physical ailments of his clients. Thousands of books and articles have discussed this material; some of the authors have concluded it is "extraordinary" (Vahle, 1987, p. 38) while others dismiss it as "unreliable" (Beyerstein, 1996, p. 147). More than half a century later, what more is there to say?

The publication of this collection of Cayce's letters provides a new source of insight into a man who has attained the status of an American folk legend. For some, Cayce's views on such topics as astrology, reincarnation, and Atlantis are cause for an immediate dismissal of his work, but others are impressed with his early endorsement and recommendation of activities that have found their way into the arsenal of many contemporary health care practitioners: massage, meditation, herbal preparations, visualization, working with dreams.

Many themes that occur frequently in Cayce's readings are no longer considered as esoteric as when they were originally uttered. The Cayce discourses insist that the potential for healing resides in each one of us; that lasting change can only come from within; that the physical body is the "temple" in which the human spirit manifests; that dreams are an unlimited source of guidance; and that the human mind is the "builder" by which people can discover and express their life "mission." Cayce advised, " . . . all *healing* is from the Divine within, and not from medications" (1173-6), a sentiment not too far removed from that of the Spanish rabbi Moses Maimonides in the twelfth century: "The physician should not treat the disease but the patient who is suffering from it."

The recommendations covered in the Cayce readings include allopathic medicine, osteopathy, chiropractic, massage, physical exercise, colonic therapy, nutrition and diet, herbal treatment, various oils, hydrotherapy, electrotherapy, and—when appropriate—surgery. After studying these recommendations, Vahle (1987) concluded that they aim to improve bodily assimilation, elimination, circulation, and relaxation. The readings "proceeded on the assumption that by restoring the normal balance in these areas, the body could, in most circumstances, heal itself" (p. 34).

These remedies and principles have become central to so-called "holistic medicine," of which Cayce was in the vanguard, and are echoed by complementary treatment regimens and alternative therapies, which now have their own journals and are even included in the curriculum of several mainstream medical schools. One in three Americans visits an alternative health care practitioner at least once a year and spends as much on this type of care as for conventional medicine. The ratio of Australians and Europeans who use alternative and complementary health care is similar (Marston, 1999). Cayce's pioneering role was acknowledged by John P. Callan, in a 1979 editorial in the *Journal of the American Medical Association*, which stated, "The roots of present day holism probably go back 100 years to the birth of Edgar Cayce in Hopkinsville, Kentucky. By the time he died in 1945, Cayce was well recognized as a mystic who entered sleep trances and dictated a philosophy of life and healing called 'readings.' His base was established at Virginia Beach, Va., now the headquarters of the Cayce Foundation."

Cayce never suggested a mechanism for these readings, although the critical event seemed to be the bout of laryngitis that terminated Cayce's job as a traveling salesman and initiated a career as a photographer's assistant. A traveling state hypnotist was unable to restore Cayce's voice, but a local hypnotist was somewhat more successful. Indeed, this success led to Cayce's first reading, one done on himself in 1900. It started with the words, "Yes, we can see the body," the same prelude that was to be used for the next forty-three years. In 1914, Cayce's young son lost his sight in an accident, but regained it after Cayce followed directions given in a reading. Later, a reading was credited for his wife's recovery from tuberculosis. In all fairness, it must be noted that another Cayce son died in 1911, following a series of illnesses, but no reading was attempted.

Cayce's two surviving sons later wrote a book, *The Outer Limits of Edgar Cayce's Power*, which openly discusses the discourses' failed predictions and misinterpretations. Furthermore, Cayce's letters relate the fiasco of trying to use his gift to try to discover oil in order to use the revenue to support his more important work, as well as such short-lived organizations and institutions as the Cayce Art Company, the Cayce Institute of Psychic Research, the Association of National Investigators, and the Cayce Hospital. They trace the lamentable falling-out of David Kahn and the Blumenthal brothers, major sources of Cayce's financial support. But they also describe how the "source" of the readings led him to Virginia Beach and the gradual emergence of the Association for Research and Enlightenment, what a 1928 letter refers to as "a place where 'the work' might be studied."

In my opinion, what Edgar Cayce referred to as his "gift" or his "power" exemplifies what Rhea White calls "exceptional human experiences" or "EHEs." Cayce apparently had several EHEs: notably witnessing his grandfather's death at a distance when Edgar was four years old and his subsequently reported repeated contacts with the dead grandfather; his encounter with an angel at the age of thirteen; and a baseball accident at the age of fifteen (after which he prescribed a poultice for himself and made a speedy recovery). Later, there were EHEs that appeared to be parapsychological: comments on the clothes (e.g., the "new red pajamas") that the reading subject was wearing at the time of the reading but at another location; details of the subject's environment (e.g., "nice smell of the fresh roses on the bureau"); and details of the subject's location (e.g., "caught in traffic due to fire hoses on the street"). Eventually, such experiences would be termed "clairvoyance" or "remote viewing" and would be brought into research settings for intensive study (e.g., Schmeidler, 1994, pp. 117-120).

According to White (1995), these unusual experiences are *potential* exceptional human experiences until they are "potentiated"; that is, until the person having the experiences accepts them as authentic and identifies with them in some way. Cayce's self-induced altered state of awareness was a remarkable phenomenon, and his disciplined use of it for purposes of the discourses demonstrates his "potentiation" of the experiences and his extraordinary devotion to what he perceived as his life's "mission." Cayce's letters provide evidence for this "potentiation." In other words, Cayce could go within the experience at will as well as spontaneously; the reality he knew was not timebound or spacebound, as was that of his peers.

Eventually, following an exceptional human experience, the person having the experience is "transformed," conceptualizing the EHE as an aspect of an enlarged repertoire of potential human activity, even though others may deny its authenticity and significance. This is an accurate description of what appeared to have occurred in Cayce's development. In a 1927 letter, Cayce wrote about "the work" and its potential for shaping people's lives, and in a 1924 letter, he wrote that he made no claims for himself and did not treat anyone—delimitations that he adhered to during the rest of his life. What White (1995) describes as the "transformative potential" of EHEs is demonstrated in a 1925 letter in which Cayce wrote about seeking for other "spiritually minded" people who understood that the nature of "the work" is to help humanity "spiritually, mentally, and physically."

White describes the role of social construction in EHEs, and it is clear that Cayce's phenomena were socially constructed to some extent. For example, as a youth he avidly perused the Bible, reading it several times. According to a 1910 *New York Times* article, Cayce's father said that, beginning when his son was about ten years old, he would present a series of lessons, often posing problems that Edgar failed to solve. However, Edgar would recline in a rocking chair, remarking, "Papa, let me sleep a while and I will know it better." After a short nap, he would usually give an articulate answer to what he had previously failed to grasp.

Cayce's later contacts with hypnotists and various health care practitioners provided additional material about health remedies that was to emerge in the readings, albeit in an original and typically more profound manner. Much has been made of Cayce's lack of medical education, but during the first nine years of his career, there was someone in attendance at each of his sessions who was conversant with allopathic, osteopathic, or homeopathic terminology. Beyerstein (1996) notes that in 1923, Cayce undertook a reading for Arthur Lammers, a wealthy Ohio printer who was an advocate of astrology and reincarnation; the discourse also confirmed these beliefs, and from that time on, echoed these themes.

White (1997) argues that EHEs provide the insight and the dynamic to move humans from a lesser to a more consciously evolved state that expands human awareness of the nature of life. The less evolved sense of self in humans is primarily identified with a skin-encapsulated separate ego-self. Exceptional human experiences, however, make us aware of our oneness with all things, the All-Self. In childhood, an awareness of the All-Self sometimes exists, but in the West, it is socialized out, usually by the time a child goes to school (p. 89). For Edgar

Cayce, this awareness was reinforced during his adolescence by his vision of an angel, his poultice-assisted recovery from a baseball accident, his dowsing work, his recovery from laryngitis during his first reading on himself, and his readings for his son's lost sight and his wife's tuberculosis. Cayce studied the readings himself, further reinforcing the messages and worldview they contained.

White (1997) describes how this social construction leads to an explanatory narrative, or what I have called a "personal mythology" (Krippner, 1986). For White, an EHE includes seven conditions, each of which can be seen in Cayce's development and traced in his letters. Initially, a person has one or more unusual experiences and decides the experiences are special and meaningful. Ordinary explanations fail to suffice, and the experiences are considered genuine and "real," despite the criticism of those who deny their importance and reality. The experiences trigger a transformative process that changes the ego-self and leads the experient to the All-Self, what Cayce referred to as "universal forces." There is a "call" to a vocation, and when others request an explanation, it is given in terms of the new theoretical narrative or personal mythology. These narratives can be life-potentiating, leading the experient to a love and service, or life-depotentiating, in which case the experient may become psychotic or may commit antisocial acts, claiming that they have a Divine mandate.

This theoretical narrative is apparent in excerpts of several readings, for example:

First, do those things that will make thine body—as it were—*whole.* 516-4

Harken to thy dreams and visions, for these may oft be channels through which ye may be known, be made known to impending disturbances, or the choice to be made for the better universality in the activities. 5264-1

[Dreams] are phenomena, or experiences for a body to use, to apply, in its everyday walk of life . . . 4167-1

Hence *intuition* is an attribute of that made aware through the suppression of those forces from that from which it sprang, yet endowed with all of those abilities and forces of its Maker that made for same its activity in an *aware* world. 5754-2

One client asked how someone could best develop her intuitive ability; the discourse advised "by meditation." The questioner asked for what purpose intuition should be used and was told, "In developing herself and aiding others." (803-1) Another client asked Cayce to "Give . . . the principle and technique of conscious telepathy." The answer was, "First, begin between selves. Set a definite time, and each at that moment put down what the other is doing. Do this for twenty days. And ye will find ye have the key to telepathy." (2533-7) However, when someone asked about developing automatic handwriting, the "source" responded, "We would not advise it! . . . Rather that of intuitive force, that may be guided by higher sources." (281-4)

The theoretical narrative that emerges from these readings is one that throws questioners back on their own resources. The discourses insist that there is no question that cannot be answered from one's own inner being when one is properly "attuned" or in a receptive state of "listening." For example, the dream experience represents a channel through which information and guidance on any subject or problem can be received. However, the readings emphasize that for people engaged in personal transformation, group discussion and support are helpful. Cayce's letters refer to the Search for God study groups, a movement promoted by Edgar Cayce's oldest son, Hugh Lynn, that has spread nationally and internationally. Because the Cayce readings impose nothing from the outside and evoke changes that come from within, these groups can provide sounding boards for individuals whose personal myths might otherwise become unduly idiosyncratic.

The nature of Cayce's experience was poorly described when he was alive. One observer described it as a "natural sleep," but Cayce's complex discourses bear little resemblance to what is now known about sleep-talking. Others used the term "trance," but this word has been used in so many different ways (hypnotic trance, ritual trance, trance-dancing, etc.) that it is virtually useless for descriptive purposes. Referring to Cayce's work as an episode "in the history of hypnosis" (Sugrue, 1952) ignores the fact that, unlike Cayce, most hypnotized people recall their experiences quite well once the session ends. The *New York Times* article also used the term "hypnosis"; further, it incorrectly labeled Cayce "illiterate"!

It is more likely that Cayce engaged in self-induced dissociation, an experience that seems to exist apart from, or that is disconnected from, the mainstream, or flow, of one's conscious awareness, behavioral repertoire, and/or self-identity (Krippner, 1997). Dissociative experiences can be deleterious, as in cases of dissociative identity disorders (when people manifest multiple identities), but they can also lead to creativity and enhanced performance. Jess Stearn (1967) reminds us that Cayce's special abilities were sometimes evident when he was fully aware, indicating that his self-induced dissociation gave him the opportunity to focus more completely on a query, to transcend the ego-self and to access the All-Self.

At the time of Cayce's death, few assessments had been made of him and his purported abilities. In 1906, a physician decided to test Cayce's responsiveness to external stimuli while Cayce was engaged in a discourse; one person poked him with a hatpin while another cut his left forefinger with a penknife. Cayce, aroused by these activities, was understandably upset and cited this incident as the reason for never again allowing himself to be tested under controlled conditions. In 1910, a Boston homeopathic physician gave Cayce 180 names to diagnose and later claimed Cayce had made only two errors. However, there was no second opinion by a skeptical physician, a safeguard that would be standard practice today. The 14,000-plus transcripts of readings on file sometimes contain testimonials, but they contain few instances of blind assessments by outside physicians and no examples of what, today, are called "control groups" for comparative purposes. A random selection of 150 cases included follow-up letters indicating success in sixty-five, but seventy-four were unaccompanied by feedback, and eleven were accompanied by letters deemed as "inconclusive" (Cayce & Cayce, 1971). In one instance, Cayce gave a distant diagnosis for a girl suffering from leukemia and recommended dietary treatment; unfortunately, the child had died the day before the reading was given (Daniels & Horan, 1987, p. 94).

Years later, I served as an advisor on a double-blind study that investigated one of the Cayce readings' most frequently cited remedies—castor oil packs. There were thirty female and six male research participants in this study, none of whom expressed symptoms of any diagnosed sickness, and who were randomly assigned to experimental or control groups. The experimental group received castor oil packs, and the control group received paraffin oil packs, which had the same appearance, smell, and feel. Following Cayce's suggested procedures, the oil packs were applied directly to the skin of the upper right quadrant of the abdomen and remained in place for two hours. Within a twenty-four-hour period, four blood samples were taken from each research participant in order to evaluate immune system functioning before and after treatment. Blood samples were processed by an independent laboratory, and these data were analyzed by an independent statistical consultant. An analysis of variance technique demonstrated that members of the experimental group showed increases in the number of total lymphocytes, especially the T-11 cells; no significant increase was detected among the members of the control group. Possible age, gender, and daily rhythm influences were ruled out. The T-11 cell increase represents an enhancement of the body's ability to defend itself by forming antibodies against pathogens and their toxins. Although further research is needed to confirm and amplify these preliminary findings, it is possible that castor oil has chemical properties that maximize the body's immune system, at least for a short period of time (Grady, 1997).

Unlike most contemporary "channelers," Edgar Cayce did not claim that the source of his information was a specific spirit but, rather, what he called the "universal forces"—a cosmic information "source." Nor did he claim that the reported cures and successful advice were due to his own abilities, but rather to the source of the discourses. Beyerstein (1996) points out that Cayce's original sessions were supervised by an osteopath who also practiced hypnosis, while his second supervisor was a physician—the same one who unwisely allowed Cayce to be probed by a hatpin and penknife. Following that fiasco, Cayce allied himself with the homeopathic practitioner who had claimed stunning success with the 180 names he had given Cayce previously. This association lasted until 1911, when Cayce, extremely ethical in his interpersonal interactions, broke away because fees had been taken from a woman before she had received her reading.

The publication of a collection of Edgar Cayce's letters will not only remind readers of his "gift," but may galvanize investigators to engage in careful, systematic study of other "exceptional human experiences" and what they may contribute to human welfare. In the first place, additional research can be done with some of the health remedies mentioned in the Cayce readings. The wet cell appliance is an example of "energy medicine," one of the outgrowths of Cayce's theory of healing. The technology is now available to study these remedies to determine their potential utility.

Advances in psychotherapy research can now determine whether the incorporation of so-called "past-life reports" is an important way of working through inhibiting behavior patterns. The discourses supported investigative work, noting, "Such experiments, such studies, such approaches, as has been given, must be rather from the regular form of activity that is presented day by day. Then, when there has been determined by such investigators or investigation that these do conform, they may be set in *any* way." (1135-3) The same reading mentioned J.B. Rhine's pioneering work in parapsychology at Duke University.

As for inquiry into specific advice given by the Cayce readings or similar material, current experimental designs use control groups in innovative ways. Psychological research has demonstrated the effectiveness of dream interpretation as a part of psychotherapy, but only after it was compared with similar procedures, such as having one group of clients work with dreams reported by other people (Hill, Diemer, Hess, Hillyer, & Seeman, 1993). Another caution is the over-reliance on people's memories; recall of an event, especially details, will often shift over time to conform or disconform a person's "theoretical narrative" or "personal mythology," especially if the "need to believe" is an important issue (Krippner & Winkler, 1996). If possible, "before" and "after" medical assays, X-rays, and physical examinations should be undertaken to confirm or disconfirm the results of an intuitive reading. Finally, even when an unorthodox healing is successful, the possibility exists that the placebo effect, the client's expectancy, and self-fulfilling prophecies were at least as responsible for recovery as the treatment itself (Krippner & Achterberg, in press).

None of the caveats contradict the material in the Cayce discourses. Repeatedly, they state, "mind is the builder." Human beings have the ability to use their intuitive capacities in the service of changing their own attitudes, emotions, behaviors, and health. The spirit of Edgar Cayce lives on at the Association for Research and Enlightenment (A.R.E.), which has its own university (Atlantic University), publishing arm, physiology department, overseas tour program, summer camp, periodicals, overseas archaeological projects, study groups, and lecture series (Bro, 1989). Cayce's spirit also can be glimpsed in this remarkable collection of his letters, which provide an archival treasure for anyone interested in "exceptional human experiences" and a truly exceptional life.

Stanley Krippner, Ph.D.
August 1999

References

Anon. (1910, October 9) "Illiterate man becomes a doctor when hypnotized." *New York Times,* pp. 56A-59A.

Beyerstein, B. (1996). Edgar Cayce. In G. Stein (Ed.), *The Encyclopedia of the Paranormal* (pp. 146-153). Amherst, N.Y.: Prometheus.

Callan, J.P. (1979). "Holistic Health or Holistic Hoax?" Editorials. *Journal of the American Medical Association,* 241(11).

Cayce, E. E., & Cayce, H. L. (1971). *The Outer Limits of Edgar Cayce's Power.* New York: Harper & Row.

Daniels, P., & Horan, A. (Eds.). (1987). *Psychic Powers.* Alexandria, Va.: Time-Life Books.

Grady, H. (1997). "Immunomodulation through castor oil packs." *Journal of Naturopathic Medicine,* 7(1), 84-89.

Hill, C. E.; Diemer, R.; Hess, S.; Hillyer, A.; & Seeman, R. (1993). "Are the effects of dream interpretation on session quality, insight, and emotions due to the dream itself, to projection, or to the interpretation process?" *Dreaming,* 3, 269-280.

Kahn, D.E., with Oursler, W. (1970). *My Life with Edgar Cayce.* Garden City, N.Y.: Doubleday.

Ketchum, W. H. (1964). *The Discovery of Edgar Cayce.* Virginia Beach, Va.: A.R.E. Press.

Krippner, S. (1986). "Dreams and the development of a personal mythology." *Journal of Mind and Behavior,* 7, 449-461.

———(1997). "Dissociation in many times and places." In S. Krippner & S. Powers (Eds.), *Broken Images, Broken Selves: Dissociative Narratives in Clinical Practice* (pp. 3-40). New York: Brunner/Mazel.

Krippner, S., & Achterbert, J. (in press). "Anomalous healing." In Cardena, E.; Lynn, S. J.; & Krippner, S. (Eds.), *The Varieties of Anomalous Experience.* Washington, D.C.: American Psychological Association.

Krippner, S., & Winkler, M. (1996). "The 'need to believe." In G. Stein (Ed.), *The Encyclopedia of the Paranormal* (pp. 441-454). Amherst, N.Y.: Prometheus Books.

Marston, R. (1999). Foreword. In W.B. Jonas & Levin, J.S. (Eds.), *Essentials of Complementary and Alternative Medicine* (pp. vii-ix). Baltimore: Lippincott Williams & Wilkins.

Miller, R. (1993, July/August). "Cayce remedies firm is booming." *Venture Inward*, pp. 23-24.

Schmeidler, G.R. (1994). "ESP experiments 1978-1992: The glass is half full." In S. Krippner (Ed.), *Advances in Parapsychological Research* (Vol. 7, pp. 104-197). Jefferson, N.C.: McFarland.

Stearn, J. (1967). *Edgar Cayce: The Sleeping Prophet.* Garden City, N.Y.: Doubleday.

Sugrue, T. (1942). *There Is a River.* New York: Henry Holt.

Taylor, D.S. (1993, July/August). "The wet cell appliance." *Venture Inward*, pp. 10-12.

Vahle, N. (1987, November/December). "The spiritual legacy of Edgar Cayce." *New Realities*, pp. 34-38.

White, R.A. (1995). "Exceptional human experiences and the experiential paradigm." *ReVision*, 18(2), 18-25.

White, R.A. (1997). "Dissociation, narrative, and exceptional human experiences." In S. Krippner & S. Powers (Eds.), *Broken Images, Broken Selves: Dissociative Narratives in Clinical Practice* (pp. 88-121). New York: Brunner/Mazel.

Preface

THE WORK. **FROM** my earliest memories these two words—which referred to the information that my grandfather received in his "readings"—have been a part of my everyday life.

I do not remember my grandfather very well, but my mother's and father's lives were deeply woven into the fabric of this thing we call "the Work," and my father obeyed its call all of his life, without hesitation or question. My mother—always reserved, gracious, and quiet—served by the hours and days of separation from my father as he traveled. Raising my brother and me alone more often than the whole family would have liked, my mother did all that was required by my father, our home, and my brother and me. It was always there, the Work, and we never questioned its existence or sought its definition because it was simply a thing that was.

This Work is many things to many people. In the years since my grandfather came to Virginia in 1925, groups have formed, people have gathered, and organizations have come into—and gone out of—existence. While my grandfather was alive, people frequently asked through the readings how the Work should be carried on, earnestly seeking a glimpse of a vision for the future. The answers were fairly straightforward, never impossible or complicated, always practical, firmly rooted in daily life, in language that blends the spiritual ideal with the material: "There is set before thee life and death, good and evil. *Choose thou!*" (443-3) Straightforward, yet also profound, mysterious, and lofty words that tugged at the souls of those who read them. Then, as now, once touched by this Work, people's lives were never the same.

This search for a vision of the Work through the readings, which began during my grandfather's lifetime, continues to the present day. The same difficulties that confronted those who actually heard the readings confront those who read the readings today. While this frustrates us and complicates our lives, perhaps it is a sign that the Work itself is still alive, still growing, still expressing itself in materiality, unfinished. Growth is not always predictable, and if the spirit of this Work is a living thing, which the readings profess and my grandfather believed, then perhaps this diversity and vision-seeking are really signs of the great vitality left behind in the printed words of a man who died in 1945.

It has been said that we reveal ourselves through our correspondence. If this is so, then my grandfather revealed himself to thousands of people during his lifetime. Perhaps, through his letters—as well as some of those written to him—we, too, may more clearly catch a glimpse of this elusive thing we call the Work.

In addition to contributing to the development of this Work as seen through Edgar Cayce's letters, I hope this volume will serve to provide a little better understanding of the man through whom this information that is called the readings came. Sometimes, famous people and the events related to their lives seem to become larger than life as time passes. Edgar's own words may help with accurate descriptions of such stories and events.

There also have been—and still are—skeptics who say that psychic ability doesn't exist and that, therefore, evidence for any psychic component in Edgar's work is nonexistent as well. These events just didn't happen, they say. Others say that, while the events were real, they were "the work of the devil," of an evil force that tricks us by providing helpful information. If these events did happen, however, the implications are huge regarding both the process of psychic abilities and many of the age-old questions about the nature of reality. Psychic abilities and some of the results contradict what were believed, at least until recently, to be incontrovertible laws of physics and physical reality, suggesting a nonphysical reality with implications about some type of survival beyond the death of the physical body and other possibilities.

Virtually all who have taken the time to actually investigate the phenomenon of Edgar Cayce have come away concluding that the psychic process—at least where he was concerned—was real, that he demonstrated genuine psychic abilities over and over. If that is true, the implications seem especially important as we try to better understand individuals who have an extraordinary measure of these abilities, and perhaps, to better understand the nature of the ability itself.

Although there are several biographies and other sources of information about my grandfather, including family and friends who knew him and who can recount their impressions and personal experiences, I hope this selection of his correspondence and early reports will provide an additional window on the man and his Work that will be helpful over the long run in trying to better understand people such as he.

Charles Thomas Cayce
President
Edgar Cayce Foundation

Introduction

EDGAR CAYCE WAS born into a world on the fulcrum point of transformation. In 1877, the recently reunited U.S. was beginning what would become a sweeping change from a rural, self-sufficient, primarily agricultural economy to a more urban, centralized, interdependent, industrialized nation. Traditional Christianity—whether Catholic or Protestant—still was the primary religion for the great majority of the population, and it had so far withstood all challenges to its supremacy.

The spiritualist movement—with its "mediums" who claimed

to talk to the dead and materialize "ectoplasm" in darkened rooms—had swept through the country in the 1850s, and it boasted more than two million American members at its height. It had peaked, however, without becoming much of a challenge.

The New Thought adherents—Divine Science, Unity, Science of Mind, Christian Science—also spread across North America in the mid-1800s. These offshoots of eighteenth-century Mesmerism promoted the belief that healing essentially is an act of will. While they ultimately retained larger followings than spiritualism, they also stabilized at levels that presented little threat to mainstream Christianity. But traditional religions soon found themselves facing another, far more disturbing threat to their faith and authority—an unprecedented revolution in science and technology that already was beginning.

Edgar Cayce was born between the advent of two of a handful of inventions that would change the American landscape in ways that continue to play themselves out even now, more than a century later: Bell's invention of the telephone in 1876 and Edison's invention of the incandescent light bulb in 1879. The world also was still reeling from the 1859 publication of Darwin's *Origin of Species*, which brought into question the entire biblical version of creation. As all the sciences began to progress in leaps and bounds, using empirical research to prove their validity, their progress was accompanied by a growing doubt in many minds and hearts about the truth of both the Bible and religion, and about the existence of God. Phenomena that eventually would be grouped under the heading of *para*psychology—extrasensory perception, the existence of a soul, life after death, communication with the dead—were quickly relegated to the trash heap of quackery and connivery by a scientific mindset that required predictable, repeatable results under controlled laboratory conditions as a prerequisite for being declared "real."

Some critics have tried over the decades to compartmentalize—and explain—Edgar Cayce and his psychic readings by lumping him in with the spiritualists, attempting to tar him with the same brush of "fraud" that brought down any number of popular mediums or by explaining away his abilities and message as a to-be-expected development of the New Thought schools. Neither was the case. In fact, there is no evidence that

Edgar Cayce directly drew any of the material in his readings—of which he had no conscious awareness as he spoke in trance—from the New Thought teachings.

A closer look at his life also shows the fallacy of dismissing him as nothing more than a latter-day spiritualist. Throughout his life, Edgar Cayce remained firmly rooted in the Protestant Christian faith in which he was raised. He was always the first one to caution his supporters—and he did so repeatedly—against trying to turn the information he brought forth in trance into any sort of "cult, schism or ism" (254-103); unlike spiritualism, the Cayce material was not a religion. While he did occasionally convey messages from those who had passed on, communication with the dead was not his goal and comprised only a miniscule part of the more than 14,000 readings documented in the files of the Association for Research and Enlightenment. Nor did he ever indulge in the theatrics of spiritualistic mediums, such as moving furniture, playing floating trumpets, or passing himself off as a spirit from the corners of darkened rooms.

Instead, Edgar Cayce—a simple, humble, self-effacing man—would lie down on the couch in his office in full daylight, go into a hypnotic-like trance, and bring back answers to all kinds of questions from deeper levels of the questioner's mind and from a kind of universal data bank that he called the "hall of records."

Timeline

1877—March 18, Edgar Cayce is born near Hopkinsville, Kentucky.

1887—Joins the Old Liberty Christian (Disciples of Christ) Church.

1890—Encounters an angelic presence who promises that he will become a healer.

1892—Quits school after eighth grade to help support his family.

1895—Meets and begins dating Gertrude Evans.

1900—Loss of voice costs Edgar his insurance agent's job; he goes to work in Hopkinsville photo studio.

1901—Hypnosis experiment restores Edgar's voice and leads to trance health "readings" for others.

1902—Gives reading that cures Aimee Dietrich, the first "miracle" cure.

1903—Gertrude and Edgar marry.

1904—Purchases Bowling Green photo studio; studio destroyed in fire in 1906.

1907—Hugh Lynn Cayce born.

1908—Edgar meets David Kahn in Lexington, Kentucky.

1910—Dr. Ketchum's paper about Edgar is read at Boston medical meeting, triggering first national publicity in Sunday *New York Times*; Edgar contracts with Dr. Ketchum for readings.

1911—Milton Porter Cayce, the second child is born; he dies eleven days later.
—Gertrude contracts TB and is pronounced terminal by the doctors; Edgar's reading saves her life.

1912—Edgar breaks with Dr. Ketchum after discovering Dr. Ketchum's use of the readings for financial gain.
—The Cayces move to Selma, Alabama.

1918—Edgar Evans Cayce is born.

1918-1920—Edgar travels, gathering supporters for his oil-drilling efforts.

1920—Edgar forms Cayce Petroleum Co. in Texas; the drilling fails to find oil.

1920-1922—Edgar travels, giving readings and lectures.

1

The Early Years: 1877-1922

I AM ASKED so often to tell my experiences leading to the development of the phenomena as manifested through me that I feel the need of presenting the facts here in a simple manner. This is not an attempt to write an autobiography, nor even set down in chronological order the curious happenings which have impelled me to accept psychic phenomena as natural experiences of my every day life. If I could sit down with you for a quiet conversation I would tell you this story . . .

I was born and reared on a farm in western Kentucky. I attended the schools in the district and was considered rather dull until I began to read. A woodcutter told me the first Bible story that made a lasting impression. He told me that he was "strong as Samson." He said that the night before the preacher talked about this strong man who was somebody in the Bible. I went to my mother with the story and asked her to tell me about him. Later I asked my father to procure a Bible for me for my own that I might read it.

By the time I was fourteen I had read the Bible through several times, understanding little, yet to my developing mind this book seemed to contain that something which my inner self craved. As I read its promises and the prayers of those who sought to commune with the One God, I felt that it must be true. I had a religious experience, a vision and a promise (a promise that to me is still very sacred). As I have read this Book throughout the years, its promises have become more and more real, and I have better understood the need for faith and prayer if we would make these promises our own . . .

Edgar Cayce, Psychic Diagnostician
Introductory publication, 1920

Spiritualism? No. I believe in spirituality . . . This Cayce you are looking at is nothing. He is but a tool . . . it is what is done through me as an instrument that counts . . . I don't count and what you think of what is accomplished through me doesn't count . . . I don't know what it is that I do, or how it is done. Perhaps Tesla hit it when he said it was like a switch that puts one in contact with the wireless of the universe, or as Edison said there was a record of the universe, and there were needles which fitted the record . . . I am not trying to get any publicity . . . if I wanted publicity I could take you out in the street and raise myself 40 feet in the air . . . I know I can do it. I am not trying to make a fortune out of this power of mine. I refused a theatrical contract a little while ago. It isn't because I am rich. I am poor, I have notes in the bank down in Selma right now. But I am using my power to help whom I can . . . and I in-

tend to go on doing whatever I can to make the world a
little brighter for anyone who is in earnest ... I will give no
readings that will in the least bring trouble or unhappi-
ness to anyone. I want to help ...
                    Birmingham newspaper article by Pettersen Marzoni,
                                  quoting a talk by Edgar Cayce, 1920

These words are the words of a young man in the first flush of
the energy and idealism of youth, spoken before the full and
crushing weight of the yoke of this awesome power settled
firmly on his shoulders. In these words were the seeds of Edgar
Cayce's idealism, which grew over the next twenty-four years
into a pylon of spiritual integrity, firmly anchoring him between
heaven and earth. His gift was to become the one unwavering
constant in his life. Despite the lifelong devotion of his wife
Gertrude, his sons Hugh Lynn and Edgar Evans, and his secretary Gladys Davis Turner, it was only this strange ability and his
final surrender to its demands that defined and determined the
course of his life. All else in life was second to "this power."

What was this power? And what was it that this ability demanded of him, that each time he set it aside to live a "normal"
life would pull him back on some invisible track that stretched
into an unknown, unseen future?

The following letter regarding reading 2480-1 shows that, as
early as 1927, Edgar knew that his ability had some higher purpose:

                                                    October 4, 1927
Dear [2480]:
   I am in hopes that you have read one of the little pamphlets giving an outline as to how I arrived at the conclusion that the information that is gotten through this
manner is worthwhile. I wish it were possible for me to sit
down and talk with you in person, rather than trying to
write—for you never know just how one will receive or
take that written in a letter, and I feel oftentimes a great
responsibility—if the work is what I am led to believe it is,
and a still greater responsibility when I realize that it may
be shaping men's lives who are to be our teachers, our

ministers, or our writers—or our everyday business man,
for I realize what we *think* we become!!

> With kindest personal regards, I am,
> Edgar Cayce

Just so, we may bicker and haggle about anything that
comes under our observation and say all manner of hard
things about it, but when it reaches in and gives ease and
comfort to our physical bodies, and our loved ones, then
and there it becomes to us something worth while, and no
matter what others may say, to us it is the *real* thing. But
to make a comparison, to show what we often mean when
we speak of the spirit of things, let's compare how the
work is looked upon, and see what is given as headlines in
newspapers to attract the attention of the general public,
and then what individuals have to say. We will then catch
the idea of what is meant by "afar off," and what is meant
when it has been brought home, as it were, to individuals.

> Edgar Cayce Memoirs, 1932

If there were questions in Edgar Cayce's own mind in the early
years about the exact nature of this ability, the verdict was even
more in question in the public mind. Consider these newspaper headlines from the time, for example:

New York Times, October 1910

"Illiterate Man Becomes Doctor When Hypnotized. Strange Power Puzzles Physicians."

Boston, R.H. September 29, 1910

"Marvel Doctor Discovered. Illiterate Youth Does Wonders in Hypnotic State."

B.G. (Kentucky) September 1906

"X-ray Not In It With This Man"

Yet, these notes to and about Edgar Cayce showed that others had no doubt about the reality of his gift:

>H.M., Artesia, Mississippi, April 11, 1919
>**The Treatment given according to your diagnosis certainly was the means of my regaining my health.**
>A.B.B.

>Selma, Alabama, January 22, 1921
>**The boy immediately began to improve and gain in weight. He is now perfectly well, and we owe Mr. Cayce a debt of gratitude that never can be paid.**
>W.L.J.

>Sapulpa, Oklahoma, October 31, 1920
>I wish I had words to express my feelings toward the 'wonder man' for I do not remember his name, but know my niece owes her life to his reading.
>F.H.D.

>Birmingham, Alabama, January 22, 1921
>I believe in Mr. Cayce and his psychic power, for seeing and experiencing is believing. I know not from whence this power comes, but I do know that he is using his power for good. Hence, it must come from good, the *all* good, which is God. May he never lose his power.
>W.K.S.

In his memoirs, Edgar pondered the real meaning of such accolades:

>These perhaps sound like some spiel for some patent medicine, yet is there not something of a deeper feeling? Isn't there something of a note that the individual has received a greater benefit from coming in contact with the power than mere healing of the body? Let us get this thought. There is not a healing of any form, unless there has come the consciousness of a desire for help, and from a higher source than that of our own consciousness. Then

that which can add the knowledge of the higher spirit must be that which partakes of the *all* good, which is *God.*
        Edgar Cayce Memoirs, 1932

Nor did Edgar Cayce go unnoticed by the medical community. Stories are still told of physicians, seemingly more successful than their colleagues, who were later found to have had private consulting arrangements with him. But such secrecy was not the case with the flamboyant and dynamic Dr. Wesley Ketchum, as evidenced by his statement that was read to the American Society of Clinical Research by Harry E. Harrower, M.D., in September 1911:

About four years ago I made the acquaintance of a young man 28 years old, who had the reputation of being a "freak." They said he told wonderful truths while he was asleep. I, being interested, immediately began to investigate, and as I was "from Missouri," I had to be shown.

And truly, when it comes to anything psychical, every laymen is a dis-believer from the start, and most of our chosen profession will not accept anything of a psychic nature, hypnotism, mesmerism, or what not, unless vouched for by some M.D. away up in the profession and one whose orthodox standing is unquestioned.

My subject simply lies down and folds his arms, and by auto-suggestion goes to sleep. While in this sleep, which to all intents and purposes is a natural sleep, his objective mind is completely inactive and only his subjective is working.

By suggestion he becomes unconscious to pain of any sort, and, strange to say, his best work is done when he is seemingly "dead to the world."

I next give him the name of my subject and the exact location of same, and in a few minutes he begins to talk as clearly and distinctly as any one. He usually goes into minute detail in diagnosing a case, especially if it be a very serious case.

His language is usually of the best, and his psychologic terms and description of the nervous anatomy would do

credit to any professor ... and there is no faltering in his speech and all his statements are clear and concise. He handles the most complex 'Jaw breakers' with as much ease as any Boston physician, which to me is quite wonderful, in view of the fact that while in his normal state he is an illiterate man, especially along the line of medicine, surgery, or pharmacy, of which he knows nothing ...

Now this description, although rather short, is no myth, but a firm reality. The regular profession scoff at anything reliable coming from this source, because the majority of them are in the rut and have never taken to anything not strictly orthodox ...

Now, in closing, you may ask why has a man with such powers not been before the public and received the endorsement of the profession, one and all, without fear or favor? I can truly answer by saying they are not ready to receive such as yet. Even Christ himself was rejected, for "unless they see signs and wonders they will not believe."

* * *

In these early years, readings were given without thought to the creation of a body of work but rather to help a sufferer—a priority that would remain with Edgar throughout his life—or to demonstrate to the professional community the worth and value of his remarkable abilities:

During this same period a Mr. Stowe requested a reading for his wife, giving her name as Mrs. H. Stowe. It was said by those present that the reply came, "There are several here—which one?" Then her address was given (for he had been married several times), and the reply came that she had only a few days to live—complications of some kind.

No stenographic reports were kept of these readings for the first few years, and then only spasmodically where individual cases were taken down to be verified for records. Practically always some individual was present other than the one conducting the reading.

Edgar Cayce Memoirs, 1932

Affidavits, such as the one in the following example, often were used instead in this era, carried from place to place and shared to establish trustworthiness and credibility. Many such testimonials, witnessed and notarized, are on file from the early years and often are used, as in the case of Aimee Dietrich (2473-1 Reports, Edgar's first published case other than himself), by the Edgar Cayce Foundation as a letter of record in place of missing reading transcripts:

Selma Dallas County Alabama
This is to certify that I have known Mr. Edgar Cayce for the past four years, and have had several business and friendly dealings with him.

I am prepared to say that in Selma he is known as a man of good character.

My attention was first directed to him as a result of his faithful church work, and I have every reason to believe that he is an honorable Christian man.

John A. Davison,
First Baptist Church, Selma, Alabama

Subscribed and affirmed before me this 22nd day of January 1921, R.C. Butler, Notary Public, Dallas County

*   *   *

David Kahn, a young grocery clerk from Lexington, Kentucky, and later a New York furniture company executive, was a close friend. He and other enthusiastic entrepreneurs infused Edgar Cayce with enthusiasm over the idea that he could use his gift to find oil, thus providing a source of income to support the work Edgar felt called to do through his gift. Throughout 1918, 1919, and 1920, he traveled extensively, gathering a group of supporters in the creation of the Cayce Petroleum Company, the money from which was to pay for an institution, perhaps a hospital, through which Edgar could carry out his work. He also continued to operate his photographic business in Selma, the management of which fell mostly on the shoulders of Gertrude and several assistants. Edgar, David Kahn, and others worked on the oil project, giving readings to raise money for purchasing oil and mineral rights by leasing tracts of land in Texas.

By the end of 1922, the strain of the constant travel and the increasingly long absences from home began to tell on everyone involved. David had sustained such heavy losses in the venture that even he became discouraged. This combination of financial losses and the emotional toll on his family caused Edgar to leave the oil business to others and return to his photography full-time. The years of chasing after the pot of gold at the end of the rainbow had not answered the needs of his gift. It was time for a change.

Timeline

1923—Edgar returns to Selma to take up photography full-time after three years of traveling.
   —Gladys Davis is hired to take down and transcribe the readings.
   —The Cayces move to Dayton, Ohio, where Edgar becomes a full-time psychic and tries to establish the Cayce Psychic Research Institute.
   —The first recognized mention of past lives is made in a reading, launching Edgar into a whole new dimension.

1924—Edgar is introduced by David Kahn to Morton Blumenthal, New York stockbroker, who will become one of Edgar's strongest supporters, along with Morton's brother, Edwin.
   —Association of National Investigators is planned with David Kahn and the Blumenthals.

2

"The Work" Becomes a Life's Work: 1923-August 1925

1923

THE YEAR **1923** proved to be a pivotal year in the history of the Work. It was the year that three major events occurred which changed the direction and the nature of the Work and which marked a major shift in Edgar's view of what his own "life mission" was.

First, it was the year that Edgar Cayce gave up the photography business and made a final commitment to giving readings as a full-time occupation, a commitment he was to reaffirm during the hospital years. Also, it was the year a new dimension—the concept of reincarnation—was added to the Work during a horoscope reading, giving birth to what would later be called life readings. Finally, it was the year Gladys Davis was hired by Edgar as a stenographer to record the readings, and she joined the Cayce family as a permanent member of the household.

In September, the now forty-six-year-old Edgar Cayce, Gertrude, and their sons were living upstairs over Coleman's Drug Store at 21½ Broad Street in Selma, Alabama. Hugh Lynn, sixteen, was enrolled in Selma High School. Edgar Evans was five years old. Edgar was established in his own business—The Cayce Art Company—and taught Sunday school in the First Christian Church.

Gladys Davis had graduated from the Central City Business College on April 15, 1920, and was employed at Tissier's Hardware. Edgar Cayce's father, L.B. Cayce, had been both taking photographs and conducting the readings. On September 9, Miss Willie Graham, manager of the gift department at Tissier's, asked Gladys if she would take down a physical reading for Miss Graham's nephew. Edgar and Gertrude were both so impressed with the quality of the transcript that Edgar offered Gladys a job as reading stenographer and transcriptionist. Without hesitation, Gladys accepted their offer of employment.

Within two months of hiring Gladys Davis, Edgar was persuaded to move to Dayton, Ohio, by Arthur Lammers, a Dayton businessman. The plan was to build an institute there as a home for the Work, so the Cayces prepared to move again. It was in his first reading for Lammers that Edgar's supporters thought he first broached the subjects of astrology and past lives (although subsequent research by Gladys Davis eventually would find one earlier reference):

One day in 1923, after [Mr. Cayce had been] giving readings off and on for 22 years and helping people, a Mr. Arthur Lammers called on [Mr. Cayce] and said he was a business man and asked [Mr. Cayce] to go to Dayton with him. He began to talk to Mr. Cayce about the sub-conscious mind and asked Mr. Cayce if he had ever asked

where the power came from. The answer was that this was given years ago but he did not know what it meant—that the sub-conscious mind of Mr. Cayce, while in the unconscious state, become active and from that sub-conscious mind could take whatever information he desired.

Mr. Lammers talked about Hindu philosophy, Yoga, and Christian Science and since he seemed to be a reasonable man, Mr. Cayce decided to go to Dayton with him. In a hotel in Dayton, Mr. Lammers asked him to give him a horoscope reading while still asleep. Mr. Cayce said he did not know anything about it. Lammers tried to explain that at least at one time, Astrology had a better reputation. However, while asleep he was asked to give the horoscope reading for Arthur Lammers. The reading startled Lammers by saying that in order to make it understandable [Mr. Cayce] would also make known [Mr. Lammer's] other experiences or lives on this earth plane which were practically involved in his horoscope. [Mr. Cayce] gave the influence of the planets,—not as set up for the chart, but the chief influences—and told what the man had been in a few of his previous lives. When Mr. Cayce wakened he was told he had given a horoscope and had also spoken of reincarnation.

Mr. Cayce was faced with the decision that day, not only of continuing to believe in his ability to help people by diagnosing their physical ailments, but of facing the realization which, for him, was a step into a higher and unknown sphere of thinking—that astrology and reincarnation are facts of the great Reality of Life. So he had two things to consider: (a) that astrology is a fact, and (b) reincarnation is a fact. He had here to accept that he had been living only a portion of Reality, of spiritual life, even though he had studied the Bible assiduously since the age of twelve. He was really at the point then when he felt he should lay it all aside, but after talking to Mr. Lammers he began to get hold of the idea that this, at least, offered him an explanation of why he had this power and why he used it. So he began to get readings of himself, to find out how he had this ability to help people, where it came from. He had to accept and know that he had been living with only a portion of his real self or he had to reject entirely his own power, which now for a quarter of a century had been proving itself to him and others as practical and efficacious. Now he had to face a theory that had been handed down from time immemorial, that *what he was* was not strange, and what he was may have been unique in the fact that, although the average man does have the sub-conscious mind, he is not able to get in touch with other sub-conscious minds.

Then he was unique.

Thomas Sugrue, *Astrological Review*, 1947

No transcript of that horoscope reading was made, yet the revolutionary idea of reincarnation startled Lammers, stunned Edgar Cayce, intrigued Gertrude, and seemed only natural to the young Gladys Davis. It introduced new dimensions into the readings. This was not the first hint of exotic and mysterious ideas such as astrology and reincarnation, but it was the first time such information was acknowledged publicly.

It was only in later years, during the indexing of the readings, that Gladys Davis placed this note in reading 4841-1, which had been done in 1911:

9/27/76 GD's note: I've just discovered that reincarnation was mentioned in Physical Reading 4841-1 on 4/22/11, with the explanation of the soul, subconscious mind, several embodiments, etc.]

...We take this body as a unit, and it is as near perfect, in a normal condition, as we will find. We have it composed of a physical, mental and abnormal, or soul. We have it obtaining [prevailing? succeeding?] in the oldest body, as its soul is transmigrated. He got it from its fathers, and fore-parents, or what is [was] given him by the Maker. We have formed its functions here and carried from one particle or body to another. It is expelled from the embryo and formed into the faculties as we have in the system, and become in the body as we have in a normal, living body—

strength, power, physical force, mental force, will ... 4841-1

This first reference to reincarnation had gone unnoticed at the time by L.B. Cayce, Edgar's father, who conducted the reading, and by Katherine Faxon, who was the stenographer. But in 1923, those individuals associated with Edgar Cayce did not miss the significance of the reference in the Lammers reading. Tom Sugrue was later to write:

Edgar Cayce did not easily accept the idea of reincarnation. His wife and son and other members of his family had finally got used to physical readings—and now something else! His eldest boy said he did not believe in reincarnation. Why? Because he did not know anybody who had ever written about it. Then his son asked: 'Why cannot we remember?' So they looked through the Bible and found enlightenment.
                    Thomas Sugrue, *Astrological Review*, 1947

Leaving Hugh Lynn behind in Selma to finish the school year, Edgar, Gertrude, Edgar Evans, and Gladys Davis moved to Dayton, Ohio, where, from November 1923 until September 1925, events unfolded which were to yet again change Edgar's concept of the Work.

1924

Once the Cayces arrived in Dayton, a new group of supporters formed, and the Cayce Institute of Psychic Research of Dayton, Ohio, was organized. On the board of trustees were Madison Byron Wyrick, a Western Union superintendent; Linden Shroyer, a Dayton accountant; Arthur Lammers, an advertising executive; George Klingensmith, a Pennsylvania construction engineer; and Edgar Cayce. On December 23, 1924, work reading 254-18 recognized the organization. Wyrick subsequently published a booklet, *A Message to You from the Cayce Institute of Psychic Research*, from which the following is taken:

Rarely do we find the application of one's God given talent so appropriately invested for the good of others as in the life of Edgar Cayce, born at Hopkinsville, KY., March 18th, 1877.

Reared in humble surroundings, ever buffeted by the finger of destiny, until in the year 1900 when through a seeming misfortune to himself (through the loss of his voice) there was revealed to him, and through him, the hidden treasure of his soul.

To choose for one's self a life of service for others is the highest mark of real character, especially in these days when many measure success according to material prosperity.

It is refreshing indeed to come upon a character so rich and full in soul development, as to permeate the very environment of his being with an atmosphere of peace, calm and tranquillity. One whose power of concentration and soul development has attained that fullness of degree, that permits him to lay aside all earthly cares and enter, as it were, upon the sacred threshold of universal knowledge and power, bringing to us information from the unseen forces of good, for practical application to the daily needs of the ills of humanity.

Psychic force, while not understandable, still remains an unseen power or dynamic influence in our daily lives. Some call it personality, others hypnotic influence, and still others believe that all psychic force is hindering rather than helping the development of the human race. To those in doubt, we say any force is good or evil, according to the intelligence of direction and the application of that force. Two of the mightiest servants of mankind (steam and electricity) contain within themselves, power of destructive forces beyond the wildest dreams of man's imagination; yet when directed properly, these mighty forces become man's most obedient servants, from lightening the burdens of the housewife to the digging of Panama Canals, and increasing transportation facilities, that the fullness of life may be enriched, according to man's will.

To understand ourselves and help others understand

"the harmony of their immortal souls while thick enclosed within these vestures of decay" is the mission of Mr. Cayce's life through his psychic force.

Blessed as he seems to be, with a soul force and psychic development far beyond the normal, the limitless possibilities for good will only be measured by time itself. Much is still lacking in his environment, for the best development of the human family, yet God in his all wise providence will accordingly in due time, provide the ways and means for the most effective application of the work for the benefit of mankind.

To date more than eight thousand psychic readings have been given by Mr. Cayce during the past twenty years. Many thousands of these readings were given gratis in order to help those who were sick or suffering from seemingly incurable disease or sickness. His greatest reward has been through the many letters of appreciation received from those suffering ones who have been helped or entirely cured, through the physical diagnoses given in the Psychic Readings.

The powers possessed by Mr. Cayce are such that the language of today does not contain a word to describe it. We use psychic for the want of a proper word. Let it suffice to say that his transition from the conscious to the subconscious stage is enthralling because of the word picture that he transmits to the conscious listeners, and presents on any matter of whatsoever nature with proper and intelligent queries. To hear or read his thesis on trips that he makes into the realm of subconsciousness gives one a clearer understanding of what is meant by the visions or dreams of the prophets, our Lord and His disciples. It permits of an understanding, too, of the realness of the inhabitants of oracles in the Old Greek temples and the bards of the separate tribes of mountain folk in the cradle of Christendom. Convince yourself by test, which is the individual's method of proof. Your conviction will give the Cayce institute its desired impetus toward its avowed aim of service to mankind.

Because of the wrong impressions created in the minds

of men through the use of the word "psychic" there is but one answer to those who doubt. Let any tree be judged only by its fruit [;] seeing is believing—results are the acid test of any effect. We therefore invite not only investigation of the readings themselves, but your careful consideration of the underlying motive of the Cayce Institute, organized with no other aim than to be of service to mankind, and do its share of the world's work for humanity.

THE PURPOSE

The Institute is organized for the purpose of giving psychic readings for the benefit of those who through sickness and suffering require an understanding of their condition.

Mr. Cayce's work and its practical help to humanity during the last twenty years gives ample testimony as to the value of the service he has rendered for the benefit of mankind.

Many seemingly incurable cases of sickness, diseases and suffering have come under the influence of his power, and have been greatly benefited and relieved of serious human ills.

In order that there be no misunderstanding relative to these psychic readings, it is here stated with emphasis that no promises of cure, or even relief, are made. Much depends upon the condition of the mind and body of the individual itself.

While there is no attempt made through this work to influence the religious inclinations of any with whom it may contact, it must be remembered that: "Faith is an effective force, the measure of which has never yet been taken."

Physical ailment in most, if not all cases, is due to living out of harmony with nature's laws. Naturally, then, to acquire an understanding of, and live in accordance with these laws, should and would do much; not only restore the sick, but guard the health of those that are not yet afflicted.

To know the Truth, and live in harmony with it, is the

great end and aim of all creation.

Shakespeare well said, "Tis the mind that makes the body rich."

While this booklet is not intended as an essay on the mental attributes, it is nevertheless very important that the work of a Psychist be judged with average intelligence and open mindedness, and that due credence be given the work according to the practical good accomplished through the psychic force.

*   *   *

Reincarnation was a fascinating and intriguing subject to this group. Suddenly all personality conflicts and, equally, all friendships were seen in a new light. A more complete picture of past-life associations evolved during this period, and questions were asked about the development of the psychic faculty, a line of questioning that would later be taken up by Morton Blumenthal, the New York stockbroker who became a Cayce supporter. In spite of their common interest in Edgar Cayce's work, however, financial hardships among members of the group soon began to take their toll on the effectiveness of the Cayce Institute of Psychic Research. Communications—and eventually financial support—broke down.

This pattern seemed to repeat itself throughout Edgar's career. A group would form, then dissipate, and he usually was left with the financial responsibility. On behalf of his gift, he often traveled at his own expense, frequently in response to well-intentioned friends attempting to promote his work. Yet somehow, he was rarely, if ever, reimbursed. At this time, he was yet again in the middle, willing to cooperate with all but at the mercy of events. He wrote to George Klingensmith:

June 24, 1924

Dear George,

Yours of the 22nd received yesterday afternoon after six o'clock. As we have moved the office from the Hotel to the home it was a little bit late in being delivered to me. Shroyer is still in the room, so he received it and gave it to

me. I know that you have been through the drubs and
have done everything possible to try and get something
done. I have not been able to get in touch with Lammers
myself but I have talked to Mr. Shroyer but I am afraid he
does not say very much to Mr. Lammers. I know there
must be changes from day to day. I doubt whether this
reaches you. I'm in hopes that you have been able to arrange some way and are already on the way home. I can't
help but believe that Mrs. Bethea [a friend from Alabama]
will make some sort of arrangements so that we will get
things started. I tried to stay at the hotel until you returned but just felt like that I was doing myself and everyone connected an injustice in having that much more
expense than is necessary with the number of people we
are having for readings at the present time. Practically
everyone we have is out of town. I believe you can call me
over the phone after midnight for eighty-five cents, provided you just call the phone number. If you will do this,
have the call reversed. It will be alright. Our number is
Main 1472-J. Don't ask for any particular one but I'll get to
the phone. Shroyer says Lammers refused to pay anything
further. Said he was not going to until you came and you
all had a settlement. Certainly a very peculiar attitude to
take at this time. Let me hear from you as often as you
possibly can, but I'm in hopes will see you real soon. With
very best from all,

Sincerely,
Edgar Cayce

June 25, 1924

Dear George:

I have yours of the 23rd and am certainly sorry to know
that conditions are so acute with, seemingly, so little
chance for getting Mr. Lammers to do anything. As I told
you in my letter yesterday, I have been unable to see him
myself. You know how well he can keep away when he
doesn't want to see you. I have seen Mr. Shroyer once or
twice. He said he had already wired you that it was impossible for him to get Mr. Lammers to do anything, and he

thought that you had made other arrangements and was looking for you at any time. He has only been out once for a reading since we have been here, as the distance is most too much for him and as we can arrange otherwise why he lets it go by. Conditions, I suppose, are almost as acute with us as they are with you, but I am hoping that something will develop real soon. I'm expecting [a] telephone call from you to-night. Certainly wish I could talk to you a few minutes. Know what was what.

I'm in hopes you can arrange some way or another very soon so you can get back here and have the thing finally out with Lammers and get what's coming to you. Doesn't seem there is much chance anyway except go to the mat with him. Let me keep in touch with you as often as possible.

Glad to say we are all well—physically. With kindest personal regards from all,

Sincerely,
Edgar Cayce

Western Union Telegram: July 15, 1924
George S. Klingensmith
Wilmore, Pa.

Can you arrange to meet me in Chicago to take charge of readings? Wire me here Southern Hotel at once. May want to leave tonight and know beforehand.

Edgar Cayce

George's response could not have been anything but a disappointment:

July 15, 1924
Dear Judge [a nickname for Edgar]:
Just received your telegram with reference to me going to Chicago to assist you and must say that due to money conditions right now it is almost impossible for me to do so.

I have really made conditions here now that nothing but law will decide it so I am for the present forgetting that

I have any money coming at all and am just about ready to start my old business up again and feel that before thirty days go by that I will again have at least a little pocket money.

I do not of course know what your idea is for Chicago any more than it might mean a new field for a time which I am sure it would and must say that I am more than sorry that I have not right now the money to get us to Virginia Beach, but I need new Psychology and a new start and in a short time will be ready for you, if you are still wanting to go through with our plans and if you still have faith in me.

I hope that conditions will ease up for you a little at least until the big work is ready.

I sure would be glad to hear from you from time to time and assure you that I have done every thing I know to do to start the ball. I have been trying my best to figure out what is wrong so that so much effort has not brought some results and can see nothing save that none of us have strong enough faith.

Please give my best regards to all and all here send their best regards to the gang.

Sincerely yours,
George S. Klingensmith
Engineer and Contractor
Wilmore, Pennsylvania

July 28, 1924

Dear George:

Yours of the 15th received. I suppose you were surprised to have my wire relative to going with us to Chicago but things had gotten in just such a shape at Dayton that it was absolutely necessary that I make some kind of move and not be forever ding-donging everyone for a few shekels to get along on. It seemed that we might do something at Columbus, so I went over. We had plenty of work but little money. While I was there I had a wire from some parties I did work for about a year ago here in Chicago. They wanted me to come immediately. I felt I did not want you to get out of touch with the work, provided you still had the faith and confidence that you have manifested by the time and money you have put in same, and that there was a possibility of our coming to Chicago, you handling the readings, and we would be able to make sufficient connections to get along financially until some other developments could open up. Hence the wire that I sent you from Columbus.

Now, I've been here nearly two weeks. There have been many situations and propositions and I would have liked to have had your version of them. Just what they are going to be, whether I shall accept any of them, [Drs. Robert and Harriet Saxman, chiropractors in Chicago] have been very lovely to me, and offer a wonderful proposition in the property that you know about, and perhaps have seen. Also they offer whole-hearted cooperation, which I'm very sure would be worth while, but under the conditions, without knowing the absolute status of the people you have conferred with regarding capital for the support of the work, it seems to me it is assuming an obligation that is prohibitive under the circumstances. Of course, I know I would have cooperation of Mr. Wyrick and his friends, and more or less the same from other connections I have made here, but I'm afraid I would wear myself out going back and forth, and that I would never make it satisfactory with my family.

Now, I have another proposition that is a tentative one from a regular M.D., and some of his associates in a financial way. I am supposed to see him today, and hear the proposition through, and the Doctors Saxman tomorrow, and then make some kind of decision. You know I still have faith and confidence in your ability and sincerity, or I would not have wired you as I did. I also have a proposition, but which means that I would be on the road for perhaps the next year or so, from the people in Columbus, who are anxious that I return there now at once. I have as yet heard nothing from Mrs. Bethea. Neither have I been able to get an expression from Bransford [John S., a Nashville realtor], so I don't know what to think or do. I am convinced from the reading Virginia Beach is the place to establish the [hospital], the question then being is the time at hand to do so? . . .

Sincerely,
Edgar

* * *

One of the most important, influential, and longest friend-ships in Edgar Cayce's life was with David Kahn. David was a boy in Lexington, Kentucky, when he met Edgar. While some records indicate the meeting probably took place around 1915, David himself said he was fifteen when he met Edgar, which would make it 1908.

As David told the story in *My Life with Edgar Cayce* (1970, Doubleday), Mr. DeLaney, a next-door neighbor of the Kahn family, had asked Edgar Cayce to come from Hopkinsville to give a reading for Mrs. DeLaney, who had been injured in an auto-mobile accident. David said that Mrs. DeLaney was greatly helped. No record of that reading remains, other than David's account. What did remain was that David Kahn became fast friends with Edgar Cayce, having more than 250 readings throughout his lifetime and referring more people to Edgar for readings than perhaps any other individual.

David Kahn also influenced Edgar Cayce to use his gift to try to find oil and traveled with him from as early as 1918 until the summer of 1923 in a vain effort to strike it rich. Throughout his entire life, he exerted considerable influence over Edgar. Per-haps it was due to David's positive enthusiasm, as he certainly was a dynamic and persuasive personality, but from their earli-est days together, David could always get Edgar's attention. David's ebullient enthusiasm and unfailing optimism influ-enced Edgar Cayce in much the same way as Edgar's own father had. Edgar found it very difficult to say no to David, even if he had wanted to, and he could always work up enthusiasm for yet another of David's get-rich-quick schemes. David got excited about finding oil, and Edgar followed him and others to Texas and Oklahoma. David was enthused about Dayton, and Edgar followed Lammers and others to Dayton. Not all those around Edgar shared his confidence in David Kahn, but the young man was nevertheless a permanent, familiar, and well-loved member of the group. In later years Gladys would chuckle and say of David that the readings (3352-1) said that you got to heaven on the arm of someone you had helped, and in this case Mr. Cayce's entry into heaven was assured!

David was warned in his first life reading not to marry until he had passed the age of 38 because he was "in that position of adoration with those of opposite sex." (257-10) In 1924, at the age of 31, he met and fell in love with a young lady by the same last name. David and Lucille Kahn were married April 17, 1927, four years short of the advice in his reading, and remained close friends with Edgar and Gertrude Cayce throughout their lives. The Edgar Cayce Foundation has copies of 195 business advice readings for David, with indications that many more were done. David Kahn always credited Edgar's readings for his considerable financial success.

It also was David who introduced Morton and Edwin Blumenthal to the work of Edgar Cayce. David had met the Blumenthal brothers in New York City. The original relationship between David and the Blumenthals developed out of David's hope that Morton and he could be successful in a joint business venture. In the earliest exchange of correspondence, we can see the differences in personalities and attitudes toward Edgar and differences in their ideals and approach as to how to carry out the Work. These differences later contributed to the lack of harmony that eventually resulted in the loss of the Cayce Hospital. Morton Blumenthal and David Kahn were very different kinds of people.

Irving Furniture Factories Incorporated
469 Seventh Avenue
New York City

June 16, 1924

Dear Judge:
    ... Morton is very anxious to join me in something that he can later recommend to his friends—when we have made a success in a small way—we can then enlarge in a broader way—and make money in the expansion—and sale of good will ...
    But this is a thing that will not wait—of all the things we

have ever talked about or entered into ... we ask them to join us—in a manufacturing proposition that has real honest merit—and I have already arranged the sale of the entire output—it is merely now the manufacturing end of it all.

As to the reading—as I said before—it covered all that I knew—and was very good—but the principal thing—it refused to give—for any personal reason—I am willing to wait and let Morton and myself [be] here at the same time. While here you will have time to look after your own affairs as we are busy during the day—and after four we can get together and take care of our matters. Now Judge this is our last bi[g] chance—because if we fail on this—I will feel that the forces do not want us to use them for business—and I shall accept their ultimatum . . . I have thought of you the first time I had a chance—so that you might share it ... take my advi[c]e—poor as it is—and take the next bus for the city—wire me time and train you are arriving. Get me an answer at once as Morton watches every train—and has the mails timed—he is a genius for work—but very strict about appointments—he has a wonderful income and necessarily must deliver the goods ...

I can not be too emphatic—don't lose a minute—but come. Morton is very square and is as myself always ready to meet the issue—and no hard feelings—but he is also willing to pay for each and every reading—so you lose no time—in your efforts ...

I hope you have mailed the girl's reading already—as she is very uneasy . . . Judge—I was flat. I took the 25.00 I send Mother every week and sent it to you—and Morton put up $50.00—I was supposed to send $50—also so understand you have received the full $100.00 in case you decide you will not come—I will arrange that you are paid for the two readings—and I will have to refund him at least $25.00—you see its not the money—I would send you $1000—if I had it—but this is a chance where you can have a reliable position and grow with the firm—and still we can be together for other things ...

Sincerely,
Dave

* * *

Eventually, Edgar Cayce received a request from David Kahn to do a reading on his intended business partner, Morton Blumenthal. Ever sensitive to the manner in which his ability was to be used, however, Edgar would not undertake the reading on David's request alone:

August 7, 1924

Mr. Morton Blumenthal
c/o Wm. Lauer and Company
74 Broadway, New York

Dear Mr. Blumenthal:
   Pardon me for addressing you but I presume, from letters from our mutual friend Mr. David E. Kahn, that perhaps you expect same. Dave has asked me a time or two, in fact has sent me a long list of questions, to give a reading on you. It has been one of my rules, and is one I feel I should in no way ever break, not to give a reading on anyone unless they desire it themselves. Of course, the person being in the right mind and capable of judging for himself.
   Now, if you desire this reading made, I shall be very glad to hear from you and to undertake it for you. I am sure, however, that from my experience it would be best to separate these questions into a purely physical and mental and spiritual reading, instead of trying to get so much mixed all in one; that is, so many things relating to outside business conditions.
   I am very sorry indeed that it was impossible for me to come to New York at the time Dave wired for me. There were so many circumstances just at the time that I could not overcome, and to be perfectly frank my financial condition just at the time was such that I could not spare the time away, nor meet the necessities of the family with the existing circumstances, but I am sure that if this reading [request] is prepared in the correct manner you will be able to get an insight into the workings of same, as well or better perhaps at the distance than present at hand. While

I feel no one exactly understands how the work is done, I do not myself, yet my long experience and under so many various circumstances I feel that I can, personally, better explain it to individuals than anyone else can. Therefore, it is better in many ways if an individual is really interested in the good that humanity, as a whole, may obtain from the manifestations, for him to be in touch directly with the work, but this may be accomplished when you have gotten a little more insight by a reading on yourself.

I am enclosing you, then, the questions as Dave first sent me. If you feel that these are as you would like to ask them, you may return them just as they are, but I will of necessity have to transpose many of them but will make the reading and the questions will be outlined just as they were asked. I feel sure you have heard a great deal of the work from my good friend, Dave, and from what he has said of you I'm very anxious to meet you in person. Naturally, also, I'm anxious to know what a reading would say about you from a mental and spiritual standpoint. However, I would never take one on *anyone* without the individual asking for same.

So, thinking from Dave's last letter that you desire the reading, I am enclosing you the regular card, with the date and hour set when this can be made. Please fill in and return with your questions at once, telling me just where you will be on this day and hour. I know your time, Daylight Savings, is one hour in advance of Dayton, Daylight Savings.

Trusting that our friendship and relations may be as satisfactory as I anticipate, I am

Yours sincerely,
Edgar Cayce

August 9th, 1924

Mr. Edgar Cayce
P.O. Box 463
Dayton, Ohio

Dear Mr. Cayce:

I am in receipt of your letter of the 7th, and I want to thank you for the kind consideration you gave the communication which our friend, David Kahn, addressed to you in my behalf. Although I was disappointed in not having the pleasure of making your personal acquaintance I am sure that at your own convenience you will afford me that opportunity at some future time. Dave has spoken to me of you in such glowing terms that I look forward to meeting you with a great amount of pleasure.

Regarding the questions Dave sent you in the matter of my own reading, I left this to Dave feeling that he was better acquainted with the circumstances, with your methods, and with you personally, and could therefore better address you than I could myself. I would most certainly appreciate your giving me a reading and am certain that due to certain personal conditions, not at all financial, you might tender me a great amount of aid. I should appreciate however, your giving me a complete reading including financial as well as physical, spiritual and mental. However you know best what to do in such a matter and rather than revise my questions I am returning them to you as made out by David Kahn and leaving to you such revision as you may deem necessary.

I sincerely hope that it will be possible for you to answer the majority of these questions and I assure you the aid such answers may bring me will be greatly appreciated. I ask, however, in order to make the matter intelligible to me that you return my questions together with any revised questions you may make together with your reading. In other words, I will receive from you, your reading, the questions made out by David Kahn and your own revised list of questions should you find such a revision necessary.

As per the card enclosed I will be in my own office on Tuesday, August 12th on the fourth floor of 74 Broadway in the firm of William E. Lauer at 10 A.M. (N.Y. Daylight Savings Time) Except for lunch taken some time around 1 P.M., I will remain in my office until 3:30 P.M. N.Y. Daylight Savings Time. I note that you have Tuesday August 12th, 10 A.M. as the time set on your card.

Allow me to thank you in advance for your courtesy in addressing me, and to assure you of my appreciation of any personal attention and personal effort you may make in my behalf.

Sincerely yours,
Morton Blumenthal

MHB/HAD

P.S. I will not be in my office before 10 A.M. or after 3:30 P.M. New York Daylight Savings time. Morton Blumenthal.

This physical reading was the first of 468 readings for Morton Blumenthal over a six-year period. He was responsible, more than any other person, for what might be called the philosophy of the readings, since it was he who introduced questions related to the nature of humanity, consciousness, and reality. These themes were later explored by several groups of people around Edgar Cayce, especially the sixty-five readings done for the Glad Helpers prayer group (the 281 series) and refined at the practical level through the 130 Search for God readings (the 262 series).

*   *   *

Alfred D. Butler, of Selma, Alabama, was a lifelong friend of Edgar Cayce's and one to whom Edgar would unburden himself, using Alf, as he was affectionately known, as a sounding board and counselor. Edgar's letters to Alf were usually very long and detailed, providing many insights into Edgar's feelings about the events and people in his life at that particular time. As early as 1916, Alf, his brother Roger, and many other members of the Butler family had all had readings.

The Cayces and the Butlers met at the First Christian Church in Selma, where Edgar had moved in 1912 to open a photographic studio and where he was teaching Bible class 7. Alf, born November 30, 1887, was only eight months younger than Edgar, and their friendship and correspondence were to endure until Edgar's death. To Alf, Edgar unburdened himself about the personality conflicts among the people at the institute and about his resulting financial struggles:

November 6, 1924

Alfred D. Butler
Birmingham, Alabama

Dear Alf:

I have yours of the 2nd and was indeed glad to hear from you. It certainly has been a long time since I heard from you and I've thought very often that I would write you but some way or another it seemed that I put it off from time and time, and you finally wrote me first. I thought sure I would write you as soon as I returned from Chicago, several months ago, for while I was there there was a medium came to see me one afternoon and she, in giving me one of her readings, described you and Rog both to me very distinctly, and said that we would be associated together before the year was out. Well, if such should be the case, I think each of us will have to get busy very soon, for the year is most gone.

Well, I have had almost a year now of giving my entire time and attention to trying to develop the work. It is quite a different thing to go at something of this kind for a little while, even for a few weeks or months, where there has been a great deal of interest created, through some reason or another, and in locating in a city where you know few people, and without any money, or any interest created, and make a life's work of it.

True enough, I have had some few people, like our friend Klingensmith, interested in the work. Some others like my good friend Wyrick, whom perhaps you heard Klingensmith speak of, and if it had not been for some such good friends as Wyrick I don't know what would have happened before this. There are certainly a great many things that have happened during the year that I would like to sit down and talk to you about. I would hardly know how to begin to write you, but as I am sure you well know there has been a something, I hardly know what, that ever since I have known you has seemed to impel me to once in a while, whenever I had the opportunity, to sit out and pour the whole thing out to you, and you in some way, through your kindness and consideration have listened, and I'm sure I can truthfully say have never failed to advise me in as good or as correct a way as any friend I've ever had. I can tell you I've felt a loss of this during the last year, for there is indeed few, if any, that I have been able to go to and advise with, as I have oftentimes gone to you in the last eight or ten years I've known you. True enough, I have several friends who have written me quite excellent, even wonderful letters; yet when the many points of consideration of business possibilities and developments come up there have been few, if any, that I've been able to go to at all.

I hear from our friend Klingensmith every few weeks, sometimes oftener. I've seen nothing of him since about the 2nd or 3rd of July. There was nothing very definite at the time accomplished by his endeavors. I am sure, however, there are a great many conditions that he started in motion that will eventually work out, provided I can wait long enough to see their development. He, perhaps, as you know, is at present back in Wilmore, PA., his home, taking a hold again of his old work and I think doing very nicely. It is something dreadful when a person is treated as George was by a person [Arthur Lammers] who interested himself in me, and in George, to get out of him all of the loose money he had, for my good friend who brought me here certainly did that very thing for George, and caused him to lose a good many dollars, as well as nearly a year's time, waiting and fooling along with him, and then finally let him drop after he'd gotten all he could get, but George is a good, clean-cut fellow and I'm sure will make his way and be an effective force among people wherever he may

go. I certainly wish that you and he and I, and a few others
I know, could get to work on this proposition in a manner
that would be satisfactory for all, but what we lack is the
money to start with, and that is the thing none of us have
and we'll have to get along the best we can.

I never hear anything from Fay [Autry, one of the earlier
stenographers], or any of her people. I did have a letter
from her mother sometime about the first of last January.
Haven't heard since. I had a letter, or in fact several of
them, recently, from Riley [Hurst, a Texan involved in the
search for oil]. He is at Wichita Falls. His girl, Lucile, married a fellow by the name of Long, I believe, near Gold-
thwaite, something like about six or seven weeks ago. It
certainly has nearly put Riley out of commission. He
wrote me several times, asked me to try to use my [psy-
chic] influence to get her back for him. Such a thing, of
course you know, was impossible, yet I have had to try to
talk to Riley almost like a dutch uncle. Some way or another it looks as if anyone that tampers with it certainly,
sooner or later, comes to where they want the effects of
what might be possible, yet often want to guide it in the
wrong direction. We've certainly had some curious turns
and twists, in this A.D. during the last twelve months.

As to how the work of the Institute is getting along, it
would surely be a hard proposition to begin to try to tell
you in a letter, and I'm just about where I was twenty-five
years ago. Wonderful prospects but nothing very definite.
However there has developed rather a different turn in the
last few weeks from anything we've had heretofore. In one
of my readings, on how to develop, it gave the name of a
man in New York [Morton Blumenthal], with his address,
so when we had written these up I sent him one of the copies. Had never heard of him before, except indirectly. Since
then he has had several readings for himself. Finally,
about four weeks ago, after much discussion regarding
the information obtained in the readings, about a certain
physical condition, he sent me a wire to come to New York.
I find he and his brother [Edwin] very nice people indeed.
They are Jews, members of the Stock Exchange, friends of

my friend Kahn. The elder of the two boys [Morton], who is thirty, unmarried and well-connected and I suppose makes good money. The younger one [Edwin] twenty-five, married and married worlds of money. Both have seemed *very* interested in the work. In the reading on the younger it said that he was psychic himself and would be able to develop same by following out certain suggestions in line of study and work. Last Sunday the elder of the two came down to see me, spent Sunday and Monday here. His idea is to work out a magazine along the line of the work. In other words, start a magazine, perhaps something like or under the caption of, "*Monthly Psychic Review.*" Just whether to make it a new publication, or attempt to get it connected with some publication already in circulation, seems to be the question, and, too, it will be necessary to have one or two more people connected with it who would be willing to give their time and life to the work, along the secretarial line for both organizations. Besides writing the matter for the book, some parts of which will have to be enlarged upon and several other articles on subject matter. We have two scenarios that perhaps will be presented to some company within the next week or ten days anyway. Of course this will be through this group in New York. Whether their connections and money will be sufficient to get one of the producing companies to undertake it or not, of course is another question, but I am sure if they could ever get one of them produced, and even though it became only partially known of the source from which it was obtained, I would have about as much work as I could well do in the next year or two. I am sure a great deal depends, too, on the development of the younger of these two brothers makes in his psychic experiments, for if he becomes sufficiently interested to want to devote some of his time to it I'm sure he and his wife have sufficient money to do whatever they would want to. This telegram from the older brother would seem to indicate things were coming along nicely. This was received this morning and reads:

"Eddie [Edwin] had two wonderful manifestations. One

probably about self. The other about your last reading. See letter following."

Now as to where this is going to lead of course a fellow could get himself all "het" up, but I'm trying to keep an even balance and to the very best I know how, and of course hope for results satisfactory, if they are right and will be of benefit and service to mankind. If not, they *should* fail.

As to the family, we are all getting along fairly well in health. Hugh Lynn had some trouble with his eyes since coming here; however, this is being corrected, though it was necessary for him to put on glasses when he started in this year's school work, so he has no trouble, we might say, save the trouble of glasses at the present time. This, I believe, will be overcome. He seems to be getting along very well in his school work. The Madam is getting along very well and is in fairly good health. She takes most of the readings now, as I have the office at the home where we live. Edgar Evans just started school last Monday and it has been a surprise, and a very pleasant one, to all of us how he has taken hold so far. Gertrude's mother, Mrs. Evans, has been with us for several weeks now, which has made it very nice for Gertrude and all of us, as Gertrude has not been able to get home this year, the first time she has failed since she was married. Miss Gladys, our stenographer, whom perhaps you remember worked at Cathon-Coleman's a while and had been at Tissier's' for several years when she came to work for me while in Selma, came on here. She has been about the first one, outside of Bill Schanz, who has ever been able to write these [readings] just as they are given. She gets 'em! Which of course makes a great deal of help and most satisfactory to the ones who want the readings. We have had to make several trips during the year, and when it was necessary she could both take and write the readings. We've been to Columbus twice, saw our friend Mr. Mohr [Frank, a midwestern industrialist], but neither of the trips there were satisfactory from the financial viewpoint, but strange to say both leads that have proven of any financial benefit came while I was in Columbus. Whether there is any connection or not I suppose would be purely conjecture. Mohr has attempted, himself, and through a friend of his, to undertake the starting of the work, as he did in Birmingham. So far, however, I've never been able to get him to cooperate with anyone else, with whom I had to rely on. Consequently I've never taken up the work. Jack Stone of Montgomery [Alabama] was here a month or six weeks ago with a view of taking hold and helping out. However, not having the financial backing as he thought was necessary, he left without doing anything definite, and I haven't heard from him since he drove through in his car, supposedly went back the same way. I do not know whether he is back in Montgomery or not. Our friend Mr. Wyrick has been working on his oil proposition in Bosque County. At first, there seemed to be pretty good cooperation between he and my friend McConnell [a Texas banker], but something came up, either between Martin [Wyrick's associate] and McConnell or between Wyrick and McConnell, that has set Mr. McConnell very much against the whole proposition. Wyrick should be able to finish his [oil] well sometime next week, and should he get developments will go in to develop Rocky Pasture and surrounding territory. I have, through Mother Moore [a Texas widow who owned the land on which Edgar searched for oil], still been able to hold some interests in that part of the country and I'm in hopes will eventually be able to make some returns to the people who invested in the [Cayce Petroleum] Company. I saw Alf Wilson on my recent visit to New York. He says he feels confident that the thing will work out somewhere, for he knows there is oil in Rocky Pasture, for he saw it himself. You, perhaps, remember him and his visit to Texas. I hear from McConnell every few weeks. They have had quite a change in their bank at Meridian. Tidwell [C.W., a Texas banker] has retired and Judge York [also a Texas banker] has assumed charge of the institution. McConnell, of course, is still the largest stockholder, taking over part of the interests of Tidwell when the change was made. Long [Joseph B., a Texas banker] writes me once in a while. He seems to be doing fine. They've never done anything with those [bank] notes that were left in San Saba. They are still held by the bank, though there are many of the leasees who have filed claims to have the leases annulled. Among them Mr. Moore, who was sold out some time ago. Several of the others have transferred their leases so that it might be used, should we be able to start operations on Rocky Pasture before December year. It was necessary, sometime ago, with the new ruling on trust estates in Texas, to file a new report with the Federal authorities. The papers were sent me by Long. I referred them to McConnell. Though he sent me his resignation from all connections with the company and wanted to have the affairs of the company wound up and close the trust agreement, I told him I was perfectly willing but he or some of the other members in Texas, I was sure, would have to put up the money necessary for those who had been connected with same to meet in Texas and officially close same. He has not referred to it since, but tells me he filed the report when I sent him the papers.

I feel very sure, from what you have said and what Klingensmith said when he was here, that you have had quite a trying time waiting on your firm to make your salary sufficient to be worth while. I'm glad to know there has been some assistance and that there's a probability of further help along that line.

Yes, there are several people that I know that are connected with the C.P.A. especially one of the firm of Smart, Gore & Company of Chicago. You look up their record and see what their standing is along that line. Mr. Gore has had one or two readings on his physical condition, and has told me that if there was any time there was anyone I wanted him to give a chance he would be glad to place them. I'm also very well acquainted with one of the boys who had charge of their offices here in Dayton. He is constantly changing people and it might be possible that, should you desire at some time to make a change and take up that kind of work, I might be of assistance in getting you connected right. From what I hear, there seems to be no better company in the country than Smart, Gore & Company...

I hear from a few of the people I knew while in Birmingham every little while. Many of them though I never hear anything from, except in some indirect way. I once in a while receive a letter from the Carolinas, Virginia, Florida, Mississippi, from some person who tells me that they heard of it from an individual they met from Birmingham, whom they themselves or some member of the family, had received direct results from the treatments. The greater number of cases that we have come from all parts of the country, and it is quite often that they have their prescriptions filled in at Sellers' Drug Store there in Birmingham. People from as far West as Washington and as far east as Massachusetts have sent their prescriptions to Sellers' to be filled. I haven't come in touch with many of the Medical profession here, as you know most of the doctors in Ohio are of the Homeopath School. However, I know Dr. Gravett very well, who for a number of years has been President of the National Osteopath Association. He and Percy Woodall of Birmingham [an M.D. and osteopath] are very good friends. Of the fifty or seventy-five cases that I have had in this district, that have been sent to osteopaths, all but two or three have gone to Gravett, or his assistant. Since coming here, he has had to enlarge his Institute. I don't mean by that to take care of the patients I have given him but seemingly it has worked together, for among the first patients that my readings sent to Gravett was a real estate man here in Dayton, and while Gravett was treating him he proceeded to sell a place to Gravett, in which he has opened an osteopathic hospital. Consequently both were very successful. Gravett in treating the man and the man in selling Gravett. His assistant, Dr. Lydic, [Lyman A.] is the one who has been treating Hugh Lynn. He is an osteopath surgeon and an eye, ear, nose and throat specialist! He has been present at several readings, with the patient, and has one on for today.

Well, I reckon I've rambled along enough until you're almost tired of reading this stuff, but I'm certainly glad to hear from you again. I hope you'll let me hear from you whenever you have the time and feel the inclination to write. You know we are always glad to hear from you.

With kindest personal regards from all of us, I am

Sincerely,
Edgar Cayce

*   *   *

William Lamar "W.L." Jones was another friend from the days of the First Christian Church in Selma, Alabama. W.L. was originally employed at the Georgia-Alabama Retail Monument Dealers Association, where a J.W. Peters was president of the Selma office. Both men had readings from Edgar Cayce. W.L. was the assistant superintendent of the Bible School where Edgar taught. They continued their friendship and correspondence until Edgar's death. W.L. continued his support of the Work, serving as a member of the A.R.E. Board of Trustees (with Gladys Davis Turner as his proxy) until 1959. In this letter to W.L., Edgar described the founding of his newest organization, the Association of National Investigators, with the Blumenthal brothers:

November 14, 1924

Mr. Wm. Lamar Jones
Selma, Alabama

Dear W.L.:

I have yours of the 19th which was just the day that we returned from New York. As always, you know I'm glad to hear from you, and I certainly appreciate your wire sent me in New York and your desire to be associated with the work we're going to try and undertake. I feel you are most anxious to hear how far we got along while we were there. [They arrived in New York on the 10th.]

With Mr. Blumenthal, his brother and I we have formed the Association of National Investigators. Everyone who cares may join in this association. The purpose of the association is to further the work that I am trying to do, to get same on a basis where we can do the most good for the most people, in a physical, mental and spiritual way. The Book [the 3744 reading series] will be printed as soon as it is possible to do so, and every little while there will be other data printed and distributed to those who are interested in same. We hope to eventually build up something of a library of matter of this kind, not necessarily wholly of the work that I do, but anything along kindred lines, and we hope to study the phenomena in such a manner that we can make it understandable to others, and that they may apply it in their daily lives. As yet, we have not asked for contributions from any individuals, but rather going along the line as I have been for the last year, and those two [Blumenthal] boys assuming any deficiency that may occur in the office expense of the work of this kind, until such time that we can put it on the basis where it will be self-sustaining, or where there can be enough of an income from the data, sold either direct from our own publication, or sold to magazines for their publication. In this way and manner create the broader interest in the work and get those interested who are financially able to contribute to such work, when they see that same would be beneficial to many peoples. This, I believe, covers the whole proposition at the present time. I, of course, will remain in Dayton until school closes, after which time I hope to be able to move to Virginia Beach and establish all of the work there, (So you [might] just as well be arranging to move to Virginia Beach about the middle of June, or first of July, for you know we got to get together.) The main office of the publisher, the institute where people may receive treatments according to readings given, or where classes may be held for the study of the phenomena, in the manner and way we are outlining from time to time. Now, what do you think of it?

To be sure, we included you in our list for the Association of National Investigators, and sometime I hope in the near future we'll make a call for all these people to get together and establish these societies in different parts of the country, and have a real work going on.

Yes, we all had a very pleasant trip to New York. While it

was awful cold, a lot of disagreeable weather, lots of snow and ice, yet we bummed around a bit, saw many things you can't see anywhere else except in New York. It was especially interesting to Miss Gladys, Hugh Lynn and Edgar Evans, though Miss Gladys had right smart of hard work to do while she was there, for we had about two readings every day, and then all the data we had to get together, and of course she had to write it up.

I certainly do wish I had been able to be there for that birthday dinner. Some of these days we'll get together on that, and then I'll have to make up for all the time I've lost. Mr. L.B. wrote me that you reminded him of it and he certainly did wish that he could have been there.

Well, be sure and let me hear from you whenever you have the opportunity. You know I'm always glad to hear. Hoping you'll let me know just what you think about the layout of the proposition [ANI], and how things are going with you, all ask to be remembered to your folks, and with kindest personal regards and best wishes,

Ever the same,
Edgar Cayce

*   *   *

The readings had repeatedly advised Edgar Cayce to establish himself near large bodies of water, frequently mentioning the U.S. East Coast and specifically mentioning Virginia Beach as the ideal location. Some of the Cayce family had visited the obscure fishing village as early as 1915, but it was not until the Blumenthals entered the picture that Edgar himself visited the Tidewater Virginia area.

The first contacts in the Norfolk/Virginia Beach area can be traced from a friend of Edgar's from Birmingham, Alabama, who, in turn, had a friend in Norfolk named Dr. Horton Held:

November 16, 1924

Mr. Edgar Cayce
Dayton, Ohio

Dear Mr. Cayce:

Recently through the courtesy of a very dear friend, Mrs. John L. Hayes, of Norfolk, I had the pleasure of meeting Mrs. Bethea of Birmingham, Alabama who told us a great deal about you and your work.

From Mrs. Bethea I gathered that you are lecturing and teaching and that you are contemplating forming a school. She also spoke of your wonderful psychic powers.

She also intimated that you employed other lecturers in your work. As you will see by the enclosure, I am lecturing along kindred lines, though I regret to say that Virginia is not a very fertile field for this line of work.

I should like very much to hear from you and to know more of yourself and your work and it might be possible that something might develop where we could be of mutual benefit to each other. Address me at the address on this letterhead.

Trusting to hear from you in the near future I am,

Cordially Yours,
Mrs. Horton Held
Lecturer and Teacher of Applied Psychology
339 W. Bute Street
Norfolk, Virginia

November 20, 1924

Horton Held, Ph.D.
339 W. Bute Street
Norfolk, Virginia

My dear Mr[s]. Held:

I have yours of the 15th and thank you very much for your letter. I'm afraid, however, that you have the wrong conception of the greater part of the work that I have been doing for a number of years, but which I have only been applying my whole time to in the last twelve months. It would be very hard for me to try and explain this to you in a letter. I have done very little lecturing; only where I have been in a city for some time, groups of people have asked me to talk to them, but I am no lecturer. I'm enclosing you one of the little booklets that has been compiled and published by a friend of mine, who has received some direct benefits. This, perhaps, will give you a vague idea.

At the present time, I am trying to write a statement regarding my experiences, and I shall be glad to send you a copy of this, even before its published, if you so desire.

My greatest hope is to some day establish an institute of learning and psychic research, connected with the institute a hospital, where the suggestions as given through the research work might be applied and all humanity gain by the research carried on there. For some reason, I have often been given in my own readings Virginia Beach. Why, I know not, as I have never been in that district. Have no friends, or even acquaintances, there, and this is the first letter I've even received from the district.

I'm sorry to hear that the people of Virginia do not respond to Psychology and its many phases, for I am sure it is very necessary that there be some cooperation wherever such an institute might be founded.

I shall certainly be very glad to hear from you and to answer any questions that the little booklet might suggest to your mind. All of my work is practical experience: as you can readily see from my writing I've never studied Psychology, Physiology, Anatomy, Mental Science, Mental Healing, or any of the kindred cults that have to do even with the work that has been accredited me by others. I make no claims for myself, neither do I treat anyone.

I am certain that you found Mrs. Bethea quite an interesting personage to talk with. To me, she is one of the greatest students of Mental Forces that it has been my pleasure to know. She has a conception of the workings of same beyond most of my acquaintances. She has seen a great deal of my work and has heard me attempt to talk to quite a number of groups of people, but I have never felt that I was even a good talker, much less a lecturer. I *have* been considered a fairly good Sunday School teacher, but I'm sure from your studies you will gain an insight as to what my work is like.

Where a great number of psychologists, and mental theorists, fall out with my work, however, is while I'm in this condition, and giving suggestions for individuals, there's often times medicines, operations, mechanical treatments of perhaps every description, suggested for the individuals, as well as the developing of the mental faculties.

Thanking you and trusting I may have the pleasure of meeting you and Mrs. Hayes also sometime in the near future, I am

Sincerely,
Edgar Cayce

EC:GD

*   *   *

The Cayces' financial difficulties also contributed to their delay in following the moving advice of the readings:

December 9, 1924

Dear Alf:

. . . Yes, I have been getting along some way since coming to Dayton. But as I said before, if it had not been for Wyrick's assistance, I don't know what would have happened. It certainly was a bum deal handed Klingensmith, and too, by the very one [again, Arthur Lammers] who was instrumental in my coming to Dayton and whom Klingensmith had every reason to have confidence in, especially as relating to the help Klingensmith was trying to give me at the time. Yet we both got the dirty deal. But things will develop from that, I do not doubt it at all. It simply takes a long time.

It is very much like a circumstance that happened while I was in Hopkinsville. As you know Mr. [304] has quite a number of brothers who live there. Their families [are] all rather large. Only one, perhaps, out of the whole bunch, had ever accredited any good to what I was trying to do.

But one of the brothers [3775] had been sick, between eight and nine weeks I arrived. The doctors had been unable to locate the cause of this trouble, having taken out most of his teeth, his tonsils, and made three or four incisions in the body. Yet no relief whatever was given. The family finally decided that as I was there, they would like to see what I would say, anyway. The trouble was located in the left lower limb, telling the condition as you know how such a thing is done. They operated next day at that place, and found just the condition as was described without any doubt. And as the family put it, couldn't any one dispute it, for they had it in black and white before the doctor ever cut in. Now it has been a long time getting into these peoples' mind the real truth of what was being attempted. But it has finally soaked in.

...I have not heard anything from the man in New York since my return home, but I understand from Kahn, who was here yesterday, that he is still working along the lines about as outlined to you in a former letter. Kahn has been on a visit to his mother at Lexington, and was on his way back to New York. I think he is making a wonderful success in the wholesale furniture business...

Sincerely yours,
Edgar Cayce

EC:GD

Miss Gladys, as she was affectionately known by the Cayces, had to make an unexpected trip home to Selma when her father died. In his condolence letter, Edgar touched on his financial situation and demonstrated his generous heart, even in strained circumstances.

December 10, 1924

Gladys Davis
Selma, Alabama

Dear Miss Gladys:
Should have gotten this off to you yesterday, but just one of those days when you never get anything done. You

know how they come about.

Wish I knew how to tell you how we have all sympathized with you and yours at this time, Miss Gladys, but I'm sure you already know that. I've had letters from several who have written, too, about why we couldn't do work for them, and they all asked to be remembered to you and to extend their sympathies.

Guess, as Mr. Shroyer wrote you, you already know that I had to haul off and have a bad spell of it last Thursday, and yesterday was the first time I've been able to give a reading since you left, except the Wednesday after you left when there were several stenos to try out for the place; only two, however, tried to write it. A Mrs. Banning did very well, so she has done three of the readings; better than most of them do, at first anyway. She only works four hours a day.

I had a letter from W.L. Jones, also from Mamie [Gray, a friend from Selma] so guess wires got there in time to make it a little better for you, hope so anyway. [Note from Gladys Davis: "Yes, the Jones and the Grays went all out to visit with us and help in any way they could."]

Now, you wired that you would be ready to come back tomorrow. Do you really want to leave them all just yet? Should you wish to stay for a little while to be of service to your mother, I think we can manage some way here. I thought perhaps you were just hurrying because you knew how much it might disconcert the work here. But we can manage if it would make it better for your mother and the others, and with Mary expecting her baby.

Of course I haven't done any more to bring in anything, but I'm sending you what I can, and you can do as you see best to do. It's only such a short time now until Christmas, and I know how lonely it will be for your mother; and with the little one coming on, you might be of help then also. But you, of course, know best about what arrangements you have made or can make for her and the others.

I'm glad to say all are feeling very well here just now. No news from anywhere—that is very good. Mr. Wyrick's proposition [in the oil fields] looked like a failure yesterday, though the reading seemed to still offer hope.

No new appointments since you were here. I'm making dates today for those skipped, to be made next week.

Now, you do whatever you feel is best, for your mother and the children.

Please express to her our heartfelt sympathies. All send our love.

Sincerely,
Edgar Cayce

* * *

Edgar Cayce had given up photography, devoting himself entirely to his psychic work. His goal was the creation of an organization through which his readings, and the process of getting those readings, could be systematically studied and evaluated. Preferably, it also would be an organization that could support itself and his family. This decision placed him in the unenviable position of being dependent upon others for his livelihood. His only source of income was through giving readings, and when there were no requests, he could only turn to those around him for money. It must have been very difficult for him to ask for help. The following letter to Morton Blumenthal combines a mixture of humility, pride, and genuine need with his clear understanding that his gift had to pay its own way:

December 11, 1924

322 Grafton,
Dayton, Ohio

Dear Morton:

Well at last I am up again and able to undertake the work again, as you will see I undertook the reading for Eddie yesterday. I am in hopes that he will be able to get something from this that will help [him] understand matters some better, am going to try and get the other readings today that you asked about. Will send them soon as can.

Yes have had a pretty bad time of it. Goodness seems that I know so little and have such poor judgment but felt just had to go see my Mother, hadn't seen her in such a long time, but taking what little money had for that and then on top of it poor Miss Davis was called home, her father's death was very sudden. Hadn't thought he was sick, only about two hours before he died the Dr. had told her Mother he was not much sick and would be alright in the morning.

My self, well, just a bit of foolishness on my part, changing trains in Cinn. Some way I got on wrong train, they let me off about a mile or three quarters out, and I just broke my fool neck trying to make it back to the station through the yards to make the train to Dayton. Made it yes, but like to have ruined myself running so with heavy suitcase and package, seemed to break the walls of abdomen and came near having rupture. Suffered awfully, while not serious, but have to take care and can't stand on my feet much nor walk far. Tuesday last is the first time have been able to get myself to sleep any more. That has helped me wonderfully and I will soon be alright, am sure. Have had some time trying to get a steno. One we have is very willing and a physician's widow, so helps a bit, but think you will see she does not get the connection as well as Miss Gladys does.

Peculiarly as it may seem, have had very few or no requests for readings since have been unwell.

Now Morton, I am going to have to ask you to help me out a bit financially if you can consistently do so. You have been so very nice I feel loathe to even ask you, but will have to ask it from somewhere. I don't want to be in the way nor manner of riding a free horse to death, but will certainly appreciate it if you can help me a bit at this time. Perhaps we can soon have things on a better paying basis. I want to get things in the shape you wish, to get to work on the line-up as soon as possible. But as I said, taking what little I had for the visit to Kentucky and then the other extra expense and absolutely nothing come in, well I am up against it. When Dave Kahn was here Monday he was kind enough to give me $50.00. He wants a reading for his sister and his girlfriend. That cash certainly came in nice and we appreciated it. Nothing new going on here, for you know, when I am "out," there is very little that amounts to much around this establishment ...

Will try and write you more tho when we get the first reading. Glad to tell you I am ready to work, hope things are fine with all of you and trust you will let me know just the status of conditions at this time and what you wish me to try and help out with that we may get going soon.

Kindly remember me to all,

Sincerely,
Edgar Cayce

* * *

1925

The year 1925 was another year of many changes for the Cayce family as events were building toward the move to Virginia Beach and the realization of a hospital. These plans were dependent upon the personal relationship, faith, and trust between Morton Blumenthal and Edgar. Letters of this period show an increasing level of respect as the two men began to discover common ideals:

P.O. Box 463
Dayton, Ohio

January 1, 1925

Dear Morton:

I am enclosing you, herewith, the readings as gotten, as suggested in your letter of the 29th, also the one gotten today on Eddie's manifestations. [Reading 137-11 regarding an emblem for the institute]

In the reading on questions for you, we have tried to go over this, and it seems to me this is one of the best that we have ever gotten. While there are some of the questions not answered as fully as might be expected, I fear it is because we cover such a large field in the questions asked. There is, however, I am sure, great food for thought in this, and I feel that you will be able to write volumes, almost, from each question, and its answer. The small change this [has] made in presenting the questions is of my own making, and not of Mrs. Cayce's. For I think she is very much in accord with the questions we are trying to get, and I believe we are *all* gaining a great deal better understanding of many things from the answers we are getting. In the first question, we have tried to look up many of these that are mentioned. We're only able to find one, or perhaps two, but if I was to try to tell you all that I have gained from this, I'm afraid I would never get through. I'm sure that we can sit down and study this over to-gether and gain a great deal from same. I hope we'll have the opportunity to do it while I'm in New York.

As for the reading for Eddie, I was considerably disappointed in this. He, perhaps, however, will be able, through the suggestion given, to get the interpretation that will prove of a great deal more benefit than had it been given wholly and entirely from here. I'm in hopes so anyway.

Some of the illustrations that are given in yours are certainly most remarkable, and a little study of these, in view of the information, surely opens up a great field, but more of this when we have an opportunity to talk it over.

I'm glad to say that we're all fairly well. The little fellow [Edgar Evans] still has considerable temperature from his cold, but I'm in hopes will be alright in a day or two.

It looks like, from the reports in the paper, that Rock Island [stock] is going away off, rather than going to fifty-three. However, this may be a temporary condition, but I've been looking for an awful slump for a long time. Its the time when oil should be going up.

Wishing you and yours the kindest personal regards, and hoping to hear from you,

Sincerely
Edgar Cayce

Mr. Edgar Cayce
322 Grafton Avenue
Dayton, Ohio

January 2, 1925

Dear Edgar:
Enclosed please find my check for $100.00 for the usual

monthly payment. Regarding your trip, in order to make it a little more convenient for both Edwin and myself would you be so kind as to arrange to leave Dayton on Friday night, January 9th at 10:53 P.M. instead of 6:05 P.M. as noted in my last letter. The train leaving Dayton at 10:53 P.M. on the Pennsylvania Railroad in the Commercial Express—Train No. 26 and arrives in the Pennsylvania Railroad Station, New York City at 5:55 P.M. Saturday evening, which time is very much more convenient for us. Regarding check for fare, etc., this will be mailed by me Monday such that you ought [to] receive the necessary money by Tuesday or Wednesday at the very latest. I will send you a check for $500.00 which I think will cover your complete expenses both to and from New York and while in New York. You understand, of course, that the two (2) rooms in the Cambridge are all paid for and that Hugh Lynn will room with me.

It was Eddie's impression that both of his manifestations have to do directly or indirectly with the institute we are forming. One of the manifestations giving him the emblem we should use for our institute; the other telling the assistance to come to you when the demand becomes so great that you cannot handle it all yourself. However, we will see how this checks up with what you have to tell us.

I look forward with much interest to the answer to my questions. Looking forward to seeing you very soon, I remain,

Very truly yours,
Morton B.

MHB/D
Enc.

January 3rd, 1925

Mr. Edgar Cayce
322—Grafton Avenue
Dayton, Ohio

Dear Edgar,
    As per my last letter enclosed please find my check for $500.00 to take care of car fares and expenses regarding

the trip to New York.

Wishing you all a Happy New Year, am looking forward to seeing you next week, I remain,

Sincerely Yours,
Morton Blumenthal

MHB/D
Enc.

P.O. Box 463
Dayton, Ohio

January 7, 1925

Dear Morton:

I have yours of the 2nd and 3rd, with enclosures, for $100.00 and $500.00, for which please accept my sincerest thanks and appreciation.

I haven't been feeling good for several days, but I am glad to say I'm feeling a great deal better this morning, and should I be feeling as well as I anticipate to-morrow and Friday, we will leave Friday evening for New York. I will wire you, however, just what train we will leave on. If there is no difference in the fare, the Knickerbocker Special, on the New York Central or Big Four, the time of its leaving here would be much more satisfactory to us, and arrives in New York practically at the same time as Pennsylvania twenty-six. However, I will let you know in regards to this.

Also received the wires this morning regarding the horoscope reading for your mother and Mrs. Miller. I will get these for you to-morrow, if I am physically able to have the time and opportunity.

Hoping then to see you Saturday evening, with kindest personal regards from all,

Sincerely,
Edgar Cayce

EC:GD

*   *   *

By early 1925, the first signs of strains between the Blumenthals and David Kahn were appearing, the result of disagreements over how Edgar Cayce's abilities should be offered to the public and how financial support should be provided:

January 19, 1925

Dear Edgar:

Just a line to supplement my letters of this afternoon. I spoke to Dave over the phone this afternoon. He is still in Lakewood but feeling some better. He has had his office call me so often telling me of people he was sending in to see me that I called him to tell him that we were all organized and any action or addition to group would have to meet with all of us before anything could be done. I told him please not to give the thing such publicity as to get it into the papers and he assured me of his sincerity of purpose and I really believe Dave means well. I told him we would thrash the thing out when he came home. I am sure if Dave is willing to give his energy, ability and some of his time and pay what little he can, he is more than welcome. He must display the right spirit, but the best one to leave this with is my Mother, who will talk to him in [the] right manner. This is just her work or what she is best at. Believe me she is going to be one of our best admission committee [members] for it takes a pretty wise old owl to put it over on her. You must have seen that while you were here, for she spares not even Eddie or I, so by the time Ma is finished with Dave I have no doubt in the world but what he will be willing to fall into line with us and display the right spirit too. Anyway if Dave writes you, you might answer him that you are now only one of the "Investigators" of your own work, or of the phenomena that manifests thru you and that any trouble is now no longer your affair alone but that of everyone in the organization.

Well I hope everything is going fine. I am doing all I can at this end and hope I am able to rush the rest of the stationery to you soon.

Surely was great to have you here and wish you were still here. I do hope to see you soon in Dayton . . .

Regards,
Morton

P.O. Box 463
Dayton, Ohio

January 21, 1925

Dear Morton:

Well, we arrived home all safe and sound, all quite a bit worn out but found everything in very good shape . . .

I don't know how to thank you and your Mother, and Eddie and his wife, for being so nice to us while we were there. We all just appreciate it and I'm in hopes that we shall be able to lend assistance in some way that will make it not in vain . . .

I'm enclosing [to] you also the transcribed copy of the last readings [900-24] we got in New York. This is quite interesting, and in some ways seems to answer a great many things I've been wondering about a long time. In trying to explain some of it to my wife, I seem to catch an insight into just what is meant, especially in relativity of force. We began also on the other questions this morning [900-25]. From what they say we seem to have gotten a "humdinger" in some respects at least. We will get this transcribed and sent to you just as fast as possible . . .

In addition to its broader mission of a hospital, combined with other programs, the ANI was organized to be a means of income for Edgar Cayce, sufficient to support himself and his family. The ANI would pay him a regular salary. The intent of the organizers was to free Edgar from dependency upon random requests, giving him peace of mind so that his time and readings could be focused in a specific direction. This early letter shows us that Edgar made every effort to cooperate in making what would have been, for him, a very difficult transition. He had to work through an organizational structure, both in giving readings and in considering the income from the readings as no longer his own personal money but income of ANI. He demonstrated that he was able to do that, faithfully turning over all monies received by him, as shown in the rest of the January 21 letter to Blumenthal:

Well, since I started this letter, some of our friends came

in and desired a reading right away, so it was taken this afternoon. I'm enclosing you, herewith, the check for $25.00 which was paid for this reading. We will list all of these to-gether and report same on the monthly report.

I'm in hopes you'll be able to send us down the other printed matter and forms right away. Practically everyone that I have spoken to are very anxious to see the first printed matter we get out regarding the intent and purpose of the investigation.

Will write you again to-morrow, in all probability. Again thank you, I am, with all good wishes,

Sincerely,
Edgar Cayce

EC:GD

For whatever reason, David Kahn did not attend a meeting scheduled to complete the organizational plans. Edgar counseled him in the following letter:

322 Grafton Avenue
Dayton, Ohio

January 22, 1925

Dear Dave:

I'm certainly sorry that I did not get to see and talk with you again before leaving New York. I was under the impression that you thoroughly understood that I was to leave Sunday or Monday, as of course the boy had to be back in school, and I understood that you also knew of the meeting that was to be held Sunday afternoon to complete the organization for the handling of the investigation of the phenomena, such as we have been thinking of, talking of, for many years, and you know I was disappointed that you were not present at that time. Although you may have felt that it was someone else's affair, still I must say that I felt that you had enough of interest in me, and in my welfare, for you to *desire* to *know* at least what was being done under such conditions, and that you felt the interest sufficient to at least want to have had a voice in it, for you know I desired it so. However, we got together, and I'm in hopes that it will work out in the way and manner that we hope for it to. I believe all are sincere in the proposition, and I, as you well know, do not want anyone to be any more sincere than I am myself, and if they are that is all that I can ask. I'm in hopes, then, that you will confer with Morton, as you have left it in that way and manner, and that you will in some way at least work with him towards seeing that we are going in the right direction.

We certainly had a very pleasant time in New York, and I appreciate the courtesy that was shown myself and family, and I believe, which I'm sure you do, that all were considered in such a way that there can be less of an aftermath of conditions that would be detrimental than there could have been under any other circumstances.

I'm sorry that the letter from the Madam and I miscarried, as regarding the remembrance as sent us on Christmas. The kindly thought was certainly appreciated, and it added a great deal to our enjoyment of that Season.

I'm writing your mother today, and suggesting that we make an appointment one day next week for a reading for her. I'm in hopes that you are feeling a great deal better yourself, with this much needed rest that you've been taking, and that you will soon be able to resume your duties in such a way that you can go about them without any trouble whatever. You know I will only be too glad to try and be of service whenever possible. Be sure and let me hear from you whenever you have an opportunity.

There were one or two persons who phoned me from your office regarding readings on themselves. I'm sorry I was not able to give these while I was in New York, but as you know I did not have the time to even complete all of the work that Morton and I had planned on this visit to New York.

I'm glad to say that we're all feeling fairly well. I'm certainly glad of the opportunity to have been with you, even for a little while, and I'm only sorry that I didn't have the chance to be with you more.

Hoping that you will let me hear from you whenever

you have the time, with kindest personal regards from all,

Ever the same,

Edgar Cayce

*   *   *

The following letter demonstrates both the practical vision and deep spirituality that characterized Morton Blumenthal, as well as the earliest efforts to organize the giving of readings in a manner that not only would support Edgar Cayce and his family ("put the work on a paying basis" as Edgar had said so often) but also would structure activities in such a way as to give birth to a permanent and lasting institution:

William E. Lauer & Company
74 Broadway, New York

January 27, 1925

Dear Edgar:

Your various communications to hand and could write reams, but just haven't time to tell you all that is in my mind and heart, but as predicted in reading the seeming barriers to our work while you were here have dropped and I seem to have pretty clear sailing. For one thing Ma has turned to be my greatest supporter. Heaven help the persons who attack or criticize me in regard to this work. She is going to get me a desk and bookcase and fix up my room into sort of a study, so all that has changed nicely. I submitted your letters to her and suffice that her opinion coincided with mine, though for entirely different reasons, that is we both approached the problem from different pathways, but arrived at the same conclusion. Eddie just jumped to the conclusion without analyzing the matter,—just said he felt such and such would be right. I have thought the matter out carefully, and we here are all of one mind on the matter, and try as we might the conclusion we arrived at is the only logical and seemingly *right* one to us. You see I haven't trusted my own judgment on the matter, altho I have my own viewpoint and idea. However, I know how you feel about the financial part and how your family feels, so that in this case I don't feel it right to impose my ideas upon you. There are a few definite facts, hot ideas or opinions but definite established facts which I should like to lay before you, and also your family, for they are, of course, vitally interested.

First: The entire success of our work, your work, lies in the cooperation of people who are *Spiritual Minded*, for these are the only people who may understand that the nature of the work is to help humanity, spiritually, mentally and physically, and that through this help must the individual arrive at that understanding whereby he may secure the help from within himself, to better his conditions physically and financially, for with this understanding will come the realization of the small importance of money, the great importance of righteousness and correct living as a means to the help desired. Man is Man, whether in the physical or spiritual—what he desires is not what he needs, and that which he needs must be comprehended and sought after, then will the whole of all life be clarified and an understanding be given him of how to live his life for his own best interests, spiritually, mentally, physically and financially. Or as has been said: "Not by Bread alone, but by every word of God."

Secondly: These people are seldom, if ever, to be found in the field of finance and big business. This is particularly true in the financial world, for anything that does not directly bear upon the securing of additional funds is not worth while, for aside from money, the things worth seeking are social position, fine homes in the proper neighborhood, yachts, automobiles and the proper people to be seen with. Don't misunderstand me—I'm not criticizing or judging, I am merely saying that among people so disposed, with such a viewpoint, are not to be found the Spiritual Minded. The door of aid is never closed to them, but a partnership with them for any purpose other than to render the aid they request, provided they need and properly request same. For example, my partners are very fine men, respected and highly considered in the community. They might forgive my extravagance for my personal pleasures, be they ever so profligate; they could forgive loss of money in market. That is understandable. They would admire and commend my seeking out a wealthy girl on Park or Fifth Avenue and marrying her, and living a luxurious life of financial ease. They know my position could give me and does give me this opportunity, but as to my devoting my life, my time, my effort, my money, to the furthering of this beautiful work, in service to God and Man—well, they would think me a Fool, a cracked nut, and might even kick me out of the firm. Shall we cast our "Pearls before Swine"?

Thirdly: The question then resolves itself into method by which those approaching the phenomena choose to use it, and you, thru whom the phenomena manifests choose to respond. Your experience has given you some understanding of how your power should be used. Others must learn how they may use it. It is an individual matter, and does not have any bearing on any outside influence or responsibility. In the very use of the phenomena: "There has been set before you the right way and the wrong way. Choose thou."

Now you'll say I've talked like a preacher, rather than like a businessman. Well, I could have taken it up from another angle, but just now I don't want to. My God, the whole thing seems clear to me now—yesterday it was so confused. I did not understand what that reading meant by the 3 requirements to secure aid. Now I do. Time and number of readings will not give that third requirement. Only "understanding" will, and our work lies chiefly in helping people who desire the understanding to acquire it—you thru readings, I thru explaining to them, even as was told or shown to me in the dream. Now do you see the thing a little clearer? That we may awaken people to think—think—think! You shall not bargain with the Lord, neither on Sunday in the Church, or on Monday in the daily walks to Life. "Thou shalt love the Lord thy God with all Thy Heart, Soul and Might."—not only in prayer and word, but in every tho't and action. Finally, "Put Not Thy Trust in Princes (of wealth, finance, or anything) but in God alone."

What I mean by all this I can't explain to you just now, but this I know. Your family must be patient, that we may proceed in every matter in the right way and have complete faith that God in His Goodness and Mercy will bring us success, happiness and prosperity. Hugh Lynn is growing up and may meet his own problems under your guidance, if he chooses to value that guidance. In my life, I chose not to value my Father's guidance and suffered accordingly but at 20 years I broke ranks and shifted for myself. I mean that many work their way thru college and if Hugh is willing to do this I will lend him every assistance, and it so happens that I may help him considerably in this direction; that is, if he wants it. You may not know it, but I secured my second year college credits at Columbia at night, working for my father in the day time. My third year I studied Economics and Sociology at night at the University of Pittsburgh, while I clerked in McCreery's department store in the day time. The Dean seemed so interested in me that he offered to give my degree if I would study 5 nights instead of 2 a week, or in other words take 2 additional subjects. I didn't do it, and at the term end they gave me my college credits sending them to Columbia where they are registered to-day, and where any time I may use them to secure my degree if I choose to do a little studying for a year under their jurisdiction, either night or day. These credits were given in spite of the fact my work in the store prevented my taking the required term and examinations. I know the development secured during those years of work and sacrifice gave me the understanding of that necessary to persist, push on to success in the business world. I attained confidence, a knowledge of hard work, of sacrifice and determination to-gether with the ability to handle and regulate the details of my life without my parents. I do not write this to brag—I am not that kind, if I were this letter would never be written, and I should not care what you or anyone else did in any matter, so long as I secured mine. I believe in God, trust in Him, am trying to use the will He gave me in the right direction, and there is an end of it. To awaken others to themselves and to the truth of life as you awakened me to the work of your life, and where I may help my humble services are at your command. So Hugh Lynn might well now be thinking of putting his hand to the throttle of his own life, that he may attain that development which will bring his life's utmost blessings physically, mentally, financially and spiritually, in the mature years of his life that are just ahead.

I am enclosing the letters to you for your own decision. If you choose, you may return these letters to me and I will write these people on some of the Association stationery, which I have kept for such purposes, telling them just how they may affiliate with our Association and help us in our work and thereby gain help for themselves and others. If on the other hand you choose to grant their requests for readings as they asked for them it is entirely up to you...

In a day or so I will make a $500.00 deposit to start the treasury of our Association and from which your $300.00 will be drawn February 1st. Of course included is the $35.00 received of which I am keeping a record. This will leave $200.00 in the treasury which may be replenished during the month.

Must close now as have spent the day on this letter. Good luck, and best to all,

Sincerely,
Morton

David Kahn soon responded to Edgar's January 22 letter to him, agreeing to follow Edgar's advice, a response that made it clear things between David and Morton still were sensitive:

February 1, 1925

Dear Judge:

...I have not seen Morton—as yet—but will in a day or so—Judge—I have to be very careful as you know—as Morton is of a positive nature with my self—and he takes the wrong attitude on things—that is from my viewpoint—so I want him to get absolutely settled in your work—where he has guaranteed at least the amount you told him was necessary—and with a clear mind—you will be able to work better—and put your plans into operation. My plans will then work out—and by the time he has the start made I will then be where I can see the entire thing thru—to *your* satisfaction. This does not mean I will not begin with Morton at once—I will—but keep him in the saddle—as he has his position firmly set—and can see it thru—so keep me posted as to what you want me to do . . .

Sincerely,
Dave

Among Edgar Cayce's constant struggles were his efforts to smooth over the conflicts within his circle of friends and supporters, efforts that usually took the form of pleading with his friends to work harder at getting along, in the interest of putting the Work first, efforts that only sometimes met with success.

February 4, 1925

Dear Dave:

I have yours written Sunday . . . As for Morton, I am sorry that you have not had the opportunity to see and talk with him more. I don't know as there's any special thing that I can say other than that I would like for you to cooperate with him in what he is trying to do, in the way he is trying to do it. Of course, I do not mean this as dictating, as you well know, and of course if his manner and way does not coincide with yours, then that's a horse of another color . . .

I do not know, Dave, whether I can get just what your idea is, as to how Morton is taking hold of this, or not; or how that he is trying to conduct it, so I wish you would get in touch with him. Then perhaps you can better understand it, and if I'm all wrong, and he's all wrong, you know I'd like for you to express yourself regarding same. I'm just sorry that you didn't have the time to be there when we were talking this thing over while I was in New York, for it's certainly very hard to do by letter . . .

Ever the same,
Edgar Cayce

*   *   *

Morton Blumenthal began taking the first steps to help Edgar realize his dream of an institution to study the Work. New applications and forms for receiving payments, financial records, internal clerical procedures, new letterhead, and envelopes were all provided by Morton to give new identity to the Work, and the first formal mailing was sent to a list of those who had previously had readings.

Association of National Investigators
322 Grafton Avenue
Dayton, Ohio

New York City   Dayton
New York   Ohio

April 11, 1925

Dear Friend:

We take great pleasure in announcing the formation of an organization known as the "Association of National Investigators" for the purpose of investigating the psychic work of Edgar Cayce, and to engage in research work in order to properly classify and comprehend the vast field of information the psychic manifestations of Cayce opens to us.

Since you are already familiar with some phase of this phenomena it is unnecessary to go into detail in regard to the wide scope of this work, or the great benefit thousands have derived from the physical, mental and spiritual aid that emanates from this source. It is the intent of the Board of Governors of this Organization to investigate, classify and verify as near as possible each and every physical reading given by Cayce, in order that definite statistics may be secured regarding the results derived from readings of this kind. We also intend to follow up and study readings given of a spiritual and mental character including the life readings and other manifestations of a like nature.

We have already begun our collection of data on information derived from the phenomena, which data we hope to co-relate and translate into readable form for the benefit of all who are interested, and submit this literature through the source of pamphlets, magazines and books. In this manner, we hope to give to those who desire, a better knowledge of the phenomena as well as a better understanding of that which the phenomena represents— the spiritual life dwelling within each and every human being.

Should you, who are familiar with some phase of this work, care to affiliate yourself with our organization, kindly fill out the enclosed card and return same to Mr. Edgar Cayce, 322—Grafton Avenue, Dayton, Ohio. A membership in our organization gives you the privilege of investigating our records in order that you may attain for yourself a greater knowledge of this wonderful work. It also gives you the privilege of joining with us in tendering to many individuals, who like you have faith in the psychic force, the help either spiritual, mental or physical that they may need and desire.

It is our intent and purpose to establish an Association Hospital to carry on in a more scientific manner the physical work of this phenomena, and also to establish organizations in the various towns and cities of the United States subsidiary to the main Association, the headquarters of which is and shall continue to be, in New York City. You may well appreciate the scope of our ambition which is so great as to require the cooperation of all who are already familiar with and friendly to the work.

If you are interested enough to enclose not only the card signed and filled out, but also a donation to our cause, your cash contribution will be more than appreciated. Funds are in great need to further our plans, and to carry them to a successful realization.

The procedure, organization and undertaking, (the latter purely research in character), are being conducted by the Association according to the laws and methods agreed upon and voted for by the present Board of Governors in New York City and headed by Mr. Edgar Cayce of Dayton, Ohio. Additional members will be admitted to this governing committee from time to time by vote of the present Board. We shall be glad to receive suggestions, advice and counsel from any who become members of the Association, both as to the procedure of the research work itself and as to the formation of a branch organization in your own community.

In affiliating with the Association it is understood, of course, that you obligate yourself in no way or manner, except as you desire. We shall expect you to lend your aid and service as far as your means and opportunity permits. We hope you will join with us in our effort to carry on the greatest service known to Man—that of aiding our fellow man by furnishing the opportunity of lightening the burdens, cares and problems of life. We anticipate your becoming an investigator of psychic phenomena, by affiliating with our organization, for you are an old friend and sympathizer of our work and we therefore turn to you for support and encouragement.

Very sincerely yours,
ASSOCIATION OF NATIONAL INVESTIGATORS
Gladys Davis
Secretary

Edgar Cayce wrote a letter to each and every individual, stranger and friend alike, who responded to this mailing. There were hundreds of responses. In each letter, he expressed his feelings about the role of the individual in his work, which was now making a transition from a private and personal activity to the work, ideals, and purposes of the new association. His answer to each individual showed he was no "respecter of persons" (Acts 10:34). In the attention to each detail, through the sincerity and earnestness with which he expressed himself in each of these letters—such as the following exchange with Mrs. Matilda DuVall [a friend of the Kahns]—it becomes clear how important each individual was to him, an importance that also manifested in his difficulty in turning down requests for readings. This characteristic of his personality remained unchanged throughout his life.

April 27, 1925

Rosaryville, Md.

Dear Mr. Cayce:

I am in receipt of the circular letter of the Association of National Investigators (which is transposed, for it should be the *National Association* of Investigators, unless you are planning to investigate the National Investigators) but it will be impossible for me to align myself with your friends, only because I happen to be about to arrange for an indefinite absence from America. I have offered this Estate for sale, and as soon as it is disposed of—which I am thinking will be in the near future, I shall immediately leave America. I was badly injured in an automobile accident—which of course was not at all an accident, but was in the Plan . . . but it has been quiet a pull for me to get about again, altho in two months has been accomplished more than usually takes place in six months.

I am to address the Practical Psychology Club, of Washington on May 20th, when I will gladly tell them about your Association, and possibly some of them may write.

I have always wished that such a Hospital as you indicate might have been built on a piece of this Estate. It is such a few miles from Washington, the center in most ways of this U.S. and the "characters" of the "floating population" of Washington, being drawn from the limits of the U.S. naturally bears its message back to that neighborhood from which it came—to Washington.

I am asking $150,000 NET for the Estate of 435 acres. This being well known over the entire world, through the countless thousands who have been entertained here, would immediately give a publicity to any hospital built on the Estate. If you should have anyone of your band, who would be in a position to buy this place, it could be made to not only support itself, but to earn much money toward the support of the hospital proper . . . which could be built on another side of the Estate. The cream of Society are the only "patrons" we have . . . if such a name might be given to them. If you will buy a copy of April St. Nicholas, you will find an article of this Dower House, which will give you some idea on its character.

If you can sell it, I will give to your Association all money you bring *over* my net price. If you sell it at 175,000 you are certain of 25,000. It is cheap at 175,000 for it is fully furnished with rarest of old mahogany, china, glass, silver etc., all of which goes with the house.

I wish you all success. Always faithfully your friend,

Mrs. M. R. DuVall

P.S. 24 rooms in house besides cellars (4) and farm etc., etc.

Mrs. M.R. DuVall
Gordon Hotel
Washington, D.C.

May 4, 1925

My dear Mrs. DuVall:

I certainly thank you for your reply on receipt of my circular letter, also for the suggestions that you have made therein. I should certainly appreciate any word that you may say regarding my efforts when you address the Psychology Club of Washington. I'm sorry indeed that I shall not have the pleasure of knowing you personally, as you are contemplating leaving so soon. I have always looked forward with a great deal of pleasure to the time when I could make your acquaintance, for I have felt that could I but see you and talk with you I believe I could give you an understanding of what I'm attempting to do in such a manner and way that it would prove really worth while, and so near in keeping with so many of your own ideas that you would appreciate my position more.

I've thought a great deal about the estate you suggest. However, starting from the beginning and depending entirely on the good graces of those I try to be of assistance to, has put me in that position of being barely able to get along, much less to acquire properties. However, the work of the Association will be such as to gather to-gether groups of people, nationally known as investigators of this

phenomenon and from this group interest those financially able to back such an undertaking, for the work is
proving a real benefit, educational, morally and mentally,
as well as physically, to a very great number of people
from all parts of the country, and as we are going about in
a systematic manner, gathering this data, we will in a
short while have sufficient of this to present to the public.
Then, I'm believing we'll be able to establish in some given
place and go along with the investigation of the phenomena.

Again thanking you for your interest, and for any word
that you may speak, and trusting to hear from you soon.

Sincerely,
Edgar Cayce

EC:GD

May 10, 1925

Dear Mr. Cayce:

I have just received your letter . . . I am answering it
while I have things to say . . . for I know I could be of assistance to you. I am lecturing on the third Monday in June
. . . whatever date that is . . . on The Chemical Nature of
Thoughts.

I quite fully understand just how you get your results,
and I am fully in sympathy with you—BUT it is wise for
you to know how to keep your own doors closed. You must
fully understand it for your own protection, for if you
DON'T know how to protect yourself, you will lose out. You
are giving of your Soul-Power, every time you give yourself for a sitting. There will come a day when you have NO
MORE TO GIVE. I am deeply in sympathy with your desire
to do your part. It is true that you do good . . . BUT—I know
humanity, and having studied for fifty years on these
things, I have a right to tell you to LOOK CAREFULLY
INTO THE REASON OF THESE THINGS THAT YOU DO.
Learn to cover your loss in soul strength . . . Avoid "breathing exercises," as you will break down the walls of your
strength sooner through breathing exercises than in any
other way. Avoid eating meat, fish. Sweets. Alcohol in any

form, and eat as little bread—commercial bread—as possible. Few potatoes, plenty green vegetables and whole wheat.

I have lately (March 6th) come through a serious automobile accident. The three doctors, one a surgeon, said it would take me six months . . . I am out and well on toward complete health. There IS a way. You have one end of it. There is another end. You must study to find it, for no one knows all of anything. Your part you play now, is only a small bit of what you could do IF you had more knowledge . . . and this is what makes me write you this letter. "It is not I—it is The Father who sent me . . . " You remember Who said this. It is as true now as it was those thousands of years ago.

It is a true thing, that "When the seeker is ready, the Master appears." When you have an intense desire to Learn, someone will come to you to teach you. I am certain you can do "Greater things than these" . . . I want you to read this letter carefully. Should there be anything you do not fully understand, or maybe not entire accept, I will be glad to write again . . . or as many times as may be necessary, for you have a great gift . . . and I believe you are using it in an conscientious way.

There are so many things I would say to you—but . . . time is not plentiful with me. My minutes are so—scarce.

There is a book. The Cosmo-Conception. Published by the Rosicrucian Fellowship, Oceanside, California. I think it is $2.50. It is a book to read by *inches* . . . always studying over and again each point APPLIED TO YOUR OWN LIFE . . . YOUR OWN INDIVIDUAL SELF.

You need it at this time. If you will send me as many of your little books as you wish to send, I will give them carefully to those to whom they will hold a great meaning. Believe, my friend, that I want to help you. I have always had that feeling, but this is the first time you have asked for help. Please believe I am deeply in earnest in EVERY WAY . . . I have given my life to SERVICE.

With very deep loving understanding, I am your Friend,
Matilda R. DuVall

May 14, 1925

Mrs. M. R. DuVall
c/o Club Mews
Rosaryville, Md.

My Dear Mrs. DuVall:

I have yours of the 10th, and there's no use in my trying to tell you how much I appreciate this letter, for I'm sure you already feel and know that, but I do want you to know that I appreciate it and appreciate the help and assistance that you offer me. I think I realize oftentimes a great deal better than I will ever know how to explain to anyone many of the things that you warn me of. Just how to over-come these, I do not know whether I understand or not. Perhaps if I can tell you a little of my early experiences in life, you will realize the foundation on which I have at-tempted to build and of the many times I have been put to the test and have put the Forces, as we might say, for want of a better term, to the test.

But to give you just a little insight into this, in my early childhood, while I know that I have as good a father and mother as any man ever had and I'm thankful to say that I can feel that it is through the efforts of the work I'm trying to do that I still have them with me in this earth plane—but during the early life my surroundings and environ-ment was not just what would tend to lead one into work such as I'm trying to do. Seemingly not so at least. But about the time I learned to read, I first heard, through people who were not concerned with such things at all, in the way and manner we usually think of such things, of the Spirit of God indwelling in man. I heard that this knowledge might be obtained from Holy Writ, though I was eleven years old, I had never heard of anything of this kind before, nor had never heard nor read a line in this book. I immediately set about to obtain one of these books. I studied it by myself. Before I was fifteen I was considered one of the best read individuals on that Book of anyone in the whole community, in fact for three or four years, though living on the farm in a very obscure way, I conducted for one of the leading denominational papers a page of questions and answers on the Book. In my simple way, I learned to rely wholly and entirely upon His promises and they are my foundation to-day. Just how or why, when I reached twenty-one and learned something of psychic phenomena through experience, that there seems to be injected rather than purely mental, I do not know. But I have always felt that the real principle must be that that will apply to the tiny tot just learning to lisp first words, or to take the first steps, as well as the individual of mature years, for seemingly to me, years as we count them in earth merely mean the various experiences that show us that the first principles are correct, and that God *is* Spirit, and He seeks such to worship Him. Oftentimes have I been privileged to gather about me groups of children and try and give them these lessons and how to apply these in everyday life, and I feel when I receive a letter from one of these this morning, though she has grown to womanhood and now has children of her own, then when such an one comes and asks that I try and given them a little better understanding of how to train their own much in the same manner as the lessons that had been given them, I feel that perhaps it is not in vain, and that God is Good and is ever ready to use us, will we but allow ourselves to be made the channel through which His blessings come.

I certainly will try and get the book that you refer to. However, will say there have been very, very few books of this character that I have ever read, save the Bible itself. To me there is no better, no higher Guide than the Words of the Master himself, and they apply to each and everyone to-day the same as they did in the Beginning, the same as they did to the ones He spoke to, for they are the Living Words and we may rely upon them.

Sincerely,
Edgar Cayce

* * *

While the ANI would not be formally chartered until May 6, 1927, the new organization was launched. There were new beginnings for the Blumenthal brothers as well:

William E. Lauer & Company
74 Broadway
New York
April 29, 1925

Mr. Edgar Cayce
322—Grafton Avenue,
Dayton, Ohio

Dear Edgar,
 As per enclosed you will note that our new firm begins, Thursday, April 30th, 1925. Will you please address all mail to me or Eddie:
 c/o Block, Maloney & Co.
 74—Broadway
 New York City

 For reading purposes my address will be:
 74 Broadway
 First Floor
In the office of Block, Maloney & Co. and Eddie's will be the same, i.e. the floor of the New York Stock Exchange.
 Will write again later,

 Sincerely yours,
 Morton

MHB/D
Enclosure

Blumenthal Bros.
Members New York Stock Exchange
74 Broadway
New York

May 1, 1925

Mr. Edgar Cayce
322 Grafton Avenue
Dayton, Ohio

Dear Edgar:
Enclosed please find the usual check. We are now about settled in our new quarters although everything is not yet exactly smooth, except it will be within the next few days. Nothing to write of special interest in this communication.
  With kindest regards to you and the family, I am

Sincerely,
Morton

*   *   *

The reasons for the earlier failure of the Cayce Institute of Psychic Research were not a mystery to Morton Blumenthal. Perhaps he recognized Edgar's vulnerability, which was the result of his great sensitivity. This sensitivity made it nearly impossible for Edgar to have anything other than the most sympathetic and nurturing of relationships with all. Perhaps it was just Morton's way. But in the kindest possible manner, he delicately began seeking ways and means to protect Edgar from being left behind by other well-meaning individuals and loose-knit groups by shielding him behind an organization that would protect him and that would also provide a certain legitimacy and stability. Morton's motive is clearly evident. In every way possible, he sought to help Edgar Cayce realize his dream:

Blumenthal Bros.
74 Broadway

May 18, 1925

Dear Edgar:

... Now about Abeler—I know him too, having met him while in Altoona. If you come to N.Y. certainly hope I am here as well and not away. I would surely be glad to see you and think your introduction to these people through Abeler would probably be great. Just a suggestion, if you don't mind—or if you do or don't want to follow the suggestion just leave it go. When requests are made for your personal appearance and like requests of unusual nature I would advise that you write those making the request that the Association will take up the matter for consideration, but that as the treasury of the Association does not permit of such expenditures and the salary the Association pays you does not allow you to pay the amount out of your own pocket it will be impossible for you to make the trip unless all expenses are guaranteed, a deposit on these forwarded in advance and then some donation, be it ever so small, made to the *treasury* of the Association, which latter shows such a large deficit. Not that I am selfish or looking for any remuneration from this—quite the contrary I far from look for an even break, but I do think it more dignified for your own sake, if the contribution is made to the Association and the latter pays your expenses, first passing on whether the donation for expenses is sufficient. You see my point—they may limit themselves to our organization—they are more than welcome—may bring you to N.Y. if you care to make the trip, but the approval of the Board of the Association (even though that is now only you and I) must first be secured. I do not mean that I want to dictate or anything like that—but I think my way lends dignity and prestige to the work ... Well I leave it to you to handle any way you see fit.

Morton

*   *   *

One of the difficulties contributing to the dissolution of the Cayce Institute of Psychic Research was prejudice. Some distrusted Jews, others the Black race, some Catholics, and some distrusted college graduates. Morton was attempting, as his May 18, 1925, letter illustrates, to build an organization through which the Work could continue in spite of individual differences. Creating an institution to formalize activities based upon Edgar Cayce's gift was a unique and somewhat formidable undertaking.

The following letter reveals how Edgar naturally joined Morton in this effort as he always endeavored to counsel with each individual, helping them to see the good in someone they disliked. It was this characteristic that made him very vulnerable in times of conflict between individuals with whom he had formed fast friendships. He was unable to choose sides or decide on a definitive course of action. [Later, in 1931 during the loss of the Cayce Hospital, this characteristic of trying to hold on to friends in the midst of the conflicts and turmoil was to place his life at risk. In a reading given on December 10, it became clear that unless his gift was used and appreciated here in the earth there were those on the other side "calling, desiring, wanting this entity's labors here. Many are calling and desirous of its entering—*soon.*" (294-128)]

June 24, 1925

Dear George:

... I certainly hope then that you will have an opportunity, on your return from Florida the next trip, to drop by and spend a little while with us. We have had many various phases of developments in the data as is gotten in the readings that have been considerably surprising to us, and among the developments is to know that our friend Blumenthal is a very close student of the New Testament and this has come through his study of the phenomena, and he certainly gives some very wonderful thes[e]s on various portions of the Life of the Christ. To me, that seems wonderful! Perhaps you haven't the confidence in these people [Jews], as a race, yet there must be individuals that are endowed with a little bit more of 'that something' that is necessary to catch a vision than others. Still,

**I know there's many of the characteristics of the prover-
bial Jew; yet I believe this man, could you but know him in
person, would convince you of the sincerity of knowing
the Truth, irrespective of creed, race or color, and though
he may be a man on [Wall Street], attempts to pattern his
life by those principles.**

**Sincerely,
Edgar**

EC:GD

*   *   *

Edgar Cayce mentioned in the following letter to George
Klingensmith that Gertrude had charge of "practically all of the
readings now" because Linden Shroyer had gone to work for
Ohio Florida Associates, Inc. Until this point in time, the con-
ductors of the readings had been a somewhat varied group.
Some were trustworthy, while others had sought types of information that Edgar would not have wanted to give if he had
known beforehand.

From this time on, a change also took place in the language
of the readings themselves. With Gertrude as conductor and
Gladys as recorder, there seemed to be a completeness that
made a rather noticeable difference in the delivery of the information. When the readings on any given subject are read chro-
nologically, this phenomenon becomes readily apparent. In the
early years, the expression was often primitive and choppy; now,
the rhythm and flow of words became much more smooth and
balanced, as if something was moving through Edgar more easily and freely than before. There was nothing new in the substance of the information, but the delivery became more
sophisticated. It was as if some missing part was now in place:

July 14, 1925

Dear George:
**. . . Yes, we all felt rather proud of Hugh Lynn getting
through with his school work here as well as he did. He's
on his vacation now but expects to settle down at something for a year before finishing his school work, and I'm**

in hopes I'll be able to give him the advantage of more school work if he desires to keep on with same, for I feel like an education is something that cannot be taken away from him, and should be worth more to him than a whole lot of money. I feel it is true that it is better to help people help themselves than to often help them directly, without their putting forth an effort on their own behalf.

'Dynamite' [Edgar Evans] as you call him, is getting along very nicely. He's still showing a great deal of his aptitude of a studious person, as was shown in his life reading, and is considerably advanced in many ways for his years, and it's very surprising how the little school work that he has had has brought this out. He often speaks of you and wonders why you don't come to see him any more.

Mrs. Cayce is very good. She has charge of practically all of the readings now, since Shroyer has gone to work regularly. He is with the Ohio Florida Associates, Inc. Mrs. Cayce's health is a great deal better than it has been, though I believe I told you sometime ago of her fall, which at the time still gives her some trouble . . .

. . . One of the phases that has developed, I'd like to talk to you about, that of the Life Readings. These differ considerably from the horoscope and I believe really do people more good. I suppose though you saw some of these while you were in Chicago, or heard some of them say something about them. But I know these would be interesting to you, for they go into the characteristics of the individual more than any readings I've ever seen before. For instance, we had one a few days ago on Mr. H.P. Salter of Nashville. Perhaps you remember him. He always asks about you when he writes. His seems to have just befuddled him so much that he doesn't know what to say. He says either we get something or other that is almost uncanny, or I am unconsciously the best reader of individual characteristics and have the prettiest way of presenting them in story form of anyone he has ever heard. He says, however, he's not yet ready to accept Reincarnation; still has to acknowledge that it makes a great deal of Holy Writ more understandable, even at the first study...

Hoping to see you sometime in the near future, and with kindest personal regards and best wishes from all here,

Sincerely,
Edgar

EC:GD

*   *   *

Having given up his financial independence in order to follow his work wherever it led, Edgar was dependent upon the generosity of others in the matter of furnishing his home. As a husband and father, he wanted to have a home of which his wife and sons could be proud, but again he had to turn to others, relying on the bonds of friendship to supply what was needed:

August 24, 1925

322 Grafton Avenue
Dayton, Ohio

Dear Dave:

I have been expecting to see or hear from you for some time, but I realize that you have been very busy...

Well, it looks like we've gotten things started to going! I don't suppose that you have seen Morton any time lately to talk to him at any length. In fact I believe he told me the other day that he hadn't seen you to talk with you for sometime. I was in New York through Wednesday for about an hour and a half. I went through to meet Morton and we to-gether went to Virginia Beach, prospecting for locating the work there. I think we found just about what we wanted and when we get moved, why we will then only be about twelve hours from New York, close enough for us to get back and forth without losing so much time, and I'm certainly in hopes that I'll be able to see you more often and when you make a run down to Washington, why you don't be but just a little ways from our place.

Now, in this move, we are going to have to fix up a little

bit more, as we will want a living room suite. Something after what you see here in this cut. We want at least the four pieces, or more if you see fit to get same in with the others. I think we want something in blue. Of course, as you well know, there are some shades that are not pretty, but there are some others, with a nice finish, that would look good. Whether one of the large chairs is a rocker, or both of them of the one kind, why we'll leave that to you. Of course we'll want the long table to go behind the couch, or in front, as the case may be, however we use it. Immediately when we saw the place and knew we had to have these things, Morton suggested that we have you attend to this, so of course he'll take care of the bill, provided of course if you don't want to contribute that much towards the Institute right at this time. Now I know that you are wholesale people and perhaps don't like to sell single suites, but I'm sure that you can attend to this and I don't know of anyone I would rather risk selecting things of this kind for me like I would yourself. So I'm in hopes you will attend to this right away and get it shipped out, so we will have it there by the time the rest of our stuff gets there, and we expect for it to leave here the last of this week. Of course if you want to put in the lamp and the other things, why that's alright. Of course you can call up Morton and talk to him about it if you want to, but I know that you know this will be alright with Morton.

These are the shipping directions: Virginia Beach, Virginia, Casino Siding, Norfolk and Western Railroad, with notification to Van Patten [F.A. Van Patten, a Virginia Beach Realtor] of its arrival, who would take care of it and have it put in the house, should it get there before we did.

I had a rather peculiar experience, which I'm sure will be quite interesting to you. I met Morton in New York and we took the boat down to Norfolk. Hugh Lynn with a friend of ours from Selma had gone through and made the arrangements so that we could attend to the business at once, so we got through that day and I came back by Cincinnati from Norfolk. When I went down to take the boat for Newport News for the train, who should I meet but

Loraine Nathan, who had been on a house party in Norfolk and was returning home, so we came on to Cincinnati to-gether. She certainly is a cute, sweet girl, of course
had a great deal to say about you and about your visit to
Chicago sometime ago. She introduced me to some
people there, Hofheimer's. She says about the most influential and wealthiest people there, so we have two appointments when I arrive already.

I had hoped that you and Mr. Lauterstein [NYC furniture factory manager] would have gotten by here before
this, but I guess it hasn't been so that you could. Trust you
won't think this is too much of an imposition, asking you
to attend to this, but I assure you I appreciate all the many
favors you have done for me and for attending to this. Asking to be remembered to your mother and the rest of the
folks, with kindest personal regards,

Sincerely,
Edgar Cayce

EC:GD

Timeline

September 15, 1925—The Cayces arrive in the Norfolk-Virginia Beach area.

September 16—Gladys Davis arrives.

September 17, 1925—The family spends their first night in their Virginia Beach home.

1925—Planning begins for the Cayce Hospital, Cayce's longtime dream.

3

A New Beginning in Virginia Beach: September 1925–September 1926

AT LAST THE long-awaited move from Dayton, Ohio, to the place where the institute of Edgar's dreams was expected to materialize, finally took place. The Cayces arrived in Norfolk, Virginia, on Tuesday, September 15, and Gladys arrived the next day. Thursday night, September 17, was the Cayces' first night in their new home at 315 35th Street. The first letter Edgar wrote from Virginia Beach was to his friend Tim Brown, a Dayton Realtor, describing the physical toll that the move took on him:

September 24, 1925

Dear Tim:

... Well, I certainly had a hard night of it when we left Cincinnati. I took one of those pills or tablets but it didn't seem to do much good. I finally persuaded the porter on the train to get me something and I took enough of that to put me to sleep. The next morning I was feeling a whole lot better. We had to spend two nights in Norfolk before we were able to get any pallets down ever, but that fitted in very well, as we met Miss Gladys Wednesday afternoon in Norfolk. But we've certainly had some time getting straightened out. So much cleaning up and re-arranging, house so much bigger, so much differently arranged and no help, why it has put us all through—but we're kind of half way straight now and will be ready for work now I hope right along ...

I surely do want to thank you for sending the battery to Mr. Wyrick. I appreciate your writing him regarding same. I had a wire from him the same day I received your letter and we had a physical reading for him. It seems the battery ought to be a lot of help to him at the present time ...

Sincerely,

Edgar Cayce

EC:GD

As the fall progressed, the family still was settling in, getting used to the different climate and new schools for the boys, furnishing their home, and making arrangements to get the Work moving along smoothly.

October 24, 1925

Dear Mr. Shroyer

Have yours of the 19th and appreciate, more than I know how to tell you, your answering me promptly, for I assure you it makes us all feel just a little bit better when we know that we are in close touch with you, and though you may be a long way off in miles, yet when we hear from you so wonderfully, we feel that you are closer with us in spirit, in mind and purpose, for I'm sure you in your heart know how near and dear you are to each and everyone of us . . .

Well, the climate here is quite different from that in Dayton—not exactly as any I've ever lived in. More like, perhaps, Alabama than anywhere else we have lived. For instance last Saturday it was about eighty-six or eighty-eight and Monday it was about forty. While that seems a severe change, its only the winds here, seemingly, that makes it cold, so far, and it usually lasts about twenty-four to forty-eight hours, I am told by the natives, then warms up again and we do not have any severe weather until about January or February, when the ocean gets *cold*. Then the wind from the East makes it cold and damp; but not a hard climate on anyone. I guess we'll know though by experience. I certainly don't want us to have a severe winter, unless we get a furnace in our house. At present we depend on one wood fire in the living room and oil stoves through the rest of the house . . .

Yes, it will be fine if you can have a stenographer there that you can put some trust and reliance in. We realize, with our little experience at Hopkinsville, how very necessary it is to have a competent one and one that you can rely on, for although I had one that had been with me many years ago, whom we thought was very good at the time, we found there was no comparison with the *real* stenographer . . . we are on the telephone and our number is 220.

Yes, Edgar Evans and Hugh Lynn both seem to be getting along very nicely in their school work. I certainly hope Hugh Lynn makes good in his present studies, for I'm sure it will be excellent training for him and a help, should he be able to take a college course, or should he go on with work, it will help him to do something better than counter-jumping or soda-jerking.

Be sure and give our kindest regards and love to Mrs. Shroyer, Donnie and George. With a greater share for yourself.

As Always,
Edgar Cayce

EC:GD

Irving Furniture Factories
469 Seventh Avenue
New York City

                                    November 2nd, 1925

Mr. Edgar Cayce
35th Street
Virginia Beach, Va.

Dear Judge:
   Attached hereto is the B/L showing shipment of your
davenport suite from the factory . . .
   I hope you will like this suite and I expect to be down to
see you very shortly now as I am planning to go South in
the next few days. Hope you are feeling fine and your
plans are coming out as you anticipated them and I certainly will be very happy to see you on my arrival in Virginia Beach. Please write me at once what you think is the
best route for me to take from here.
   With kindest regards to you and your family, I am, as
always
                                    Sincerely yours,
                                    David E. Kahn
   DEK/RS

It wasn't long after the Cayces' move, however, that new signs
of strain among his supporters began to show, a worry that was
compounded for Edgar by his ever-challenging financial situation.

                                    November 26, 1925
Mr. David E. Kahn
c/o Irving Furniture Co.,
467 Seventh Avenue
New York City

Dear Dave:
   Have yours of the 20th and needless to say was very glad
to hear from you . . .

It was too bad that you couldn't come down with Morton when he was down to see me some weeks ago. He told me that you expected to come up until the last minute. Then that some business came up which prevented your making the trip. We certainly enjoyed his stay here. I think he's a fine fellow. We seem to be getting along very well. Just at this time, it would have been very well for you to have followed some of the suggestions that he gave you, regarding the trading on the market, as he was following out some leads that were given him, verified in the readings, and I believe have proven quite successful . . .

Sincerely,
Edgar Cayce

115 West 35th Street
Virginia Beach
Virginia

December 10, 1925

Dear George:

I had been in hopes that we would at least have a line from you when we heard from Shroyer last, as you were there with him, but we haven't. Neither have we heard from Shroyer now in some time. I am in hopes that things are going fine with you. I had a line from Frank Mohr. I don't know whether you met him or not. He said he had seen Shroyer in Miami and that Shroyer told him that I had made about twenty-six thousand dollars the first two or three days I was here. I can't even imagine where he got it from, but certainly would like to know.

We would all like mighty well to hear from you, if you feel inclined to write. We hope you haven't forgotten us. While we haven't anything new, still the same old struggle, with *wonderful hopes*, and we hope you'll let us hear from you too,—won't you?

With kindest personal regards from all,

Sincerely,
Edgar Cayce.

EC:GD

December 14, 1925

Dear Mr. Shroyer:

I had wondered why I hadn't heard from you before. I don't know how to tell you how your letter of the 9th affected me. I don't believe I've had anything that has upset me as much in a long, long time, for I can so fully appreciate the circumstances under which you are placed through the same sources. However, I was very lucky at the time, to have you and some other very dear friends to rely on, and through their efforts and yours things gradually changed a little bit. Why, though, haven't you said something to me before? You *know* I will be more than glad to try and make the reading. Please wire me collect what day or evening I will find you in your room, giving me the room number, of course, as you know.

Things haven't been easy here, though I had a letter from Frank Mohr, telling me that you had told him that I made twenty-six thousand dollars the third day I was here, when, as I told him, I had not had hardly twenty-six dollars contribution to the work since I had been here. I can't imagine where it started, unless it was Mr. Lammers. I am in hopes though that yet things will work out. Mr. Wyrick is still working on his well. They are now over six thousand feet deep. The readings have finally made the statement that in such and such a depth they will be through to the full production, and not just development area as has been given in all heretofore. I know it has been a long hard pull, but I hope yet for success there, and should this terminate properly, and in our favor, I believe things will be easier for you and I and the rest of us, for I can never forget how much I owe you. It only hurts that I can't do something right now to help when you need it.

Blumenthal is running along just about the same way as he did in Dayton and hasn't made any step yet to either publishing any of the data we've had or anything towards the spreading of the work as we feel should be. Nor towards starting of the manufacture of the Ipsab [an iodine-based gum rub]. He promises, however, to do this the first of the year, but we know of course this has been promised for nearly a whole year now, but I know he has sustained some losses in his operations. We find it a great deal more expensive here to live than in Dayton. Consequently, with lack of contributions from outside sources, that contributed by Blumenthal has not been sufficient to take care of personal needs.

Yet I find myself wishing for you to be here. We might work out something. I would be very glad for you to tell me as much of the conditions as you care to. You know I will hold them in the way and manner that you desire, and it might be of help in our trying to work out some plan . . .

All send our love and best wishes to you, Mrs. Shroyer and Donnie. Let us hear as often as possible.

Sincerely yours,
Edgar Cayce

*   *   *

1926

It's clear from Edgar Cayce's correspondence that by the beginning of 1926, he was very aware of the friction between Morton Blumenthal and David Kahn and was making an effort to explain each one to the other, with an eye toward reducing the tension through mutual understanding. Subsequent events would show that his efforts apparently didn't have the intended effect and may even have unintentionally exacerbated the situation.

115 West 35th Street
Virginia Beach, Va.,

January 1, 1926

Dear Dave:

. . . Well, I'm in hopes you get to see Morton and talk with him. He's a magnificent fellow—a wonderful man, but he has been going through some hardships of late, but I believe he's bigger and better for having to go through them, for the old adage still remains, "Yet we learn obedience by the things for which we suffer." And Morton is learning his lesson and knows he has to pay for indiscretions, yet his bigness makes him use those as stepping stones for higher things and he'll have a message some- day that'll startle the world, and many in the years to come will call him blessed . . .

Sincerely yours,
Edgar Cayce

*   *   *

Hiram P. Salter, Gertrude Cayce's uncle, was a supporter of Edgar's Work, as were most members of her family. Salter had several readings, as did his wife, Lillian Gray Salter. There are no copies of these earlier readings. Like many whose lives Edgar Cayce touched and who came to believe in the Work, Salter did what he could to spread the word:

March 4, 1926

Massachusetts Mutual Life Insurance Company
Springfield, Massachusetts
H.P. Salter, Special Representative
Suite 1125 Stahlman Building
Nashville, Tennessee

Dear Edgar:

. . . I want to acknowledge receipt of the reading on Mrs. Jakes . . .

There is another thing that might not be amiss. Since this is so different from the general trend of things don't you think it would be well to write and give me a list of persons, their names, addresses and nature of their ail- ments that any doubting Thomases may if they wish ei- ther write or wire . . .

You know the best data to give me and if you will let me have this in duplicate to have an office copy I will be obliged and of course will appreciate it at your earliest convenience.

Love to all and best wishes as ever,

Yours,
H.P. Salter

March 8, 1926

Dear Mr. Hiram:

I have yours of the 4th, and I thank you very much for same and for the interest you are taking concerning the welfare of others and the interest in the work that I am trying to do. Perhaps I lack aggressiveness, for if people do not desire to try to receive benefits from the suggestions given, I don't wish to force it on them, nor even try to persuade them. I don't think the Master ever did. I don't know whether I would know how to begin to give you a list of people that you might find out about, that you might have first hand information. I'll give you the names and addresses though of some of the recent ones, and I'd certainly like for you to have these on hand ...

Sincerely,
Edgar Cayce

EC:GD

Tampa Terrace
Tampa, Florida

April 27, 1926

Mr. H.P. Salter
Stahlman Bldg.,
Nashville, Tenn.

My Dear Mr. Salter:

Some two months ago I answered your letter relative to Edgar Cayce's work. I thought perhaps I would hear from you. Since writing you and looking over your letter again, I feel that I did not give you all the information that you asked.

First, I want to say that I spent two and a half months with Mr. Cayce in Birmingham, Ala., and heard him diagnose between three and four hundred patients and all of them, when the treatment was followed as per Mr. Cayce's instructions, received the help that Mr. Cayce said they would, and in many cases permanent cures. Others were helped. Not all of the cases that he diagnoses can be permanently cured, but if he says they can and follow his instructions, they will be.

My own personal experience, in 1915 I went stone blind. Mr. Cayce said in a reading in 1911 from an accident I had in the mines on the 7th of July, 1911, that if I did not have the correction made in my spine that he suggested, that it would eventually cause my system to become loaded with uric acid poisoning and I would lose my sight. As I remember, there were three doctors present—Dr. Ketchum of Hopkinsville, Ky., laughed and said that that condition could not cause blindness in the future, but in April 1915, I did go blind. [Mr. Cayce] also said at the time that the only remedy to gain my sight would be sweats or Turkish baths. This will advise you that I took seven hundred Turkish baths and sweats in two years, gradually regaining my eyesight until I could again see perfectly and wonderful health in every way, and not a cents worth of medicine. Other members of my family, one especially, the doctor said could not live but three or four days. I wired Mr. Cayce. Six hours later he wired me what to do. We stopped two medical doctors that were waiting on her and suggested she could not live but two or three days, and called in a homeopath doctor and an osteopath doctor, with suggestions to treat her lightly. One week from the time that we began the treatment she was able to witness a wedding and sat up three hours, and is living to-day. That's over three years ago.

I could enumerate many cases similar but I believe it is not necessary.

I trust that I may hear from you at a future date telling me of some of the remarkable cures that you have experienced.

Yours very truly,
Frank E. Mohr
P.O. Box 4123
Tampa, Fla.

*　*　*

Even though David Kahn was well aware that Edgar Cayce was employed now by the ANI, enjoying some measure of financial stability, and engaged in plans with the ANI Board in the creation of an organization, he nevertheless wrote Edgar an enthusiastic letter bursting with news of how he was putting important and wealthy people in touch with the Work, arranging for independent readings and deals within deals. Of the nine items outlined in his original letter, only the ninth item has been excerpted here:

April 30, 1926

Irving Furniture Factories, Inc.,
269 Seventh Avenue
New York City, New York

Mr. Edgar Cayce
135 West 15th Street
Virginia Beach, Va.

Dear Judge:
    Wonders seem never to cease. I have been working for you today it seems, so I thought I would notify you of the conditions as they have happened ...
    #9. Mr. Martini [a Brooklyn radio and manufacturing executive] was in to see me last night. He called me this morning for your address and you will hear from him on a reading in which I am especially interested. As he is one of my closest friends in New York. It is at my insistence that he asks for this reading. His brother is a leading photographer and I may work out a proposition whereby you will have a beautiful cottage within twenty minutes of New York where you and your family can be near everything, have a substantial income from photography, the income of which we may work out in our own business, and also where you may be near enough to New York to work on the things I have in mind.
    I do not know how you feel on this latter subject but at least it will be submitted to you.
    It certainly is wonderful how things are developing at the Beach. I am still planning my trip and there must be some reason for my withholding it, but we know that when the

time comes, I will present myself. I should like very much when you get a chance to take care of that reading of mine but first I would suggest to work out these few that I have mentioned because they are important for the future.

With kindest personal regards and anticipating a prompt answer from you as to what is going on at the Beach, believe me

As always
David E. Kahn

DEK:BBS

In his response, Edgar reiterated the decision, made in 1923 when he moved to Dayton, of giving up his photography business to follow the Work wherever it led. He spoke with simple faith and in a humble manner, gently but firmly reasoning with David, not able to do as David wanted him to, yet making every effort to hold onto this man who had been his friend since the early days:

May 4, 1926

Dear Dave:

Replying to yours of the 30th . . .

Ninth: Now, as regarding the photograph business, I think this is very wonderful of you to have kept this in mind, and to have made some study of conditions, and at least worked out in your own mind a tentative plan for the necessities and the like; with reference to the future, however, I am sure you realize I made a very decisive step when I cast my whole lot and that of my family on the outcome of this work. If I am to believe the readings, this is the place to work from, and it will be shown me from time to time, as to how to go about to receive that which will be necessary for the propagation of the work, and if the work cannot be made self-supporting, don't you think there's something wrong with the work?

Or, if people who receive benefits from the work, cannot see that it is their duty to see that ones that do give out such are taken care of, there is something materially wrong with the individual, and something wrong with the way it is presented.

Further, in connection with this, Morton was here Sunday a week ago, and is trying to make arrangements for a permanent place here. So, all in all, I think it must be worked out from here. Don't you think so? Please understand, however, I appreciate your kindly thought and your bearing in mind the needs of myself and those necessary to take care of the work—but we'll talk over these things further when I see you . . .

Sincerely,
Edgar Cayce

EC:GD

At a time when an understanding of what Edgar was attempting and a "vote" of confidence in the "undertaking" at Virginia Beach were needed, this letter from Thomas B. House Sr. must surely have helped Edgar in a number of ways:

Virginia Beach, Va.

July 26, 1926

Dear Mr. Cayce:

You asked me to express my opinion concerning the work you are doing. I believe I was asked to do this by someone else sometime ago. At the time I think I wrote, "He does it, I know. How he does it I do not know." In other words, I do not know what I do know about it.

But you know, Mr. Cayce, I have had reason to give the phenomena considerable study, as the first experience with same was in my own family. When other physicians had disagreed with me as respecting my wife's condition, the reading at the time (the first I ever saw) set things straight. Later, one was given for my son, that proved most satisfactory. Since then, from time to time, and under quite varied circumstances, I have had occasions to see the good results where suggestions as given in the psychic readings were followed very closely. This phase of the condition is the hardest part of it for the layman and for the practitioner to follow out, for unless such a place is established where the suggestions as given can be followed very closely, and under the supervision of someone who has more than a passing interest in the results that are to be obtained, the best results will not be gotten. Of this I am thoroughly convinced, after having watched the readings from day to day, also the reports from individuals in various parts of the country; for where the individual is awakened to the determination to follow out the suggestion *to the last detail*, they are the ones who report the greatest results with same.

I assure you, then, it is gratifying to know that there is the possibility that very soon such an undertaking is to be made at Virginia Beach, for I verily believe, with the establishment of such a place, suffering humanity will have access to a means of gaining health in body and mind, such as yet has never been opened in this country.

I shall be glad to lend whatever assistance that I may, and be glad to answer any questions that might be asked me concerning same.

With kindest regards and best wishes,

Sincerely,
Thomas B. House, M.D.

* * *

There seemed to be no end either to Edgar's inability to convince David Kahn and Morton Blumenthal to get along or to his financial worries:

July 26, 1926

Dear Dave:

. . . Dave, I wish you'd get in touch with Morton, and next time keep your appointment.

I certainly would appreciate it if you could, and would, get that fixed up about that dining room suite. We are sorely in need of something of the kind . . .

With kindest personal regards from all,

Sincerely,
Edgar Cayce

EC:GD

August 13, 1926

Dear Edgar:

Enclosed please find check of $2000.00 which secures us the deed to property. So is the first milestone is, or will, be passed . . .

Regarding the Board, I think this ought to be a circle within a circle. That is the Association should be made up of a wide group, possibly as many at present who choose to identify themselves with the whole work and whom we think worthy and of proper character. This whole should then constitute the governing board of the Association as a whole and should be divided into different committees or governing boards—thus, one should have complete responsibility for running and conduct of the hospital, another for publicity, another for lectures etc. Each board would have its own Chairman and sub-committees to conduct the numerous details and would meet as often and when it saw fit, but once a year, in Virginia Beach the governing board should meet to receive reports from the various Boards and discuss in the whole the general future course. The various Boards can be formed as necessity calls for them. Right now I think the Board of Governors to control the hospital institute should be made up of those capable of working intimately to some extent at least on the premises. One who could only see us once a year, unless of a big financial benefit, should serve on the whole governing board, rather [than] on the one that conducts the every day affairs of the hospital. I would say the governing committee of the hospital should be:

1. Dr. Thomas E. House as Chairman
2. Someone in Virginia Beach to serve as Secretary
3. Edgar Cayce if laws will permit
4. Morton H. Blumenthal
5. Anyone else you select who will be interested enough—more than once a year
6. Edwin D. Blumenthal (if he will serve)
7. Any others you select that fit the bill

The whole governing Board might be so constituted:

1. Morton H. Blumenthal (temporary President)
2. Edgar Cayce (temporary Vice-President—if all ok legally)
2a Any other you choose to serve as 1st, 2nd, 3rd etc., Vice-President
3. Dr. Thomas E. House (treasurer)
4. A capable Secretary of your choice
5. All the rest who will join in our work whether able to be with us at all or not, just so they are in sympathy with our work and will work for it as best they may in whatever location they may be in.

You see the whole includes the Institute Board and is only responsible to it in a general way, for the institute will govern itself and conduct its own affairs, working however, harmoniously with the whole Association. The whole excludes none—the Institute includes those capable of active service in the hospital field and that will concentrate their attention on this work principally. The same people may be both at present but I would have the organization this way if you can, for later we may have a different story and in years to come many may consider it an honor to be on the governing committee either of the whole or on one of [the] sub-committee boards. You note I have made myself temporary president—thus I hold that position only to facilitate organizations and a permanent election.

Must close,
Morton

August 17, 1926

Dear Morton:

I have yours of the 13th, with the check for the payment on the place. They have to wait on the signature of the deed, as the lady who owns same was out of town, but I'll try to get it all in shape as soon as possible and send all the papers to you to be fixed up . . .

Now, I don't know, Morton, whether I can explain this to you in a letter well enough for you to get what I'm driving at or not. Perhaps I could do a whole lot better if I was talking to you in person—perhaps its really better that you see it in black and white so you can see how the thing would look to the other fellow. Now, I think you are exactly right as regarding the governing Board, save as I said before— Dr. House would not be known in the corporation except as an employee of the Association, and at least three of the managers must be residents of the county in which this is established. I may be wrong—I believe the attorney will serve as one of the officers. I will want you to remain [in] office as the president, or the manager, or chairman of the Board, no matter how it would have to be made. He says we should have at least ten to fifteen incorporators, and we may have them from as many states as we like, but at least enough to conduct the affairs of the Association must be where they can be consulted by the physician in charge as often as is necessary. The attorney also says go ahead, get your money to start your work. He can get the corporation papers all through in less than a week—all of the cost will be less than $50—that's filing of papers before notaries, county authorities and state authorities, with a charter from each to do business.

Now, taking this all into consideration, I have thought possibly that the best way was to make a direct personal appeal (which I have never done) to our mailing list and people we have done work for. The letter, as you will see, would all be written personal . . . as a form for those whom I am not personally acquainted with, or haven't had special correspondence with. What do you think of it? Of course, where I know them, we will dictate special things as respecting that individual. The card, as you see, is changed considerable as respecting the amounts. This may be all wrong, but if we do not make it something of this class, I'm afraid they'll get the idea we're too cheap and it'll be hard to get $50.00 from two thousand people, unless there were some large contributors . . .

With kindest personal regards from all,

Sincerely,
Edgar Cayce

EC:GD

August 19, 1926

Dear Edgar:

... Enclosed please find $150.00 check. Will send balance a little later as am a little tight just now.

Believe your ideas regarding pamphlet ... [are] good. Will submit them to a printer or ad man to have this done ...

Must close,

Sincerely,
Morton

August 26, 1926

Dear Edgar:

... Am having a man work on the pamphlet ... As it is they will cost $300.00 without the cards or envelopes ...

I am sending $70.00 for $5000 fire insurance policy, Sept. 1 $282.00 is due the Guarantee Trust as I understand it and I will send that. It sure is a high rate, but must do for the time being. We will pay both Ferebee and this loan off soon as possible.

Am afraid I can't broach Eddie on another $1,000 for heating just now. I know it must be done and should be done right, but can't just now, but may if I just can make it in market a little later. One way or another I'll have it done somehow before the real cold weather sets in if I have to pay it out of my own pocket. For the present we'll have to let it wait. We've made progress—we'll continue to and the one good thing about our progress is that altho slow we are sure we are moving in the right direction and therefore the ground we gain we hold. We'll move along, I'm sure.

... As soon as possible we'll have to have an organization meeting preferably the end of September for then we'll have or might have some money in and Dr. House will be nearer ready. All for now. Kindest regards,

Sincerely,
Morton

September 2, 1926

Dear Edgar:

Enclosed please find check. Won't hold you up this month as I know it tightens things. Sorry to have to last month, what with the property etc. With printing of pamphlets, cards etc., this job will cost about $400.00—not that I in anyway regret the $400.00 or consider it of any value in the light of the value we are trying to achieve, (the institute) but it is the getting of it just at the time you need and want it. However there is nothing to worry about as it always is secured one way or another, thanks to Him who seems to thoroughly be able to furnish that necessary . . .

So far as I am concerned, unless its Dr. House's incomplete registrations I don't see why, with Croker and Van Patten you don't go ahead and *rent* the most practical house for the purpose to be used for the institute. While the money is being raised by the letters and subscriptions. I'll guarantee the 1st year's rent. I'm not positive when I'll get the money but then I never am. I don't know—but I'll get it. Go ahead! Then as money comes in we'll buy the equipment and hire orderly and nurse. But is the doctor ready? Push right on. Don't let a thing like not having the money scare you. I don't—I never have it—always biting off more than I can chew and while I sometimes get indigestion, the power of creation, whose creative work and ends I seek, plows thru to the rescue. If you think that is fiction just review the past.

You never explained to me who you could see in Florida or what you could do there to raise funds. Maybe we could manage for you to go down there and also come to N.Y. and talk to Mr. Lauterstein [a New York City furniture factory manager]—explaining what we *are* doing, not plan to do, and how we expect to grow and how we need financial aid. He can verify anything thru me if he chooses. What do you think of such a trip to N.Y.? I think it would pay in the first place and I should like you to meet Mr. Levy [David, a New York clothing manufacturer] and before leaving explain and appeal to him. I think it would bring results—*now!* Let me know what you think of this. Don't forget to send me a copy of the form of subscription card.

Nothing else for the present, except the following dreams that seem to bawl me out, so to speak, good.

Sincerely,
Morton

P.S. Out of enclosed would appreciate your giving Kellam the $25.00 we owe him for examination of title.

September 4, 1926

Dear Morton:

While I have so many things to write, I don't know whether I can cover them all just as I should or not ...

Dr. House has all of his credentials ready to file Tuesday. These will be attended to at that time—then we hope to get busy and try and locate a place and get things started in the right direction, and, as you say, it will be a great deal better to approach people in person or by letter with what we are doing, rather than what we expect to do ...

As for the Florida proposition, this is the one that I told you about when you were here—about the dream telling me we would be presented with a proposition that I wouldn't think favorably of, but were I to use it and handle it correctly much good might come from it. This is being handled, as perhaps you remember, through Mr. Mohr. Who has been interested in the work for a number of years. What I have been trying to do is to get in personal touch, direct, with these people, rather than through an agent. The readings seem to indicate that this eventually will come about, and that when it does I will be able to gain thereby sufficient for a nucleus to build about. Mr. Mohr is still here, and while he requests readings of a very material nature, readings *on* this indicate that it will work out for the best good of all—and that is our only reason for holding on to the proposition at all, for we take a reading now and then to try to see if we're handling the proposition right ...

* * *

While frustrated by events at the mundane level, however, Edgar Cayce must have been encouraged by the way in which their personal experiences with the information in the readings were winning the confidence of members of the early group.

August 18, 1926

Dear Edgar:

The enclosed (dreams of Adeline) are very interesting and will be of great interest. You know the readings long ago said my first pupils would be my loved ones about me. They are not easy ones and Adeline has been quite a rebel. She insisted that all the light business given in the readings was bunk. Then came the first vision with her mother. Now she is not so sure—in fact more inclined to believe. Poor kid—she wanted to know if reincarnations weren't often quick. She wanted her mother back again to tell her, you see, even if as another person. What little children we are, and so I recognize the wonder of your psychic work, that has brought real mind maturity—note I say mind, not intellectual, although the latter has furnished the means or instrument.

More interesting are the events surrounding the second vision. Adeline took 3 osteopathic treatments for her wrenched back, then decided to take no more. I tried to persuade her and she grew angry with me, although she has backache. Night before last I prayed that the psychic activity in the One Mind, that was aware of the condition in Adeline's psyche [her mother] appear and prevail upon her to do that which was best for herself and the forming child. In other words I asked the Lord to join with me in this endeavor to better facilitate His creation. The wonderful response came as the second dream indicates.

Then Adeline cried and said she wanted her mother. I told her to pray to the Lord as her mother—to call the Lord, "Her" and that her mother would come. Adeline said she was tired of that talk, but when she went to sleep her mother came in vision. Now all the king's horses and all the king's men couldn't keep Adeline away from the osteopath.

I cannot force her to anything, of course—should not try, yet when she attempts to meet me on the grounds—to beard the lion in the den, she meets complete defeat. She doesn't want to believe the readings, yet she does want her mother. I tell her how she may reach her mother and she does reach her just that way and her mother confirms the readings. For the time Adeline is subdued. If not convinced, she is wondering—wondering—wondering. "It is funny how things happen to and for you," she said. "Not with a grand show or hurrah," I replied. "When everything looks the worst, conditions quietly and surely change—even more than that desired is granted." "It is uncanny," she answered, still wondering . . .

We will return to 161 W 75 N.Y. in 2 weeks and I then hope to resume more consistent work on this. It is too important to neglect and will mean too much to all of us to leave off, for it will bring public recognition of the *right* kind to our entire work.

I hope those letters will get out soon, that we will get started without too great a further delay and that I will get to see you soon. Do you recall that Sept., is astrologically my bad month? I'll have to be careful for the last time things were fierce. I seem to be able to foretell conditions a little better now from within myself—the foundation trouble for example, and therefore should be fore-warned and better prepared . . .

Kindest regards to all,

Sincerely,
Morton

Timeline

1926—Hugh Lynn leaves for college at Washington and Lee in September.
  —Carrie Elizabeth Major Cayce, Edgar's mother, dies in October.

1927—Construction begins on the Cayce Hospital.

1928—Discussions begin about a university.

4

Building the Hospital:
September 1926-November 1928

A~ important C~ family milestone was reached when Hugh Lynn left for college at Washington and Lee. The Cayces' financial ability to send Hugh Lynn to college came about in a rather interesting fashion, given the family's chronic shortage of money.

In 1926, Princess Anne County (now the City of Virginia Beach) was in the process of developing a road to connect Norfolk to Virginia Beach by extending Virginia Beach Boulevard all the way from Norfolk to the oceanfront. The Cayces had paid the required deposit for their share of the cost from money provided by Morton Blumenthal, only to have it returned to them by the county, pending further developments in the project. Tim Brown and Morton Blumenthal had both discussed this matter and several other issues related to how best to supply the needs of the Cayce family during this time of preparation and planning for the new organization and hospital. Brown wrote Edgar on September 8, stating that he and Morton were in agreement that "no proper return to you for your efforts is now being made—but as soon as the Association functions as a going concern—then there will only be a percentage of readings given without payment . . . am enclosing a note to Hugh Lynn—will you please give the members of the Cayce Household my kindest regards . . . " Morton also told Edgar not to return the money but to use it to help Hugh Lynn. This returned deposit enabled Edgar Cayce to pay Hugh Lynn's tuition. Hugh Lynn's sense of humor later prompted a number of wry remarks about the road's opening also opening the road for him to attend college.

Edgar wrote to Brown:

September 13, 1926

Dear Tim:
   . . . I want to thank you, too, for your kindness to Hugh Lynn. No doubt he has already written you as to the matters concerning the "opening of the road"—this will be delayed, as I understand, for some little time—possibly there will be some mix-up about it, and they returned the amounts deposited to them who purchased them. This was the thing that made it possible for Hugh Lynn to start in school, and I certainly appreciate your kindness and thoughtfulness of him. I am in hopes that I can arrange so he can go on and finish. He started off last night, and of course you know how his mother and all of us miss him, even though he has only been gone a few hours—yet we realize that he is to make his own way in the world, and he must prepare himself for it. I'm glad that he has the ambition to go ahead, and I appreciate your assistance in help-

ing us to help him get started ...

Sincerely,
Edgar

EC:GD

* * *

Edgar's first letter to Hugh Lynn at college was written exactly one year after the Cayces arrived in Virginia:

September 15, 1926

Dear Hugh Lynn:

Of course, there doesn't very much happen here, but we feel sure that you will be interested in what little does happen, for a while, at least. I'm sure, also, that you will enjoy studying over the enclosed reading [294-81]. I'm anxious to know what you think of it, and just how it will fit in with your actual experiences there, from day to day. You must be sure and let us know, for you know we are real anxious, and if there has ever been a time when we could actually put our finger on the truths that are presented (if they be such), this is one, and while it seems to be a great responsibility upon you, I'm sure you are equal to it.

(Q) Sunday morning, 9/12/26. Dream regarding [341] and telling him that 117 of the people he would meet at school were subjects of his in the Egyptian period, and that he was in a position now to serve them.

(A) In this it is seen that the time, as known to man, is rolled back, as it were, and there is the vision of those who were in their various places—some of menial, some of exalted. And now they come together again in this change, when he who was their lord and master, as it were, in the earthly sense, joins their number. The supplication that is given to that lord and master is to show, through service and contact, that the lordly position is only a trust, that the service to the great Master may be the better shown in this physical plane. The entity will, little by little, then, single, as it were, these out. Many being the professors and the teachers in the various ways. Many in the everyday associates. Some will be drawn close to—others drawn, as it were, as antagonists to each other: These are to be drawn again into certain conditions as arose during those periods under which their connections arose in that period. Yet the entity should show self as master of the situation, and as worthy of the position as will be accorded through same . . . [294-81]

Well, Uncle Tom [Thomas B. House Sr., the husband of Carrie Salter, Gertrude's aunt] went back to Kentucky this morning. He found after he got his papers that there wasn't a chance for him to qualify in the State before the 7th to the 10th of December, and in getting up his reports to present to the Board, both the Medical Board and the State Educational Board, he felt it would be a great deal better to talk to the people in person than it would be to try to write letters about it. Then, of course, with Aunt Carrie and Thomas in Kentucky, he had rather spend his next four or five months with them than here—but I assure you it makes things lonesome and quiet around. I have to play solitaire now instead of Guardsmen. Mother said, though, tell you that she and Miss Gladys ventured out last night and went to the Roland Theatre—that she didn't bump into any cars, and hadn't broken the car up as yet.

We're anxious, of course, to know your impressions of the school, the class of people you are associated with, and the town in general. I didn't before looking it up to-day know that it was as small a town as it is.

You will be able to see about how I'm getting along physically.

Everything is mighty quiet at the Beach. I haven't seen any of them at the office as yet. We haven't gotten the papers about the property as yet. I'm sure we will though in the next day or so. I'll see Van Patten then if I don't before.

Well, let us hear from you. With best love from all,

Dad

Hugh Lynn responded with his first letter home from college:

W&L

September 21, 1926
Tuesday—Late Afternoon

Dear Dad,

Well it is almost time for dinner and I don't know whether or not I will have time to finish this now.

I believe I am fortunate in still being able to say that everything is going along O.K.

The reading on the dream of yours was more than interesting and you know that I am always interested in any unusual readings. I surely believe that the dream is going to work out just as stated. It does seem rather much of a job for me and one that you may be sure I am finding interesting, though hard. To some people's way of thinking I have not gotten in with the right crowd. Perhaps not but I believe so. They are not, I know, the most popular men on the campus, but some of them are extremely interesting and some are so helpless in some ways. Some time when there is time I shall write you in detail concerning some of them ...

I find that most of the jobs are well filled and nothing is open right now. I am going to be on the look out for something. After the first few days of checks, checks, checks I find that expenses run just as you make them! I find that there are several mistakes that I made in buying clothes, but one learns by experience. My hat and cap are of no use, my shirts need to grow collars, my ties louder, etc. These things though are of little matter when there are so many nicer things to think of.

We have our first football game here Sat and I believe it is to be a good one. The football team is in good shape and bids fair to play some good games.

I am finding all of my courses more interesting each time. Different perhaps from high school but more interesting in many respects.

Have just come back from several sets of tennis, I have been playing every afternoon for the past week.

Well I see that six thirty has rolled around and the mere sound of the word eating sounds good to me. Will—pause—to be continued—

7:15 P.M.

Well dinner is over, the room is more or less full of fellows talking and singing. At seven thirty we all settle down to study. It is rather hard to stick to a program but it can be done.

Sure glad to hear that you are feeling better and hope you continue to.

Write and tell me all the news you know, I am anxious to hear of happenings at home.

With love,
Hugh Lynn

*　*　*

Edgar Cayce's relationship with his mother, Carrie Elizabeth Major Cayce, was one of the great stabilizing relationships of his entire life. Not only did she give him unconditional love, but the manner in which she treated his extraordinary abilities from his earliest childhood gave him confidence in himself and his unusual gift.

She, in turn, had complete confidence in her "boy." She helped him understand that he and his gift were one, that he was a child of God exercising the power of God. Because of her, he understood from the beginning that his gift was not his but lent to him by God and that he was not acting for himself when he exercised his powers but acting on behalf of God. Without this spiritual anchor, it would have been very easy to have been lost in self, turning his talent back to rend him. His mother's constant admonition that he should seek God's will gave him the compass that was to guide him through adolescence until he could "take the wheel" himself. He was to return to her absolute confidence in him as a source of strength when he had to accept reincarnation as an aspect of his public work, beginning in Dayton in 1925.

Edgar Cayce's letters to his mother reveal the great love he had

for her and the closeness they enjoyed. Sarah and Ola were his
two sisters. Ola and her husband Jerry had just had their first child:

September 30, 1926

Dear Mother:

Just a little note to let you hear from me, and to enclose
you a few snap shots that perhaps you may find interesting. They were some views taken on the day that we made
the trip that I told you about in my last letter. You will see
what each one is marked on the back of the picture, so it
will give you some idea of what the places looked like, and
I am sure some of these days you will enjoy visiting these
places personally, for sure we'll take you to see them when
you come over to see us.

Well, how are you feeling to-day? I am sure that you
miss Sarah and Ola, and especially the baby, since they
have come and gone. I know you was glad to see them and
to have them with you for a while anyway. I certainly
would like to see that baby. Who does she look like? Is Ola
as crazy about it as one would expect her to be? How does
Jerry take on over it? Tell me all about it.

Nothing specially new here. The only thing, I guess, is
that Dave was kind enough to send us some pieces for our
dining room. They are very pretty, and we appreciate them
very, very much. When we get the chairs to the suite it will
certainly look very nice. It's the walnut veneer, square
table—gate leg table I believe it's called, buffet, china
closet and serving table. We expect Dave down possibly
Sunday. It's a sample suite you know that they had on the
floor there in his show room, but is very nice—only one or
two scratches on it coming down.

We hear from Hugh Lynn pretty regularly. He seems to
be getting along very well, though you know he's one of
the kind that tries to make the best of the situations as he
finds them. I know that it's not any too pleasant, for he is
barely having just enough to get by with. I am in hopes we
will be able to keep him here, for if he desires an education, I know we ought to try to see that he has the opportunity to get it ...

I haven't been very well, but I'm glad to say I'm feeling a whole lot better. I'm afraid I'm getting lazy—not having enough to do. Too much mental work and not enough of physical exercise. I know you would like, though, to see the place around here. I have a few chickens now, and a little gardening space, so I putter around with them once in a while. We have some mighty nice turnip greens and turnips coming on—mustard and spinach. Of course our chickens are all young ones and haven't gotten big enough to commence laying yet. I'm in hopes we'll have some eggs this Fall and winter—have a very nice place for the chickens, though not a very large run. I hope they'll do good.

It's rather lonesome after having so much company during the summer. Only the four of us here, but it's very nice, and we keep awfully busy with our work. In fact I'm so far behind that it's very hard to keep up with a lot of them we'd like to do when serious cases come up, but we are having requests from people all over the country. We are honestly surprised at some of the requests that we have from different parts of the country.

No new developments with any of our prospective propositions, either in the wells or from the individuals. Everything running along about the same. Still hoping for something to happen that will make things easier in a financial way.

Give my love to Sister and to Pa, and bushels and bushels of love for yourself.

Your Boy,
Edgar

*   *   *

Not being able to provide Hugh Lynn with money above and beyond the bare necessities during Hugh Lynn's college days was always painful to Edgar Cayce. It was a part of the price he paid for dedicating his life to his gift, and he was aware that his family also paid a price, each in their own way. Gertrude sent Hugh Lynn homemade baked goods as often as the budget

would allow. While both Edgar and Gertrude were very grateful
that their son was in college at all, it is nevertheless easy to see
that they would have provided more if they had had it to give.
Edgar was very conscious of what it was like to be unable to afford the "social side of life":

October 12, 1926

Dear Hugh Lynn:
   Was certainly very much pleased to have yours of recent date. I certainly hope that you do get along alright. I
certainly hope that your being unable to spend money as
freely as some others doesn't work too much of a hardship on you. I felt that possibly that was one of the reasons
that you hadn't joined one of the fraternities. I wanted to
be sure, of course, and that's why I asked you about it. Possibly it will be just as well in the Spring term, if you can. I
know you want to look after the social side of life as well
as the rest, but not to the exclusion of all of the rest—but
you don't want to be known, of course, as a "cheap skate ... "
Well, I hope you don't find that lingua de Espanol gives
you too much trouble. I'm sure it requires a great deal of
your time and attention. Possibly though this keeps you
thinking of things that prevents you from thinking of others that would not be as edifying as this. Keep well balanced! That's the main thing—you'll make it alright.
   Well, I think the Generals [the W&L football team] gave
a pretty good account of themselves with Princeton the
other day, did they not?
   Well, I hope you like your job! And that it works into
something that will be worth while ...
   Well, we sure do miss you, and want to see you—but we
hope things are going alright for you. We'll do the very best
we can, and we hope you'll do just the same.
   Let us hear from you whenever you have the opportunity. I want to get this off. I believe Mother is mailing a
little box this evening. You know we are interested in everything that you are, and the little details or little
troubles or worries that you have are ours, and we like
for you to tell us about them whenever you want to. I

know that is one thing that has made me love you so much—that we could always sit down and talk to each other about anything and everything that ever came up in our lives.

With very best love,
Dad

* * *

As the year was approaching its end, Edgar still struggled with David Kahn's difficulties with the Blumenthal brothers and with a new concern—his beloved mother's declining health:

October 19, 1926

Dear Dave:

I have yours of the 14th, regarding the reading for Mrs. Klee's son. We will get this just as soon as it is possible. Just what day, I can't say, as we are so far dated up and often times its mighty hard to break in and not disrupt the whole works . . .

What in the world has become of you, anyway? Here you have had us looking for you every Friday or Saturday for three or four weeks! . . .

Hugh Lynn, I believe I told you, is away at school. Morton was down to see us a week ago last Sunday. We were looking for you the same day . . . We have our campaign for our institution going. Its another thing I've been hoping I'd have a chance to talk over with you. You have had some pretty good ideas and theories as to how to conduct a mail order campaign, and I am sure you would have some worth while ideas concerning this. When are you coming down???

Very bad news from home. Mother is not getting along well at all. We have been very, very uneasy for her for several days. I just wish that I could go over and see her. I'm afraid I never will again.

Give my love to your mother and the rest of the folks. Let us hear from you whenever you have the opportunity, and again thanking you, and with kindest personal regards,

Sincerely,
Edgar Cayce

EC:GD

The death of his mother on October 25, 1926, in Hopkinsville, Kentucky, greatly affected Edgar Cayce. He would speak of the loss of his mother throughout the rest of his life and later would write of experiences with her "from the other side" that were a source of great personal comfort. The *Kentucky New Era,* Cayce's hometown newspaper, published the following obituary:

PEACEFULLY
PASSED AWAY
Death Last Night Of
Mrs. Leslie B. Cayce—
Funeral Will Be
Wednesday.
October 26, 1926

Mrs. Leslie B. Cayce peacefully passed to her heavenly reward at 12:15 o'clock last night at her home in the Pennyroyal apartments, after three years illness.

She was born in this country on June 23, 1855. Her maiden name was Carrie Major. On June 10, 1874 she was married to Mr. Leslie B. Cayce. She is survived by her husband and the following daughters and one son: Miss Annie Cayce, of this city: Edgar Cayce, of Virginia Beach; Mrs. J.J. Crume, DeLand, Fla.; Mrs. W.A. McPherson, Nashville, Tenn.; Mrs. L.J. Hesson, Chicago, Ill. Her children

were all with her when the end
came, with the exception of Mrs.
Crume, who had been to visit her
mother about a month ago. Mrs.
Cayce also leaves six grand children.

Mrs. Cayce was a woman whose
good deeds and noble character
made her a favorite in a large circle.
A Consecreated woman, universally
loved by her church members,
her neighbors and devotedly cared
for in her three long years of illness
by her family.

A wide circle of friends deeply
sympathize with the husband and
children in the loss of a splendid
wife and mother.

She was a member of the Church of
Christ of West Seventh Street.
Funeral services will be held Wednesday
afternoon at 2:30, conduct-
ed by the Rev. Horace Kingsbury,
of this city, and Rev. Petty Ezell,
of Nashville, Tennessee.

After services from the West Seventh Street
Church of Christ, the remains will
be laid to rest in the Riverside Cemetery.
The pall bearers will be Parker
Clardy, Hugh Major, Arthur Bowles,
John Metcalfe, Granville and Kenneth Cayce.

Once he returned home, Edgar responded to a letter from Tim
Brown, in moving words:

November 5, 1926

Dear Tim:

Yours of the 26th just reached me to-day, being forwarded to me from Hopkinsville, it having been sent to my Uncle of the same name. Hence the delay. I want to thank you very much for same. We all appreciate our friends more than ever at this time, and often feel like that but for such friends it would be hard to go on. With all of our conception of Life, and with all our understanding, it's hard to give up Mother. And to know that the voice that we loved is stilled in death. It makes us all cry out, "After death, what?" And while from our understanding we know only a transition, and only the body that passes, yet we have come to so love those bodies that give us existence until we even doubt our own selves. We know that she lives and has access to the larger life, being One with that power, that force that gives life, yet it is hard for these little minds of ours to gain that conception of this oneness of our heavenly Father to that extent that it will bring the comfort, the solace, the peace, that we desire. But, had I no other reason, almost the last words of my mother would be sufficient to make me determine to do and give the best of my life for others in the work I am trying to do. In this I find some comfort, yet the experience has been so appalling, I find it hard, hard indeed, to make this old body go to work. I want to dwell on those words, I want to dwell on the messages that she gave me as almost from the other side—but its up to each and everyone of us to make the most of what we have in hand to-day, and do with our might what we find to do, using whatever talents we have been given or have developed in the earth plane to magnify Him, to make His laws, His goodness, our God, known in the world.

Tim, I want to thank you for your kind offer, and if it is not asking too much, I would appreciate it if you will help me a little at this time. Of course, we are never prepared for such emergencies, and running continually at a very, very low margin, I find myself particularly embarrassed at the present time. I'd certainly appreciate it.

On my way back to Virginia Sunday, I stopped at Staunton and Hugh Lynn came over from Lexington and met me there. We had several very pleasant hours together. He certainly has appreciated the letters you have written him from time to time. He seems to be working hard, yet doing well under the strain. I certainly appreciate your writing to him occasionally.

I found them all pretty well on my return. I haven't been able to take up my work as yet. I just can't get myself together. I'm in hopes though that I'll be able to start in again the first of the week, for we have many urgent requests on hand. I haven't been even able to get my mind to-gether enough to go into the mail—until yesterday, and I find I have stacks of it on hand.

Let me hear from you whenever you have the opportunity. Let me know about Walter's father.

I see the earthquake came in California [see reading 195-32] almost on schedule, but I believe no particular damage was done. I'm glad of that. The wave in Japan seemed to have done the greater damage.

Again thanking you, and assuring you of my appreciation of your letter and your friendship, and with kindest personal regards from all,

Sincerely,
Edgar Cayce

EC:GD

November 6, 1926

Dear Dave:

. . . I know only one who has experienced such can understand what it is to have their mother to leave them, even if it is to go to Heaven. We feel so little, so weak, so helpless, in the face of death. Perhaps I, of all people, should be able to understand and grasp something of the larger meaning, yet I know that nothing in all my life has been so hard to meet—nothing that has been so hard to understand, and so hard to try and force myself to go on and meet the present day affairs. Being the only boy, and being with my mother the few days before she passed away, and seeing so much of information that has been obtained from unseen sources manifested, exemplified, experienced, perhaps has been just a little too much. I don't seem to be able to pull myself to-gether and to meet the every day conditions. We all know we must go on. He would have it no other way, she would have it no other way, yet *how* seems to be the great question ...

I find my desk piled up with correspondence, which so far I have been unable to even force myself to touch—but tell your mother I will write her as soon as I can ...

Again, thanking you, and with kindest personal regards,

Sincerely,

Edgar Cayce

EC:GD

* * *

Requests for readings for friends and readings to accommodate friends continued to present challenges for Edgar. Always having to balance between the preservation of the all-important personal relationships in his life and the need for the "decency and order" (254-60) that were the avenue through which an organization would come into being, he was, perhaps, unaware of the stress under which this placed him.

November 23, 1926

Dear Dave:

We were very much disappointed Saturday when we didn't see nor hear anything from you, after having yours of the 16th—but I'm sure some circumstance arose that prevented you from making the trip at this time.

Yes, I find it very hard to get settled back to regular routine work Dave. I realize that hard work and time are the greatest panaceas for such conditions, yet I believe being able to get out, meet people, go places, do something that physically tires me—rather than thinking, thinking, thinking—would be better, for as I told you before, I find myself dwelling too much on the last few days, and especially the last few hours spent with my Mother.

I want to thank you, Dave, for the check from Mr. Hawkins. We haven't taken the reading, for the simple reason we haven't known just where we would find him. We made an appointment for him, sent him our regular appointment card, and just to be matter of fact—if he can't do it *our* way, we can't do it at *all!* I don't like his attitude. But we shall be very glad to be of help if possible, if he'll come down and be just as reasonable as you infer that he expects us to be.

We also received the letter requesting the reading for Mrs. Lauterstein, and I certainly appreciate your interest, and we trust that we may be of help. We wrote her, making the appointment for the first possible time we had available. You know we can't give a reading every few minutes, or hours—for continuing at the work day after day, our experience has taught us that we must have some regularity, some system, and ask others to conform to that if they desire the work. We have of course, many requests on hand. Being away made them pile up, as well as forced us to defer appointments already made. Necessarily, these had to be taken care of before we could make new ones, and I don't think its anything but just and right to take care of them as we receive them. Certainly there may be exceptions. We make these whenever we are aware that the circumstance justifies us in doing so . . .

With kindest personal regards,

Sincerely,
Edgar Cayce

EC:GD

*   *   *

In the following letter to his cousin, Fannie Cayce, Edgar revealed his mother's last words and the details of her final hours. We also get a picture of the Cayce home as it was in 1926 and how Virginia Beach itself was changing:

December 8, 1926

Dear Cousin Fannie:

Yours of October 24th was on my desk when I returned from the saddest mission of my life. My Mother passed away on the 26th of October. I was with her several days before the end came, and while we knew that it must be, yet we were not prepared for the actual happening. I have found it very hard indeed to take up life in the same way since. I found it very hard even to keep up with my correspondence, or to even let those know whom I feel would sympathize with me under such conditions—of my great loss. Mother had been a great sufferer for a number of years, and in very bad health for the last three years particularly—but, as she said to me a few hours before she passed away, "Son, you have kept your Mother alive for three years. You can do no more, but you must use the gift God has given you to help others." I know that she was one of the most wonderful Mothers that ever lived, and she lived the most beautiful Christian life, and I know that she has gone to her reward. I know to be absent from the body is to be present with the Lord, yet it is hard indeed for us at all times to see this side and to fully realize the consciousness of anything except the great loss that we sustain in her going. While I had not been with Mother for a number of years, still being the only boy I was always very close to my Mother in heart and mind. There are five of us, as you possibly know, and we live in as many different states. One in Chicago, one in Nashville, Tenn., one in DeLand, Florida, and one in Hopkinsville, Kentucky, I in Virginia. All are married except the oldest girl who is with Father in Kentucky. To she and to my Father perhaps comes the greater loss, for they had been constantly with [mother] for a number of years, and it makes them feel it keener that her presence is missed so much in the home ...

I don't know, cousin Fannie, whether you ever visited this part of the country or not. We are within a day's journey of some of the most historic places in America, those covering the period from the first settlement at Jamestown to the present day activities of our commercial

America. Norfolk and Newport News being, as you know, one of the most, if not *the* most, important seaports in the U.S.A. The little town of Virginia Beach is just starting, and although we are close to all of this commercial world, it is very much a place of recreation, rest and will be one of the chief of the health resorts in this country and perhaps in the world. It has long been known that the sands of this Beach are the most health giving of any perhaps, save those of Abba-Baden. It was only just a few years ago though that the resources of this peninsula have been exploited, but I believe that within the next five or ten years there will be a resort here perhaps second to none; at least equal to or greater than Atlantic City, for the resources are so much greater in many respects than Atlantic City, though Atlantic City's closeness to the greater centers will always make it a desirable place.

Our little home here is not so imposing, but a very comfortable place. It is built so that I have my office and work room in the home—the office and work room being on the lower floor, but so situated that it is accessible either from the front or side entrance. A large living room in the front, with a nice wide porch all screened in. Dining room back of living room, kitchen and pantry back of that. Nice hall through the center—wash room on the lower floor, with four bedrooms and bath on the second floor. My secretary has rooms with us, which makes it very nice for our work. I am only able, as you know, to give two readings each day, which requires about forty-five or fifty minutes each. The rest of the time I have for recreation, or the handling of the correspondence, which in the last few months has been very heavy—but I usually piddle about the place—I don't keep a hired man, but attend to the furnace myself— have a little garden, a few chickens, and am preparing for a lot of flowers, I *hope*. We had some very pretty ones last year, and I am hoping for a lot more the coming spring and summer. Altogether, I think we have a very pretty little place. I don't drive the car or the flivver myself—my wife does. I am just hoping that you all will find the opportunity to get this way sometime in the near future. We would certainly enjoy having you very much, and I am sure all of you would enjoy the historic points and the beauties of the surroundings. We have a very large hotel [the Cavalier] that will be open here in the spring—of course there are dozens of smaller ones at the Beach. There is a great deal of improvement going on. Most of our streets will be paved by the early spring, and we will have two or three paved roads to Norfolk, which is eighteen miles West. We are little more than a stone's throw from the ocean front. Personally, having always lived inland, I like it very much better than the ocean front. There will be about five miles of concrete walkway built along the front this spring. This will give a nice promenade for visitors, as well as a place for the rolling chair. Altogether, I think we have a nice place, nice surroundings, and I am in hopes by the early spring we will be able to begin the operations for the opening of the institute, which has so long been my dream—to be better able to serve suffering humanity. I want to send you a picture of the plans as soon as they are all laid out. We have some beautiful grounds selected, or that have been contributed to the building of the institute, and I believe we will be able to do a great work for humanity.

We are not musicians much in our family, though we have quite a nice radio, and I certainly enjoy the programs we are able to get most every evening. Of course [we] get everything from Boston to Chicago, and as far west as Denver—Dallas, Little Rock, New Orleans—Memphis, Birmingham, Atlanta, and somewhere we can get a good program most every evening.

I'm always mighty glad to hear from you, cousin Fannie, and I'm in hopes that you will let me hear from you whenever you find the opportunity. Please remember me to Earle and Lillian, and with love and kindest personal regards,

Your cousin,
Edgar

EC:GD

* * *

Edgar Cayce shared details of day-to-day events with Hugh Lynn at Washington and Lee. In this letter, we can see some of the difficulties he faced in dealing with requests for readings. Having to honor the appointments already promised others when confronted with a request from a friend as a favor placed him under considerable strain. In addition, there always were the ever-present financial issues, and Edgar's supporters also were frequently thinking up new ventures into which to draw his psychic abilities:

December 14, 1926

Dear Hugh Lynn:

Sugar, I don't mean to bother you with the little things that come up, but I think it's well that we all understand how things come about—that's why I told you about what might be the outcome of things at Hopkinsville . . .

Morton sent me one hundred yesterday. I don't think Morton means to make it hard, though Mother is very much of the opinion, I think, that Morton got "miffed" at what I said about a letter I wrote, and is taking this manner of showing me that he's going to run it or not play at all. While I don't feel that way—Mother may be right. Anyway, it makes it rather hard for a *holiday* season. But we'll manage along some way until this well comes in. Mr. Wyrick has gone to Texas. Things are progressing, and *might* come off before Christmas, if the reading can be relied upon.

Had a wire from the people in Florida wanting us to come down right away. I haven't answered it but will by letter. Of course we couldn't do such a thing right now. They claim they didn't locate the treasure they were looking for. I also had another letter from a man in Florida, wanting me to come *right away*. He proposed to pay all expenses—wanted me to locate some oil. He gave me rather a full outlook of the oil situation. It looks good to me, though you can very well imagine what Mama and Mother had to say when the fellow enclosed a copy of a letter that he wrote to A.D. Noe [a Hopkinsville hotelier] insisting that Noe get in communication with me at once

and bring me to Florida with him. I haven't heard from Noe as yet—possibly won't. But it makes the outlook for the oil in Florida look good. This man claims one well a day or two ago blew the crown block off the top of the rig.

[**Editors' Note**: Edgar Cayce kept in contact with countless people throughout his lifetime, and often those who had been with him from the very earliest days of his career would find that the bonds of friendship held them to him over the years, from one venture to another. This was the case with Frank E. Mohr of Columbus, Ohio, who had conducted some of the earliest readings, who traveled with Edgar at times, and who knew many people who had used Edgar's gift to find lost objects, oil, and treasure. A businessman with many interests, Mohr moved from Columbus to Miami, Florida, in 1926 to set up a real estate business. There, he became acquainted with Thomas J. Peters Sr., a Miami businessman. Mohr's brother-in-law, Willard A. Wilson, who had been in the coal business in West Virginia, also had moved to Miami and had the major financial interest among the group in commercial development of Bimini Island.

Peters' Miami partner in his real estate rental and investment business was A.C. Preston. Because of Mohr's interest in Edgar Cayce, Preston wrote Edgar, asking him to come to Florida to give readings on the development of Bimini and on oil and treasure locations in Monroe and Dade Counties. Edgar, Gertrude, and Gladys arrived in Miami on Feb. 2, where they stayed at the Halcyon Hotel as Preston's guests. While there, they visited with the Shroyers, who had moved to the area, and Edgar gave more than thirty readings during the twenty-nine-day visit, including readings on health, dreams, oil, lost treasure, and the Bimini project. Unfortunately, seventeen of the Monroe County treasure readings (series 1274) are missing from the archives. The Cayces and Gladys returned to Virginia Beach on March 4.]

Well, Dave spent Sunday and Monday with us. The usual hubbub of things when he comes around—though I think Dave is settling a whole lot, but he had a good deal of talk. He brought a man by—another member of the N.Y. Stock Exchange, who has a sister living in Norfolk—a Mr.

Marquess or something like that. He wanted a reading, but didn't get it. I felt like it was best to just let them know they couldn't run in and get anything they wanted and put somebody else off, when we have had a body like Tim waiting now for about four weeks for a reading. I talked to [Marquess] and his sister for about an hour or so, and they saw a reading on Morton's wife. He seemed to be really impressed—said he'd get in touch with Morton as soon as he got to New York, and that I would hear from him again. Anyway, there has been at least three people in Norfolk that have tried to make appointments since. Somebody called last night and two were here to-day—but, as we told them, we already had more than we could do and would take them on as soon as we could.

Dave promised to send the chairs. He will—but *when*?

I think Eckin is getting along nicely now [after a burn accident], and I'm in hopes he'll be able to walk alright by Christmas. He's missing it though not being able to get in and see any of the things in the stores. Mama [Elizabeth E. Evans, Gertrude's mother] and Mother went to-day. I'm afraid they had a bad day of it, but from the reports in the papers it looks like its about the best one we're going to have for some time. When will you get home? Saturday or Sunday, or will it be the first of next week? You want anything extra or make it up while you are here? We'll spread out what little we got as best we can, and make the best possible of it.

Let us hear from you.

With love from all,
Dad

He also wrote about the Florida proposals to his father, L.B. Cayce:

December 21, 1926

Dear Pa:

Just a little note to let you hear from us. I'm certainly glad to know that you are feeling some little better, and I feel very sure that with the treatments you will continue to do so. I am having to take some treatments myself—the man I think snatched me around most too severe yesterday, and I'm so stiff in my neck and back this morning I can hardly move. But I hope I'll be better when the reaction sets in or by the time he gives me another one or two ...

Edgar Evans is some little better I think, but is not going to be able to be on his feet, even by Christmas, which will make it mighty hard for him—as well as everyone else in the household.

I had a letter from Sister yesterday, and also one from Sarah, I sent a package home—hope that you will get it all fixed so Sister can take it out to the cemetery. It makes me feel mighty bad to think that you and Sister will be there alone—I know how it will make you both feel. I wish it was so that you could be with some of us, or some of us could be with you all—but we can't just at this time, and we will have to make the best of things.

No special news from Blumenthal or Wyrick. The people in Florida want me to come down right away—but I don't know yet what to do—whether it would mean anything more than just the trip or not, I don't know. I suppose it would depend on my ability to make these people understand what I want, and then to get it. Of course it would mean practically moving the office, for whatever period that I stayed there. Whether this would be a wise thing or not, I don't know. Of course, I couldn't go until Edgar Evans is able to get out and around—then he should be in school, for to remain out another month possibly might prevent his making his grade—and that wouldn't be good at all. So what is the best thing to do, I don't know. What would you suggest ...

Let me hear from you whenever you have the opportunity. Wishing you a Merry Christmas, and may the peace that passeth all understanding abide with you.

Your Boy

*   *   *

One of the major components of Edgar Cayce's vision of the Work was the opening of a hospital, where people could get treatments for their health problems, based on their readings.

Planning for the hospital included a chief of staff with qualifications that would satisfy the Virginia accreditation requirements and pave the way for acceptance within the community. Although Dr. Thomas B. House of Hopkinsville was later selected by the readings (254-35) to fill the chief of staff position, this letter shows the attention to detail that Morton Blumenthal brought to every phase of the project:

December 29, 1926

Mr. Van Patten
Virginia Beach,
Virginia

Dear Mr. Van Patten:
    We have secured the services of Dr. Joseph L. Rothfeder of New York City, who is willing to take charge of our proposed hospital in Virginia Beach and is willing to work with us and with any Norfolk physician who cares to go on the Staff. For the time being Dr. Rothfeder will take charge and run the hospital as an open Institution permitting any Doctor who chooses to bring his patients there. It is possible that Dr. Rothfeder will have Dr. Rubin, a dentist, accompany him to Virginia Beach. Not only will this be beneficial to those who seek the benefits of the Hospital but I believe both of these gentlemen will do credit and be of benefit to the community. Both gentlemen of course, will need some place of residence but the essential thing I am writing to you about now is the renting of a twelve to fifteen room house to be used as a Hospital, which we will equip in proper fashion and which it is possible will need some alteration as regards additional baths. I would appreciate your sending me the plan of a house or houses that you believe would be available and proper for this use, the rental of which, of course, to be as small as possible. I would very much appreciate your help in this matter and I know you will do all in your power to secure for us the lowest possible rental required by an Institution of this character. I am sure a Hospital will mean very much for the community and also much benefit to the sick.

The reason I want the plan is that we are getting in touch with the American Medical Association, with one of the heads of which Dr. Rothfeder is a very close friend and the Doctor would like to take up with him the best method of planning the house for hospital use. The Doctor and I will then come down to see you in order that we may get together on this matter and start definite operation. I feel sure it will only be a matter of a short time after we have started in this small way that we can bring men down who will endow the Virginia Beach Hospital, such that we may build a large and creditable Institution.

Thanking you kindly for your cooperation and with kindest personal regards, I tender you the Season's Greetings.

Yours very sincerely,
Morton H. Blumenthal

*   *   *

1927

Even as plans for the hospital progressed, Edgar was still saddened by the loss of his mother, and he shared his feelings with his old friend from the First Christian Church in Selma, Alf Butler:

January 14, 1927

Mr. Alfred D. Butler
Box 2363
West Palm Beach, Florida

Dear A.D.—

Hadn't expected to be quite so long in replying to yours of the 28th, but I seem to have gotten started off on the wrong foot this year, for the first ten days of the year found me about as sick a bird as you ever saw. Don't think I missed pneumonia very far, but I'm glad to say that I'm feeling alright again, and we are all on the improve ...

I have had some very sad experiences since I last wrote you. My mother passed away on the 26th of October. While we knew that the end was near—of course we are never prepared or willing to give up our loved ones. I was able to be with her a few days before the end came—was very thankful and very glad this was possible. Her last message to me I feel would be a great incentive to anyone, to say nothing of the reports that we get almost daily from people in some parts of the country. She told me the morning before she died, "Son, your mother is going to die. You have done all that you could—you have kept her alive for three years, but you can do no more—but you must always use the gift God has given you to help others, even as you have helped your mother." It seems mighty bad that we are all so far separated, as to be of very little comfort or help to each other. One of the girls, as you know, has never married. She it was that was with Mother and Pa, and Pa is still remaining with her. Another one in Chicago, one in Nashville, and one in DeLand, Florida, and I here. All were home at the time except the one in Florida. I'm sure you remember Mother. She visited me, I think, two or three times while I lived in Selma. Of course, to all of us our mothers are the most wonderful women in the world, and I'm sure it is justly so. My mother seemed to me to be an exception, even, to that rule—and while I know that she is in heaven, still we have all felt a great loss and an emptyness that is hard to fill. Following this, on my return home, our little boy, Edgar Evans, had the misfortune to get very badly burned. Standing in front of the fire his night clothes caught, and the left leg on the back side, from ankle to hip, was badly burned. He has gotten along very nicely—no special complications with it, but his leg is badly drawn and he has only in the last few days begun to use it in any way. He is hopping about now or using crutches. I am sure when it has healed entirely that he will gradually gain the full use of the limb, but it has certainly been a very trying ordeal to him, as well as the rest of the family. Perhaps it isn't well, ever, to experiment—but if experiments there must be, I suppose its with our own, rather than others, that such should be. We have never had a physician even to look at the place. Not because I think I am a physician, but the child's aversion to doctors, and his whole soul's confidence in what the readings say—so these we have followed very closely in this condition. I have consulted physicians, to be sure, for I am not solely an unmindful man—but he has gotten along nicely, though it has been tedious, and a very trying condition for all ...

Well, let me hear from you whenever you have the opportunity. All here send kindest personal regards to you and yours.

Ever the same,
Edgar

*   *   *

As the new year progressed, Edgar's friends still urged him to make the Florida trip, as he explained to Hugh Lynn:

January 20, 1927

Dear Hugh Lynn:

Just a little note to let you hear from us, though I have nothing new or exciting to write about, and I'm sure you are too busy to be bothered much with long letters—but I presume you like to know that we think of you once in a while, and are hoping that you get along alright, and you'll make the grade with your examinations and won't have trouble with same.

As yet, I haven't heard anything from Morton—consequently I haven't been able to send you that little slip [money], nor able to attend to a lot of other things around here that I'd like—but it'll all come along in good time, I am sure, and I hope everything will work out alright.

I'm mighty glad to say I'm feeling a whole lot better than I have been for a good long while, physically. The weather has turned off warm and real pretty, and of course I commenced piddling around and digging around outside. I don't know what I'd have the back yard looking like if they'd give me enough time. I hope it won't look too much like a mare's nest. The chickens are doing pretty well, though several of them look like they've got the 'pip' or something worse, I don't know what. I guess it'll be the survival of the fittest—perhaps I just have too many in such a small place—its kinder like our flowers were last summer—some of them naturally choked the rest of them to death . . .

Morton wrote us a very nice letter about his idea of the reading we had on the Florida proposition. He thinks its the right thing to go—the only thing he seems fearful of is that our stay might be prolonged.

Dave has gotten two or three more people interested, so he says. One of them we are to take a reading on pretty soon—I don't know, he may be like the doctor. We haven't heard anything more from him since the reading we had on him. As they express it in Texas, I guess he's "blowed up."

Mother says tell you that she's baking a cake, so you may be on the look-out for it in the next day or two—in fact. I think she's going to try to get it off so it'll go out this evening or to-morrow.

Eckin is getting along pretty well, I think. Still has trouble with getting his leg to go off every time he starts to use it, and makes him limp right badly at times. I guess that'll work out alright though after a while.

Miss Gladys had a right bad cold—lot of trouble with her throat and tonsils. Had her hair all curled up—I don't know whether that curled up the tonsils or not, but she got a permanent a few days ago. We all went to the show the day she was in town—pretty good show—went to Keith's. Saw the Egyptian—he's certainly a wonder. The picture was Milton Stills in "Unspoken Love" I believe, or some such name—desert picture. I got my suit—I like it alright, except the vest, they never did get that to suit me, but I think I'll have them to fix it over when I get the opportunity—either make it to fit or make a new one. They left long points on it that I don't like at all. The coat and trousers, though, look pretty good—*I* think, at least, and its a little bit different from anything I've had in a long time.

I know you are busy, but let us hear whenever you have time. Take care of yourself. Love from all,

Dad

EC:GD

P.S. You should see my curls, Hugh Lynn! I'm crazy about them! "Muddie" has an appointment to get her permanent next Wednesday. G.D.

Wednesday Night,
March 9, 1927

Dear Hugh Lynn:

Well, I have wished quite often that I could talk over with you the circumstances and conditions as surrounded our stay in Florida—but as I can't talk to you I suppose the next best thing is to try and write you ... So, we have had a good trip! It was a wonderful experience for us all. It got us out of the rut. It made us see things differently. Its one thing to have a little theory that you wind around and around, and around and around, and wonder what it would be if it had a chance. And another thing to go out among people and find that there are many, many, seeking to have some theory of the vision they have seen explained to them. Its one thing to have received information concerning places and conditions, and another thing to hear those who have made such things a study for a lifetime and tell of their experiences, of conditions that exist and have existed in these places the information has been given about, and we awake to the realization that although our world is centered around a little room and a little lot, fifty by a hundred and twenty, yet our *real* world is thinking, studying, wondering, about the same things that we are gaining information concerning each and every day. Its not that it makes one feel self-satisfied—not that it makes one feel he should be puffed up. Rather that deep longing to be able to *disseminate* the real truths that have been gained in such a way and manner that many more may be benefited by them. Again, when we see the successes of those who have striven in various ways to accumulate this world's goods—then, when we are close enough to these to see how their inner lives, how their very souls, are affected by this worldly success—again we have the lesson that will prove helpful and beneficial, by having passed through the experience of contacting such conditions in their many various phases . . .

It was good to renew old acquaintances and friendships, and good to make new ones. It was fine to be with Mr. Shroyer and Mrs. Shroyer again. They seem to be getting along nicely, doing well, and I find his interests just as keen as ever—and, as he expressed it, he finds each and every day that he is finding the opportunity to apply the lessons of yester year in the conditions of to-day. I was glad to meet Alf and his wife. It seemed funny to see Alf with a wife—but again we see that deep seated confidence, hope, trust, and the manifestations of the lessons as gained in our work to-gether—though a failure as it might have seemed at the time—but so deep seated, the condition, that he would be willing to lay aside *everything*, could he but have the opportunity to be associated with the work daily. It was satisfying in a great way to see Laura, her mother and father again, and to have the father say: "I *know* I've got one of the best girls in the world, for she received the right principles and the right training under Edgar Cayce."

Well, we got home Tuesday afternoon. Mama [Gertrude's mother] met us at the boat, and while everything seems rather dull and leaden like—when away from "the land of sunshine"—yet it is good to sit in the corner and muse a while . . .

Brother, your mother says that she will write you just as soon as she can—and you may be sure that there will be a little box along by the time your birthday rolls around. I picked up one or two little things—they don't amount to anything, but thought possibly you might like to know that you were thought of—and oh, how often we did wish that you were present! In fact, I believe we wished for you so often that the whole crowd asked that you come on a visit to see them—they'd like to know what manner of man you are—that once ruled them with such an iron hand! I'm sure they would really and truly love to have you spend a few weeks with them, and I know they'd make it pleasant for you . . .

I was by the bank to-day, and am sending you a little

slip, which indicates that I stopped by on a good purpose. No doubt you will be glad to see it. We *didn't* know where it was coming from, but I found it in the mail this morning. Not much—but I'm in hopes it will enable you to get along for the time being, and make good on the opportunities that you are having in contacting so many minds that are *thinking*.

Write to us when you have the chance. I've got some hard problems to meet—but I believe I'm better prepared to meet them than I have been in a long time. *How*—I don't know.

With best love,
Dad

P.S. Eckin started to school this morning. It's right hard to dump him off into fractions, but he'll come—I believe.

EC:GD

*   *   *

The following tongue-in-cheek exchange between Edgar and Hugh Lynn gives a glimpse of the playful affection which bound the father and son together:

Washington and Lee University

March 15, 1927

Association of National Investigators
Virginia Beach, VA

Dear Association:
I found the results of my last physical reading so beneficial that I am writing you for a check reading. I have heard that you are all now pretty busy, but I am in hopes that you will be able to get this for me as soon as possible.

I have had a little trouble lately, probably resulting from my diet—overeating—as it is essential that I continue to meet classes—and while I am at present in the best of health if the conditions remain I shall not [be] so: For some two weeks now things have been growing worse. It takes a lot to move me—the above in several senses—from the idea that I need a reading to set me once again on the *active* path of life.

You will be able to locate me at my office at 222 Lee's Dormitory, if you think necessary I can be in *any* afternoon. I shall be in said office on Thursday and Friday afternoons from three to five on both of these days.

Again let me impress upon you the fact *if possible*—I am in a hurry.

Now please do not understand that I am dying or anything like that, I am feeling very very good, on this day before the 16th, but I am anxious to know how to handle the conditions that are arising.

On second thought, I shall be in my office, 222 Lee's on Wednesday afternoon also.

Hoping that you will be able to assist me on one of these dates.

I am as ever and always a most devoted member.?

Hugh Lynn Cayce
P.O. Box 145
Lexington, Virginia

P.S. Ask about my eyes also. *Diet and exercise.*

March 22, 1927

Mr. Hugh Lynn Cayce
Box 145
Lexington, Virginia

My Dear Mr. Cayce:

Yours of March the 15th, with a request for a physical reading, was received, and this was taken and sent to you on the eve of my departure on a business trip to New York City. Not having an opportunity to write you at the time, I felt perhaps it would be well to write you and assure you of our appreciation of your interest in the Association, also to assure you of our interest in your welfare. I have found, by experience, such prescriptions as given in your physical reading are at times very *active*, and at times cause some discomforture and nausea. However, usually they prove very effective, and the recuperation from such purging usually brings a fellow round in a pretty good condition. I'm certainly very much in hopes that you have found, by following out the suggestions as given, that you are feeling much better, and I certainly trust you will soon be perfectly well and alright. We shall certainly be pleased to hear from you concerning this, as we are indeed most anxious to serve whenever possible, and are always anxious to have reports from those we try to help.

Feeling, too, that your interest in the Association would lead you to desire to know the progress we are making, and as my recent visit to New York was in the interest of getting the Association work started, I thought possibly you would like to have me tell you about same.

In the first place, I'd like to say, I had a most unusual but quite an agreeable experience last Saturday evening. You know, we have several people in New York who are very deeply interested in our getting the work started, especially in getting the institute established, Mr. Morton H. Blumenthal, a young broker there, a Mr. David E. Kahn, sales manager for The Federal Furniture Company. Both these young men, as you may see from their names, are of Jewish descent, but are excellent young men, and it is quite out of the ordinary to hear Mr. Blumenthal—even in a conversation with brothers of his religion—declare the Christ to be the Son of God and the Savior of the world. But, particularly, what I desired to tell you—about the experience I had Saturday evening—Mr. Blumenthal, Mr. Kahn, and myself, were invited to a dinner dance at the Pennsylvania Hotel—quite a formal affair. We arrived a little late—soup had just been served, but we were met by the president of the club—the occasion being the annual banquet and dinner dance of the Flushing Business Men's Club. Mr. Bosky (a leading attorney of New York), president of the club, conducted me to his table. I was introduced around, and very soon there were gathered around our table *quite a number* of people, wanting to know if this was not Mr. Cayce of whom they had so often heard, and had so long desired to see and know personally. I found that there were in this gathering (of two hundred and fifty or more) some twenty-two or more for whom I had given readings—some as far back as ten or fifteen years ago. Some that had just been given last week, and one or two who now have appointments for readings. All of these claim to have received great benefits, some having been saved from operations, others from various conditions had been helped. It was certainly quite an interesting experience.

As you know, too, there has been some correspondence regarding having a physician there in New York [Dr. Rothfeder]—who is quite prominent in medical circles—to take charge of the institute work here at Virginia Beach. I had the opportunity of meeting this man, and with Mr. Blumenthal, Mr. Kahn, Mr. Marshall, Mr. Bosky, Mr. and Mrs. Lauterstein, Mr. Armstrong and others, talked over the possibility of getting the institute started at once.

It was the consensus of opinion of all that this should be begun at once, and that plans should be made to raise whatever funds that were necessary, and start in to work just as soon as this could be done. There was the discussion of renting a place as temporary quarters, but I believe it was finally decided that money spent for rent could be applied to temporary buildings for the summer that would enable them to get started sooner, and that such money would be landing to the establishing of better facilities than trying to arrange a dwelling in residential section.

So it was decided to have the doctor to communicate with the Board of Health of Virginia at once, which he did at once by wire, and to have plans submitted for the erection of an institute, or buildings of a temporary nature that would lend themselves to the perfecting of the proper way of handling and taking care of such work, just as quick as possible.

Several plans were submitted by Mr. Armstrong (An Englishman, who has been associated with such work with men like Sir Oliver Lodge and Sir Conan Doyle) also others were submitted by members of the American Medical Association, and suggestions were made by some of the professors from Columbia who were present at the meeting—though did not hear all of the discussion.

All in all, it seems very encouraging, and very probable that by the first of July we will have the institute in operation. I'm sure from your interest in the work of the Association, that this will be most gratifying to you. It is understood that I am to take the month of June as a rest. During that time, several of the officers of the Association with the doctors and nurses will be on the ground looking after the erection of these buildings—which will later be turned into summer cottages on the grounds of the Association, while the main building is being erected these will be used as temporary quarters. I think this will work out alright. I'd like to know just what you think about this, and would be glad to have any suggestions that you may have to offer.

I hope you will let us hear from you as regarding your own physical condition, and I hope to write you again soon.

Cordially yours,
ASSOCIATION OF
NATIONAL INVESTIGATORS

It was a happy sign for Edgar of acceptance into the community when he was asked to teach a Sunday school class at the Presbyterian Church. He was eager to share the news with Hugh Lynn, even though his letter ended on a more contemplative note:

April 4, 1927

Dear Hugh Lynn:

Another of those nice dark gloomy days. Possibly it may be the same way in your country—I don't know. If so, I'm sure you'll need something to cheer you up. I don't know whether I can write one of that kind or not. Possibly, if I *am* able to do so, it will do me as much good to write it as it will do you in reading it.

Well, the first thing, I guess, I'll try to tell you the news.

Perhaps your mother has already told you, but of course we are very apt to tell it in different words—and while it may be the same thing maybe it won't sound just alike. Well, I started off teaching the Sunday School Class yesterday morning! Mr. Ramsey, of the Presbyterian Church, you know, has asked me several times to take a class up there. It seems that they have no teachers. So he gave me what is supposed to be the adult Bible class. He has a very small congregation, I think, in the first place. I have never seen more than fifteen or twenty there at any one service. They are to hold a meeting, however, beginning next week. Yesterday we only had four in the class—your mother, Eckin, and a man and his wife, but I think I'll like it. Your mother said that I got along alright. You know its been so long since I have tried to talk of anything of the kind on my feet, I realize I am quite a bit out of practice, but I am in hopes that I will improve. I wonder if people will think it is a peculiar combination—I, a member of another church, engaged in a work that I am, with some ideas expressed by same that are so foreign to the tenets of the Presbyterian Church, teaching a Sunday School Class. I understand Mr. Van Patten is a member of this church, and one of its officers. He, with some other man, I believe, is at present putting on a sub-division near Washington, D.C. I don't know why, but I'm anxious to have Mr. Van Patten in the class one time. No doubt he will be ready to ask me some questions, I *hope* I'll be able to answer . . .

Another funny thing! Yesterday afternoon, Morton called me over the phone. The doctor is supposed to be down here somewhere—Rothfeder, but I haven't seen him. Morton asked me if I had seen him, and what was new—and when I told him I was teaching a Sunday School Class he seemed to be as much pleased as if I had been talking to you or one of my own family. Your mother told me to tell him that I was just fixing up a class for *him* when he comes down this summer. He said, yes indeed, he'd be mighty glad to speak to them! And he thought that was just the finest thing in the world, and he felt sure that all would be benefited by same. Very nice thing to say, and I suppose it will be some sensation, for I am contemplating trying to work up a real good class, and I am thinking of trying to get the Virginia Beach Weekly to write the comments on the Sunday School lesson for the paper. What do you think of the idea? This would give me an opportunity, when we are able, to have outside speakers to address the class, to announce it.

Well, don't let it get your goat that you failed to make the honor roll when you tried this time. You remember that verse we need to quote once in a while, "When a man thinketh he standeth, take heed, lest he fall." Possibly you might apply this to your history at this time. But just buckle up your belt a little tighter, and put it over next time—but I think you did fine, and I'm mighty proud of you. You won't let up because spring is coming on, but you'll show them that you can do the thing right. I don't know—possibly you remember you used to say that when you ate too heavy you couldn't study or remember—possibly that's been the trouble—you've been eating too much lately! You didn't say how those three little capsules worked with you. How are you feeling these days?

Well, I guess you do think that we are kind of short on our letters, but I have so little to say, that when I go to try to spread it out over so many letters, I don't get very far with them, and we have had so much correspondence to get up in the last few weeks, that I know I have neglected writing as I should, and, too, I suppose another thing—I didn't have anything to *enclose*, and having gotten in the habit of always putting in something, I feel like I'm not just ready to write unless I can, and you know I'm always thinking I'll have it to-morrow.

By the way, don't think because I haven't mentioned anything about your letter written me on my birthday, that I didn't and haven't appreciated it. I felt very much like I've heard Uncle Lucian say a time or two—I didn't say anything, for I didn't have anything "fittin" to say. I had turned my mind rather inwardly, and was searching out my own inner self, to see if I had treated you always in such a way and manner that you were fully justified in saying the nice things about me that you did. You know, sometimes I feel that I'm trying mighty hard to live right, do the right thing, by each and every one—try to look at everything in the right way—try to look at every proposition in that same light that I believe the other fellow would look at it if he was in the same position, or if our conditions were reversed. Sometimes I'm not pleased with myself at all. So, when someone that I know really has so much right to expect considerable from me, says something so nice, I have to take stock of myself, to see whether I am behind or before the cart. But I appreciate it, and I will appreciate it just as much if you rake me over the coals once in a while—if I *need* it! Of course I hope I don't, but it's those that we love, and those that love us, that are able to see our faults as well as our virtues, and the real friend is the one that tells us of our errors and mistakes, as well as of our good qualities. I'm often reminded of the little story about the fellow who was walking in the snow, unmindful that anyone was following, when the little fellow called out, "Dad, don't step quite so far. I can't make it."

Well, let us hear from you when you have the opportunity. You know we are always glad to hear, for—as you know—we never start our day's work, in reality, until the mail comes.

> With best love from all,
> Dad

*   *   *

As the summer went on, construction began on the hospital site, and Edgar continued his efforts to get David Kahn and Morton Blumenthal to see eye to eye.

August 16, 1927

Dear Tim:

I ought to be ashamed of myself for not having answered yours of the 23rd and August 4th, but it looks like I've had so much to do that I *have* neglected my correspondence considerably . . .

As you know, we have called another meeting for September 3rd, at which time I am in hopes that Mr. Wyrick will be here—also Bradley [Franklin F., a Chicago businessman]—and that we will be able to get all of the trustees lined up in the right sort of way, each one contributing as best he can to meet the needs of the present time. I would give a great deal if you just had the chance and the time to be here at the present time. There has arisen a very peculiar condition and situation. Maybe it doesn't mean anything at all, but—if I am not far wrong—were it handled in the proper way—it might mean a great deal for the institution. In fact, it is the first contact with a family or group that the readings have told us *would* be interested in the undertaking, and that when they were there would be no cause to worry about money or finances—and I have it in my mind some way or another that you know these people. Do you know—or know of—a Charles W. Coe [a California rancher]? In fact, I believe his interests are pretty well divided—a great many of them being in California. Of course you'll be here for the meeting. While I know it may be working sort of a hardship on you to give so much time to this at present, but it is *needed* so much to get things in the right shape right now, that you'll just *have* to be here! I gave Kahn a talking-to while he was here, but I have done more harm than good possibly—as it seemed to make he and Blumenthal get cross with each other. This will eventually work out alright, but all the more necessity of our keeping closer together if possible and getting off on the right foot while we're trying to make some plans about starting with the building—for more and more we can see the real need of the institution; for if we are to judge by the requests that we have from people desiring to come here to be treated according to the suggestions given—there will be no trouble of the institution taking care of its own self once it's put in operation—and add to the ability to get others to contribute...

They started yesterday [August 15th, 1927] on the grading of the [hospital] lot. After we go over the ground with

the architect again—after having the lot staked for us—
I—also the architect—came to the conclusion it would be
much better to make a two-story house rather than
spread it over so much ground, and it would make it
cost—so the architect claims—four or five thousand dollars less. With the drawing of the new plans, I sent them to
the doctor. We expect them back this week. Then the architect will get up the specifications, and hope to have the
bids ready for us at the next meeting. So all the more necessity of your being here to see that we make the right
decision about it . . .

Sincerely,
Edgar Cayce

EC:GD

*　*　*

Personality conflicts around Edgar escalated, and sharp differences began to emerge as they had in the days of the Cayce
Institute of Psychic Research of Dayton, Ohio. The break between David Kahn and the ANI finally happened. As had occurred so many times before in his career, Edgar's welfare and
his dream became the battleground:

August 13, 1927

Mr. Edgar Cayce
115 West 35th Street
Virginia Beach, VA.

Dear Judge:

I have received this week, application for membership.
This is strictly confidential between you and myself. At the
present time, you know my circumstances and the conditions under which I am laboring. Write me and let me
know just what kind of membership you want me to take
out at this time and how you want it paid.

I still have not had time to write you in detail about the
reading but I shall do so in the next day or so. You see, I am
working day and night on account of Mr. Lauterstein be-

ing in Europe and Mr. Isaacs in N.H. for two months, so of course, it keeps me stepping and I have had no culmination of our agreements.

When I deposited $700.00 with Morton some time ago, it was his intention, so he informed me, to use the information he received to build up the $700.00 where I could give you a $5,000.00 donation, but after six months, I received a letter from him a few days ago to please send another $400.00, so it looks like I am going in debt instead of making any money. Therefore, I am going to sell out my stock interest and attend to my furniture business, and by the time the hospital is in shape, I hope to be able to give you at least enough beds to furnish the hospital. (Morton sold me out with about $200.00 loss today—I said another $200.00 so to date it has cost me $400.00)

Please say nothing to Morton at all about of what I am going to give. Whatever I will give to the hospital will be to Edgar Cayce and nobody else, and Morton cannot expect to tell me after all these years, what and how I should conduct my personal affairs. There is one person only can do that and that is Edgar Cayce himself, because I know that whenever you tell me something, it is just as I would tell you and there is no side-issues in the matter.

My entire intention has been, when the hospital was completed, to furnish as much of it as I could, at least furnish the beds that go into it.

However, regardless of what Morton thinks, my interest will always be with you as long as you have anything to do with the hospital.

To prove to you that no one can in any way influence me for or against you or your work, today we gave your address to three different people for readings. I have written four or five letters this week as the records will show, to various people besides discussing you with several others.

Money may mean something in the success of the Institution but not everything. Were it not for the labor that you and I have put out in the past years to build up respectful attention to the quality and sincerity of your efforts, I am sure Morton could in no way induce anybody to give five cents and at the present time I am not so sure that he is going to be able to do all the things he thinks he can do. He can give up his own but when it comes to inducing others, that is a different story.

I have had nothing more to say to him since our last conversation. Adeline and Lucille met on the street and they will remain good friends because they have nothing to do with our affairs.

As to coming down Sept. 3rd, I have sent you my proxy already and I am not certain whether I can get there or not because most of our office take vacations at that time, but I may get there at a later date or a little before; one or the other.

I am arranging to send the chair that I promised you and the Madam this week and I hope you will like it.

With kindest regards to you all, believe me,

Sincerely yours,
David E. Kahn

*   *   *

In the middle, trying to make peace and hold the project together, Edgar Cayce responded to David with a sincere letter filled with the same quiet, reasonable approach characteristic of his relations with everyone. What a strain it must have been on him to act as peacemaker amidst sharply clashing personalities—all of whom he respected and honored as his dear friends and all of whom played such important roles in the Work.

August 19, 1927

Dear Dave:

Have yours of the 13th . . .

Regarding the application—it's hard for me to say, Dave, just what is the right thing for you to do—for, as the reading distinctly puts it, you should choose yourself as to what your attitude should be, or will be, and no one has the right—or should assume the right—to dictate to you in any way as respecting it—your attitude or your views about the work or the phenomena. We may reason together concerning same, and by such reasoning we may both be able to arrive at a conclusion that would be most satisfactory—and I think you should take some class of membership—but that's entirely within your own conscience, and I don't want to assume the responsibility of saying what you should or should not do. Naturally, being incorporated, and having set out a definite plan, we want to try to work that plan. The plan—if it proves alright—will be the very thing. If we have chosen the wrong plan, we'll want to change it as soon as we see that we are in error. Now that plan calls for memberships to the Association to obtain information through its sources. When anyone becomes a member, naturally they see you are one of its officers, and it is natural for them to presume that you are some specific class of member—as to what class, its none of their business—that's with you and your own self. That's why I believe, with the good work you have been doing—and have done in the years gone by—become a booster for memberships to the Association—we will get wonderful results! If you are not in sympathy with this manner of conducting the work, why that's entirely different.

I know you are kept very busy, and I know you've got your hands, your heart and your mind full of your own business and business associations and relations—that's why I have tried not to bother you any more than was absolutely necessary.

Of course, I say nothing to anyone about what any other member of the association—or anyone else interested in seeing the work furthered—what they do for me or for the work. That is just as the reading gave you—a matter of individual consciousness, but it does not prevent all of those so interested working along toward one common cause, or one common good of the phenomena and work itself. We believe—and have believed for years—the institute plan the best way. I believe, from the requests we have nearly every day, and from the general air that we feel that is so hard to put into words, that this *is* the best way, and that if we had the place at the present time it would not only pay for upkeep but would be a means to induce others to come in and help us out in a way and manner that nothing else could or would. I believe you have agreed with me that the institute was the right thing, and I know you're going to help in the way and manner that seems the very best to you. *I* know you have been the one most instrumental in getting Morton interested in the work—but now that he's gotten so interested, there is no *use* in falling out with him because his plans and ideas are not in accord with yours. Each of you can give and take. You don't have to fly off the handle at all—but, each can work *in his own way* to the common good of all!

As regarding what you deposited with Morton, I have nothing whatever to say. If I have ever given any information that was to be used to make that seven hundred dollars even *eight* hundred, I don't know it! I *do* know I have *never* given Morton any information in a reading respecting Chrysler Motors—by questions being asked about what that particular stock was going to do! But I can't help but feel that he will work the thing out some way or another that will really be satisfactory to yourself. As to whether there has been a loss—and it has been sold out or not—I don't know, for he has never mentioned it to me that he even had any of your money to speculate with.

I know you will always be glad to try and influence people to have readings made by me, if I conduct *myself* in the way and manner towards you that merits same—and I hope and trust that I may always do this—for, as you *well* know, it is my wish and my desire to *use* and *be used* for the help and service of others whenever it is possible . . .

Sincerely,
Edgar Cayce

EC:GD

August 31, 1927

Dear Dave:

I had thought that possibly I would answer yours of the 22nd in person, as I felt you might be here before this time. However, I think I answered the greater part of this in my last letter—and at that time I sent you the application for membership, and in this mail am sending you several of the pamphlets. Possibly it would be very well for you to read this entirely through. As you will see from same we set definite rules in the by-laws, rules and regulations, regarding the readings ...

You may be correct, Dave, regarding the initial reading, but if you will remember, before we had the rules and regulations set up in our Association, there was considerable discussion about this very point, and we took a reading—you were present and heard the readings, and it gave in this that memberships to the Association where individuals had had reading was $15 a year, and $10 for each reading. The first application for a membership with a reading should be $20. You remember we all agreed that this would possibly make initial readings fall off somewhat. So far we can't say there has been such a great depreciable number of requests. Possibly not as many as we had in April and May, but very near as many as we are able to take care of, with the requests for readings from those who are already members.

With the trustees, our membership now is near thirty-five or forty, and I'm in hopes that we will be able to add to this continually. I think, as I suggested to you and Lucille, that as soon as you all get located—and it is convenient for me to come to New York—I want to come and spend ten days or two weeks, and I believe by meeting people personally, talking to some of those for whom we have already given readings, we will be able to increase our membership and possibly be able to get some real nice contributions to the Association, will be a real definite work, and from the number of requests we are constantly having, I don't think that if the institution is once established there will be any doubt about its taking care of its own expense and possibly building up a fund that would broaden it's scope of work ...

Hoping I will see you all real soon, and with kindest personal regards from all,

Sincerely,
Edgar Cayce

EC:GD

Timeline

November 11, 1928—Cayce Hospital is dedicated.

1929—Dr. House dies in Dayton.
    —October 29, the U.S. stock market crashes.

1930—Dr. Lydic named to head the hospital staff.
    —Atlantic University opens.
    —David Kahn and the Blumenthals fall out; the Blumen-
    thals withdraw their financial support.

February 28, 1931—The Cayce Hospital is forced to close.
    —Planning begins for the formation of the Association for
    Research and Enlightenment, based on advice from the
    readings.

5

The Cayce Hospital Era: July 1928–March 1931

1928

JULY 29, 1928

An article in *The Weekly* newspaper :

Construction on Cayce Hospital underway. Cost is $100,000—building is situated high on sand dune near 105th St. Is first unit, others may be added.

The National Association of Investigators has let a contract for the construction of a thirty bedroom hospital at

Virginia Beach. The new building will be known as the Cayce Hospital for Research and Enlightenment and is of concrete and shingle construction, four stories in height. Besides the thirty bedrooms, it will contain a large lobby and dining room, a lecture hall, library, doctor's quarters and spacious porches.

The total cost of the investment, including ground, building and equipment will be approximately $100,000. Plans for the structure were drawn by Rudolph, Cooke and Van Leeuween and the contract awarded to the United Construction Company of Norfolk. Rapid progress has been made during the past two weeks, the concrete foundation walls being almost completed.

The site of the hospital will be one of its most attractive features. Rising from a high sand dune, probably the highest elevation between Cape Henry and the Beach it commands a view of the territory for many miles around. The property measures 150 by 300 feet along 105th Street and extends between Holly Avenue and the boulevard. The present building is the first unit and will be followed by others as the occasion demands.

The Association of National Investigators was incorporated May 6th, 1927, in the State of Virginia. Although founded upon the psychic work of Mr. Edgar Cayce, and although the immediate basis of its formation was to further foster and encourage the physical, mental and spiritual benefit that thousands have and are deriving from Mr. Cayce's endeavors in the psychic field, nevertheless, the larger and more embracing purpose of the organization is to engage in general psychic research and also to provide for the practical application of any knowledge obtainable through the medium of psychic phenomena. In the matter of specific application, the Association seeks to render psychical aid to the sick and ailing through its hospital, and also to disseminate and exploit for the good of humanity knowledge obtained from its research work through the lecture hall, library and other educational channels.

The Association Hospital will furnish those who seek

physical readings and desire to secure treatment exactly as prescribed therein the opportunity to gain same at the hands of competent and sympathetic physicians. The hospital is to be conducted along only the most modern, scientific, as well as ethical lines. Every comfort and service for room, board and treatment will be such as is customary to an Institution of this kind, and all moneys so paid except the physicians' fees will go towards its maintenance.

Other headlines about the dedication of the hospital—the culmination of part of Edgar Cayce's lifelong dream—appeared as the publicity campaign bore down on the all-important date of November 11, 1928:

Virginian-Pilot
Friday, October 30, 1928

Cayce Hospital to Be Opened Armistice Day

Dr. W.M. Brown, of Washington & Lee, To be Speaker at Beach

Virginian-Pilot
Monday, November 9, 1928

Cayce Hospital to Be Dedicated Armistice Day

Building Four Stories High Containing 30 Bedrooms Cost Approx. $150,000.00 . . .

Morton Blumenthal, of New York, president of the Association of National Investigators, and Dr. Edgar Cayce, the secretary are also on the program of addressees.

Cayce Hospital at Virginia Beach Opens Next Month

Formal Dedicatory Exercises For New Institution Conducted Yesterday

Thirty Private Rooms
Contained in Structure

Virginia Beach realized another ambition yesterday with the dedication of the new $150,000 Cayce Hospital at One Hundred and Fifth Street and Atlantic Boulevard. Owing to inclement weather the exercises were held inside and hence limited the number of those in attendance. A large number of Virginia Beach residents and many visitors were present, however.

The principal address of the afternoon was delivered by Dr. William H. Brown, of Lexington, professor of education and psychology at Washington and Lee University. Dr. Edgar Cayce spoke on "Why and How We Came to Have an Institution of This Character," while the introductory remarks were made by Morton H. Blumenthal, who presided. The invocation was by the Rev. Frank H. Scattergood, pastor of the First Presbyterian Church.

The Cayce Hospital, named for Dr. Edgar Cayce, is owned by the Association of National Investigators, incorporated under the laws of Virginia in 1927. The structure was begun June 19th of this year and was constructed by the United Construction Corporation of Norfolk.

Officers of the association are Morton H. Blumenthal, of New York City, president; Thomas B. Brown, of Dayton, Ohio, vice president, and Dr. Edgar Cayce, of Virginia Beach, secretary-treasurer. The hospital will open some time in December and will be conducted by a competent staff of physicians and nurses under Dr. T.B. House, formerly of Kentucky but now of Virginia Beach. It will be used in addition to regular hospital work as a headquarters for research work in medicine and surgery.

The hospital building is a three-story structure of stucco and shingle finish with thirty private rooms, wards, doctors' offices, library, dining room and living room in addition to all modern features.

Following the dedicatory exercises yesterday after-

noon, the hospital was thrown open to the public for inspection and a large number took advantage of the opportunity.

Virginian Pilot
Monday, November 12, 1928

* * *

In June, Edgar Cayce was giving a routine physical reading for case 5642. It was 11:00 a.m. At the beginning, as soon as he was unconscious, a message was volunteered to him from his deceased mother:

EC: Mother!
Mother is here—and you haven't written Sister yet, and told her—Sister wouldn't like it, Brother—and she'll feel hurt! Write to Sister, tell her, and Sarah and Ola and Mary—they will all want to have a part, and they'll feel just as you do—and after while when everything is straightened out it will be so nice for you all, to think that Mother will be right with you! Be a good boy. Write, Brother! Talk to Mother. Be good to Papa. He will be home before long. But write to Sister—and tell the children Mother loves them all. 294-114 R4

In an additional note, Gladys Davis wrote, "On awakening EC remembered the above as a dream, but also his voice was heard saying these words; hence they are recorded as a psychic rdg."

The message refers to a fountain contemplated at entrance to Cayce Hospital, which EC had planned as a memorial to his mother. She was telling him that he should let the other children have a part in the memorial by contributing to the cost of it. (294-114 R5)

October 30, 1928

Dear Mary:
Sister [Annie] no doubt will tell you about my experience, but I want you to know it too. You know how anxious

I was to have a place where "the work" might be studied, not just in a haphazard way but seriously, and you know too how anxious Mother was that we should have it. I had often felt that I didn't know whether I cared to succeed unless Mother knew it, but I know she knows! I had tried to plan something that would be in memory of Mother—the fountain, which is as the fountain of living water, which seemed to me the most appropriate thing for such a place, and I had thought I would put that. When I had gone about to have the basin prepared for this, for the first time [since she passed on] Mother came to me and talked, while I was asleep of course, and we went through the building. Possibly it was a little bit of a selfish motive, and I know Mother wouldn't like that—yet I didn't want to burden any of you—but after the experiences yesterday—a copy of what was said I'm sending you, for I am sure you will know it was our Mother talking. I wasn't conscious of it until after it was all over and the others told me about it. I want to go ahead and have this done. If you all want to send any little thing towards it, it's alright—whether it's little or much, or what—because I had planned, of course, to take care of it all myself, but I know now that you all want to be known in it anyway. Let me hear from you about it. Sister [Annie] will no doubt talk with you about what we would put on the little plate. Any suggestion you have to offer will be mighty nice.

Give my love to Will and the children. I know you are all glad to have Pa with you. Wish you all could come back with him.

With best love from all,
Brother

1929

In April 1929, the hospital marked what Edgar Cayce considered its "formal" opening. The staff had been working hard to get everything squared away, and Edgar was still pondering designs for the fountain in his mother's memory. But he was eager to share his excitement and satisfaction over the realization of one of his dreams with his good friend, W.L. Jones.

April 29, 1929

Dear W.L.

I am sure I owe you an apology for not answering your letter of sometime ago, with the drawing [for the fountain]. We have been so very busy, though, trying to get everything in shape, and then so much to look after, and I haven't since seeing the drawing—been pleased with my idea; consequently, I have let it sort of rock along, to try to get it straight in my mind. I am of the opinion now, W.L., that it would be too much like a monument, rather than a fountain. Don't you think so? I don't believe it would look good—don't believe I would be satisfied with it. Might be better if I made it in a much smaller thing, but that would make the figure so small that I don't believe it would look good. In fact, I've almost come to the conclusion the idea wasn't worth much *as a fountain.* It would be a *beautiful* thing to have as a marker on the grounds or as the top of a pedastle [sic]—but as a fountain, I believe it's the wrong idea, and I don't know what I will do about it. Anyhow, we will forget about that for the time being, until I come to some definite decision about what I want to do with it.

Yesterday we had our first of the formal addresses by Mr. Blumenthal. This marks, we might say, the formal opening of the institution. While we have had quite a number of members there, quite a number of local people taking treatments, yet we had such a goodly number for the lecture and I think everything went off fairly well. I wasn't feeling as good as I might have been, but I suppose it was more from excitement at seeing a dream come true, than anything else.

Now, respecting your reading—we won't be able to get to this before the afternoon of the 14th, W.L. Will that be too late? Then, you know we will have to know where you are just at the time. I would like for you to make out a list of questions. We have so much that we have had to do—spending so much money. We seem to be outgrowing ourselves, even before we begin, in some respects.

I hope this time will be satisfactory, and trust we will be able to help.

With kindest regards and love from all,

Ever the same,
Edgar Cayce

Having reached the actual dedication of the Cayce Hospital was a major achievement for the Cayces and the ANI, but it still was just the beginning of the work that was needed to make the hospital a going concern. A review of the correspondence records throughout the hospital years shows that the seeds of discord which eventually closed the hospital were sown early on in the relationship between David Kahn and the Blumenthals. Those differences grew until factions formed, battle lines were drawn, and both the ideal and truth were lost.

Each one connected to the events had a different perspective—or as Edgar Cayce himself might have put it—a different experience. It was not possible for anyone to have the whole picture, save the readings.

The personality differences between David and the Blumenthals that contributed to the breakup of the ANI created factions and groups with decided philosophical differences. Some saw the hospital as a charitable institution, others as a "proposition that would have to pay for itself." The irritation between David and the Blumenthals, especially Edwin, grew to such dimensions that the Blumenthals began taking a stronger and stronger position in an effort to counteract David's actions which, unfortunately, placed Edgar in the middle.

Edgar was caught up in the forces swirling around him as well as everyone else. Requests for readings from those he had known from his earliest days conflicted with the schedule for the hospital. The Blumenthals felt that David was using his personal relationship with Edgar to go around the system, but their protests to Edgar were few in number, never acrimonious, and always rather gently voiced. David's letters to Edgar have quite a different tone. The limit on the number of requests that could be fulfilled in a day always meant choices had to be made. The Blumenthals felt Edgar should choose the long-held dream and ideal of the hospital over accommodating David Kahn.

February 5, 1929

Mr. Edgar Cayce,
115—35th Street,
Virginia Beach, Va.

Dear Edgar:

Enclosed please find check for $1200, the regular monthly contribution for February, as I don't know whether Morton sent this to you or not. If he did, will you please let me know for our records. The other check, $1424.18, to be applied on the payment of the additional five lots on the ocean front adjoining our present property, as outlined by Van Patten.

I am sure you feel as we do, that this is very valuable property for the Association, and in order to help the cause along, as, of course, we always want to, this money is being sent by Morton and I personally and not from the Association account. I just state this so that it will keep your records clear.

When speaking to Van Patten I tried to be emphatic, that we wanted the title guaranteed, as I think that is important. If you think so too, will you please see that he has it done.

As usual, I suppose the details of acquiring this new property will fall on you. My understanding is, $1000 mortgage to be due in one year, another $1000 in two years at 6% interest. If this all seems satisfactory to you, go ahead and close.

I hate to trouble you too much, as I know you must be swamped with work after your vacation. I surely am. Strange that we both returned on the same day, and I hope your visit benefited you as much as mine did me.

There are [so] many things I would like to talk about and write you about, but I will save you the trouble and call you on the telephone within a day or so.

If there is anything I can do, you know that you can call on me at any time.

I hope that you and the family are all well and that I shall see you in the near future.

Sincerely yours,
Edwin

February 9, 1929

Dear Edgar,

I have wanted to write to you for a long time and much has turned over in my mind that I should like to discuss with you, so here and now I want to make my apologies for this stationery, the writing if you are unable to read it, and the letter if it turns out to be a book or sermon, and annoys or bores you. So much for that.

In one of the beautiful readings you have given the phrase "Forward March" was unexpectedly given [254-46]. That it seems to me might be a big part of life; not merely in a physical sense, but in its meaning as a whole. Is this, not that which we are endeavoring to do in the Association. We owe a great debt. We have allowed ourselves to be spiritually awakened, we have had a path chosen for us to travel. Of our own accord we could never contract this debt, but we have been allowed to make it. It is a debt of gratitude for the help we are enabled to enjoy thru our own development, our own righteous desire of being at oneness with the "One". But then what are we to do with this help received, the Divine awakening? Yes you know the simple answer help others *serve, serve, serve* always keeping in the ways, and serving in the manner of, 'He' whom has given His all to us in his image. Given us all, but left us delicately to choose right from wrong.

Having been given our opportunity how shall the debt be repaid? That too will be with His help if we will only permit, and the supreme efforts shall be thru our institution. In giving to mankind that which we have learned and are ever striving to learn. Thru the institution will come our message, and we pray the good, we know to be everyone's if they will only accept it.

This clumsy jumble of words was prompted by a letter I wrote Dave suggesting we expected him to see to the donation of the furniture. For I note in your report you have received invoices, however that may be just a matter of forms, and I have written to Dave telling him what we expected.

I took the liberty of telling him our work might at times

seem a great effort a sacrifice and strain, and who among us knows it more than you and Morton. You especially whose life has been devoted to the cause, you under all difficulties, hardships and sacrifices have enabled yourself at this date to be the means of our very expression of truth. You have indeed been faithful. And always remember Edgar, when things look bad, when you are blue, when you are worried when you might have a feeling of "Oh what is the use" remember you now at this time are just on the threshold of truly answering that question. Your studies, and observations are going to be a demonstration to physical man of what life is and what we should do with our earthly experience. Does that mean you and I and all of us are to sit back put our feet on a desk and say well here we are come and learn from us? Certainly not. Does it mean we are to broadcast our doctrines? Certainly not.

But it does mean we shall and must live a life exemplifying what the truth is. What the truth teaches us. In our own lives, in our own actions must the proper vibrations exert themselves thru us. We all have our share to do to create the perfect balance. Just see Tim putting into scientific demonstration of that one force Stansell motor, that which Morton is putting into philosophical teachings. Surely there is balance. We must give to those who seek.

We have much work before us Edgar and truly it can only be done with God's help. We must not delay in starting the classifications of the information at hand as given in the reading on the work. While on the subject would suggest when you have the opportunity to take the reading on the functions and duties of the various committees it will be most helpful.

Was indeed sorry to hear you were suffering from "neuritis" but hope that is now a matter of history. Yes, what is history but the arrangement of men's experiences as related merely to change, as we know everything is in constant change, and that is why time plays no part in the subconscious time being merely the change.

No doubt Van Patten told you I wrote to him. What is your opinion of the new property. Morton is at a loss to understand why the building and loan wants bonds for twice the amount of money they loan us. I don't understand it either. Do you.

You must be pleased with the progress you are making at the hospital. I am anxious to hear how things are progressing.

The only reason I can think of for writing this letter is the great necessity for us to carry on to our goal. To complete that which we have started. To assure you of the part we all want to play. Or as you have said "Forward March."

My best to all,
Edwin

February 20, 1929

Dear Edwin:

I have yours of the 9th, and I don't know how to answer. I wish I could talk with you concerning many things that come up at times. It always looks like we are in such a hurry when we do have the opportunity to get together, or we have some special matter in hand that we want to talk about or discuss, or have gotten something that is worrying us and we want to get it off our gizzards. It seems to me that, could we all have seen the man that left here last evening, we would feel that our work here is not in vain. You know our first patient came down for treatment on the 11th, from Philadelphia (Mr. [470]). He had been told that he was in a pretty bad condition, and he was—but to see the man steadily each day getting better and better— it is even better than Mr. Curie could say. After his first day here, I think he averaged putting on a pound and a half each day in weight. He went home yesterday feeling alright, in fine shape, ready to take up his work again and go on making the very best of everything. He said to me, "Mr. Cayce, I've known you and your work a long time. You have saved me, I am sure, many a day and night of suffering—but I understand the purpose of the institution better than I could have possibly understood it had I not come to see—I understand the heart of many of those of your associates. I would like to know each and every one of them personally, and to personally thank them for what they have done for me, and for what I know can and will be done for others if they will only do as I did—come and let the work be carried out to the letter just as given—then they will get the results as I did." That's possibly the answer to *many* of the things that have come up. There are several others taking treatment—new ones every day locally and out of town trying to get in. We will be open possibly by the first. We are waiting on the linens and a few other little things that are needed to get straightened out.

Yes, as you say, "Forward March" is and has been *ever* the real pith of the information that has been given. I have often thought of how many times it has insisted to Morton, in his earlier days especially, that "in the doing of this you will get understanding—commence!"

Last Sunday afternoon there were quite a number of people out from Norfolk to see the building. Among them was a family that I have known ever since I've been here—one of the business men (book and stationery) of Norfolk [Mr. William Freeman of Wm. Freeman & Son, stationers]. They came in and were astonished to see the undertaking. While, as he said, he had known me for three years—nearly four—he hadn't known what it was all about that we were undertaking to do, but he thought it was very wonderful—a very marvellous [sic] work. The next day (Monday), I was in to see about some matters—dropped in to see him. He took me by the arm and carried me off upstairs, and he told me this:

"Mr. Cayce, you know we only have the one boy—he's in the business here, and his mother and I realize it won't be long before he will be in charge of everything. It has been rather a burden to us that he has constantly gotten farther and farther away from what *we* have been brought up to think as the Church, or old theology. He has no patience whatever with the ministers of the day—this one, that one and the other, constantly seem to be a bore to him. But when we were discussing you and your work last night, he turned to his mother and his wife and said, 'Now that, to me, is religion! *That* man I would like to do everything possible to see that he succeeds, for the life—the people that come in contact with him—tell the tale without his preaching anything.'"

That is possibly saying the same thing, Edwin, as you expressed in your letter. That I know, and you know, is the great trouble of the world at large today—people preach what they would *like* for others to believe, but what they do not *act* themselves. Yes, it is our lives, our walks in and out before men, that tell the tale—just as it was with the Master long ago. It wasn't that he was not criticized. It wasn't that he followed in the footsteps of those that had been teachers before, for he didn't—for, as he said himself, "John came neither eating nor drinking nor associating with the rabble, yet they said he was of the devil. I come eating and drinking *with* you all and you say I have a devil,"—but His life was such that we, through exemplifying that simple gospel of "Have no other gods before me, and love your neighbor as yourself", will make ourselves gain a better understanding of our relationship to our Creator, or to that Creative Energy we call God, and to that *created through* that Energy we call our fellow man! So we *must* carry on. I just hope and trust that I may be better able to serve than I have in the past. I have tried—possibly not as hard as I should have—but have tried to do the right. Not that I profess to be good, or even moral, but I *do* think I *am* sincere and live what I believe!

I received the letter yesterday with the notice from the Guaranty Title & Trust Co. I will attend to this. It is the payment on the property where I live. Morton knows about it, but I don't know that he has told you just what it was.

I believe, truly, the property that has just been acquired practically doubles the value of that we already hold.

I also received this morning the check of $2000 towards the expenses. That will help us considerably in getting up this month's bills—some of them we must meet—some of them we will possibly be able to hold off for a while yet. You can't imagine how very busy I'm being kept. We have two or three readings every day, except Sunday—and we have had to put in Sunday recently, as you know from that sent you (and I hope it helped matters out). Our first check for the Hospital was $35. The patient stayed at the hotel, of course, and this was for his treatments. Very good beginning, especially when we know the man went home highly pleased. He did a good deal of work around the Hospital after the first few days. Helped us set up beds, rubbed off furniture, moving it about, etc.

The grounds are beginning to look real good. This we have had to spend a lot of money on, but—as you said sometime ago—we don't want to spoil the whole thing by being penny wise and pound foolish respecting this part of the work.

Hope you will have the opportunity to get down to see us sometime in the very near future, and with kindest personal regards to Ruth, the little lady Peggy and yourself, I am

Sincerely,
Edgar Cayce

EC:GD

Nor was the increasing animosity among his friends the only time bomb waiting to disrupt Edgar Cayce's dream. The stock market crash occurred October 29, 1929; 16 million shares changed hands. By the end of 1929, stock losses were estimated at fifteen billion dollars, and losses through 1931 were estimated at fifty billion dollars, affecting twenty-five million people. Six months before the crash, in March and April, both Morton and Edwin Blumenthal had had warnings from the readings about the market:

> . . . unless another of the more *stable* banking conditions come to the relief—a great disturbance in financial circles. This warning has been given, see? Mind these are all in the position of being an influence in market conditions, and may turn *either* way, as the conditions come. 900-425

> . . . were these to be allowed to run without a check in *ei-*

ther direction, there must surely come a break where it would be *panic* in the money centers—not *only* of Wall Street's activity but a closing of the boards in many centers, and a re-adjustment of the actual specie and moneys in these centers. 137-117

October 27, 1929

Dear Edgar:

. . . As you know, the market went to pieces and we all took a beating. I lost $175,000.00, some of which was profits, and for the present I'll be unable to raise any cash. However, by hedging and trading we will, as given in the readings, be able to make some turns and once more be of service. It is nice to know that we are receiving guidance in these matters, and I am only sorry we had to take severe losses, but as I explained to Morton, it is merely a test for ourselves and we will either gain or lose, depending on how we accept that which we now find as been presented to us.

[Edwin]

The Blumenthals weathered the financial storm, bent, but not broken or broke.

*   *   *

The New Tomorrow, voice of the ANI, was the brainchild of Thomas Sugrue and Hugh Lynn Cayce. Conceived as a quarterly publication, only two issues were published, December 1929 and April 1930. The following is an editorial celebrating the hospital opening as the culmination of Edgar's many years of work, but it also was an editorial that would prove to be bitterly ironic within eighteen months:

Love dies, hope dies, the things of beauty fade;
Alone the ageless soul, aloof and wise,
Leaves to the grave this senseless, fading jade,
Flitting to other lives, and other skies.

T.J.S.

EDITORIAL

"There's a divinity that shapes our ends, rough-hew them how we will."

On Sunday afternoon, March 31, 1899, in the living room of a little house in Hopkinsville, Kentucky, three people watched a man who could not speak[,] talk in his sleep. The watchers were Mr. and Mrs. L.B. Cayce and a layman, the sleeper was Edgar Cayce. The words spoken by the latter as he slept comprise what is known as the first reading ever given by Edgar Cayce. Its results were immediate. When he went to sleep Mr. Cayce could not speak, his vocal chords were paralyzed. When he awoke they had returned to normal functioning, his voice was natural and clear.

It is a far cry from that little house on the bleak March afternoon of a dying century to the Association of National Investigators, Incorporated, and the Cayce Hospital, at Virginia Beach, Va. It is a far cry indeed, and the vagaries and whims of human frailty carried the cry farther still, ere the inexorableness of Time and the certainty of Fate brought Truth to the harbor of Faith and Love. Yet nothing worthwhile is won without struggle, and the pain and disillusion of Experience bring a greatness to the soul, a sweetness to the heart, and a clearness to the ideals that set us firmly on the King's Highway and direct our footstep toward the Kingdom of God.

It was a long, hard road for Edgar Cayce, from the first fairy voice of childhood to the first ground broken for the Cayce Hospital. Man through his opaque mist of materialism sees little of the world beyond his length, breadth, and thickness, and because of his own conceit the attempts of truth boomerang from a solid wall of self. How difficult it is to make people understand something they cannot contact with the senses! How discouraging it is to see truth misinterpreted and misapplied, used as the individual sees fit, to suit best the desires of his own nature! How long to the goal it seems when the road is so winding and rough, so studded with stubble, so littered with deadwood, so cluttered with debris!

To conquer self was the first task, and perhaps the hardest, for as Polonius said: "This above all: to thine own self be true, And it must follow, as the night the day, Thou canst not then be false to any man."

To convince himself that he was not a freak of nature, not an unconscious fraud, not a spiritual charlatan, was first of all the work of Edgar Cayce. For years he lived in self-conscious embarrassment because of his strange peculiarity, for years he feared to give the aid requested of him because he did not know nor understand the thing he did. For years his life was a mental torture, a seething indecision, a labyrinth of ideas, ideals, misbeliefs and disillusions.

From the left came a cry of service, from the right a whisper of gain. Which way Parnassus? No answer came. Time passed, and the mind that could not know of itself, learned from a world that clutched at stars and dragged its soul in mud. Reality stumbling skyward in the illusion of smut taught a lesson etched in pain and failure. The answer became obvious.

"Though I speak with the tongues of men and of angels, and have not love, I am become as sounding brass, or a tinkling cymbal. And though I have the gift of prophecy, and understand all mysteries and all knowledge, and though I have all faith, so that I could remove mountains, and have not love, I am nothing."

To Edgar Cayce had come an ideal, to him was shown the truth. And so he lived, and so he lives, and so he will live forever. He survived the cries that branded him charlatan, quack, spiritualist, clairvoyant, hypnotist, fake and fraud. He survived the misunderstanding, pain, disillusionment, loss of friends and attacks of enemies. He survived the purgatory of ignorance to conquer himself and others, finding peace and happiness in the knowledge of truth and the possession of an ideal.

It was at the September meeting of the American Association of Clinical Research in 1911 that recognition and hope first was given for the work. This meeting was held in the rooms of the Society of Natural History in Boston, and a paper describing the phenomena, written by Dr. W. H. Ketchum, of Hopkinsville, Kentucky, was read. The opinion of the Association was voiced in the sentiment that the work deserved further study and was deserving of commendation and support.

From this first bit of official recognition, this first gleam of hope that he was something more than a freak of Natural law, Edgar Cayce formed the purpose and ideal of his life, a purpose and ideal which is now that of the Association of National Investigators, and which is expressed in a single word—Service.

It was natural that Mr. Cayce should conceive of a hospital or sanitarium, where the people he diagnosed could be treated as he prescribed, under physicians in accord with the work; and it was natural that he should go to his own peculiar source of information for advice concerning it. The first reading taken on the establishing of a hospital approved of the idea and outlined the method of going about such a venture. On February 11, 1911, it advised Virginia Beach as a site for this hospital. On June 19, 1928, the first ground was broken for the Cayce Hospital. What happened during the seventeen years elapsing between the creation of the idea and its material culmination?

It is a long time between the idea and the creation, the dream and the reality. In 1911 Edgar Cayce began working toward the establishment of a hospital. On February 11, 1929, the first patient was treated in the Cayce Hospital at Virginia Beach.

There is not much use in reciting the hardships of those seventeen years. Let us pass over them lightly, as we passed over those years before the faith and ideal became visualized. From Hopkinsville, Kentucky, to Selma, Alabama; from Memphis, Tennessee, to Birmingham, Alabama, and westward and the loved ones who followed him. It was a hard road, and a long one, strewn with bitterness and broken hopes. Yet always the faith remained, the ideal was firm, and the readings repeated the admonition, go to Virginia Beach.

Why was such a wonderful work so difficult to begin?

Why was such an ideal so hard to attain? Nothing is worthwhile until we fight for it, what comes easily is seldom appreciated. Though the faith and the love were firm, the mind and spirit and body had not yet been sufficiently tried and attuned. Those associated did not understand, there was not the harmony of an organization, in short, the time was not ripe. Many people and groups of people took up the work and planned to establish a hospital. Each was unsuited to the task it seems, and eventually they dropped it. The time was not ripe, the vibrations and conditions of the Universal forces and the earthly conditions were not properly adjusted for the happening of such an event. Time passed. It seemed to Edgar Cayce that things were going round in circles. The thing he saw so clearly, the thing he desired so earnestly, was but a misty haze in the minds of others. Patiently he waited.

At Dayton, Ohio, in January, 1925, the first germ of an idea was born for The Association of National Investigators. From that time on, like a babe in the mother's womb, it grew slowly toward an inevitable culmination. Conditions had become right, people had come in accord, and Time had slipped into place. The rest was merely adjustment and readjustment, smoothing out details and making arrangements. The result was a certainty, the dream a reality, the desire a gratification.

In September of 1925 Edgar Cayce and his family moved to Virginia Beach, establishing a residence at 115 West 35th St., an address grown familiar to many since then as the office of the Association and the place where all readings are given. Here the work was continued in the old way, obviously. But all the time the Association was planning the culmination of one dream and the beginning of another.

On May 6, 1927, The Association of National Investigators was incorporated. On June 19, 1928, the first ground was broken for the Cayce Hospital. On November 11, 1928, the Cayce Hospital was dedicated. On February 11, 1929, the first patient was treated in the Cayce Hospital. The dream is a reality, the ideal is achieved, the *work* has *begun*.

The world goes on unheeding. The waves of the ocean have not ceased their beating, the season its changing, the sun its rising, the world its evolution. Only something has happened. Something definite has begun, something tangible has taken form, and a small group of people look toward a new horizon. The world whirls on, unknowing. Meanwhile we work. Someday the world will stop its mad racing to listen, and heed. Time only knows when it will be. For the present let us make sure we will be prepared. Let us take up our happy burdens and start forward, trusting the others to follow where we show the way.

The time has come for beginning what this publication purposes to do. We have formed the nucleus, laid the foundation on a strong rock of suffering and final understanding, and we are ready to promulgate and project the truths we have learned to the world at large. That they will reject with laughter and scorn is natural, that they will eventually accept and approve is inevitable. The purpose of this publication is not didactic, explanatory, or even that of propaganda and exploitation. It is merely to record in systematic fashion the advances and achievements of this association. Journalism is the world's contemporary historian, and as a specific journalist it is the purpose of this magazine to reflect and record the work of our organization. Though primarily for our members, it is inevitable that it will fall into the hands of those outside, who will wonder and question its meaning and contents. To those people we extend an invitation to inquire and study our work, to visit our offices at Virginia Beach, and to join with us in a brotherhood of searchers for truth, for ourselves, for the world, and for God.

To the members of the Association who will receive this first issue we ask the tolerance of innovation and the assistance of co-workers. It is your magazine, open to your views and suggestions, and we will gladly welcome and appreciate your criticism, contributions, and general support.

The New Tomorrow
December 1929

* * *

1930

As 1930 began, Morton Blumenthal continued to pour money into Edgar Cayce's Virginia Beach projects in astronomical amounts.

January 10, 1930

Mr. Edgar Cayce,
115 35th Street
Virginia Beach, Va.

Dear Edgar:
    Enclosed please find check in the amount of $8,000.00 to cover budget sent to us.
    Will you be so kind as to make a check out to Dr. Brown in the amount of $800. To cover January appropriation for the University.
    Nothing else new since I spoke to you over the telephone.
    Trust you and the family, and all our associates are in the best of health, and remain

Sincerely yours,
Morton

MHB/MS
Enc.

In spite of the stock market crash, the Work—and the demands for readings—continued. Edgar Cayce needed someone to make administrative and financial decisions for him, and he also needed for all parties involved to abide by the decisions so that he could work in peace and quiet. In this letter, he made it very clear where he stood on appointments for readings, still expressing his willingness to cooperate with all.

Adding an ominous note to the group's dilemma was Morton Blumenthal's failing health, which brought Edwin to the forefront. Edwin was naturally more protective of his brother than he was concerned for Edgar Cayce. On January 11, 1930, Morton left for vacation by boat from New York harbor for France. Dr. Theodore J. Berger had been treating Morton osteopathically and reported the following to Edgar:

> ...They were in a great turmoil up at Morton's with all the preparations for sailing. Their boat was late in arriving and they do not sail until midnight tonight. Morton's local head and sinus trouble has entirely cleared up but he is in a very fatigued state. He is tired out and his nervous system is at a low ebb. His vacation will do wonders for him. I am to go up to treat him for the last time at four o'clock and then I hope to see them off at the pier tonight...

Edwin lacked the benefit of the long-term relationship between his brother and Edgar, as well as the sort of absolute trust that Morton had in the readings. In spite of all the turmoil surrounding Edgar and his hospital, however, Edgar tried his best to keep things moving in the right direction and to meet the demands of those around him:

> Wednesday night, January 22, 1930
>
> Dear Tim:
>   Yours of the 16th received ... I am hoping your work is showing some results with the motor developments. You've been working pretty hard on it, but you shouldn't overtax yourself and not be able to enjoy the fruit of your labor...
>   As regarding the appointments—we all may have been some hasty in things that were said, but there's one thing, Tim, we will never be able to set down a rule as to the readings. While I have quit making any more appointments, except as they seem to have a definite something to do with the developing of our plans—and am not even accepting any more memberships (where they carry readings) until I am able to make some definite arrangements about it—for we are doing ourselves, the Association and the work, and most of all the individual, an injustice in making an appointment for a reading months and months

in advance when they may be depending upon something that might be given immediately, and it is best that they seek information through other sources, for of course, we will have to give more and more time to those who are in the hospital, or who are really making arrangements to come to the hospital—being limited as we are with the ability to carry on faster. Of course, as others [psychics] may be developed [as recommended in 254-54] (and of course they are), why it will be carried on in possibly a much more satisfactory manner—get [readings] off whenever they choose, and get ones in when they want them—irrespective of what may have been promised others; but it won't be done that way through me. I could have sold myself for a few crumbs long ago . . .

Yes, I think Lydic is doing some wonderful work. I think he is quite an executive, as well as a good doctor. I'm afraid it is a little bit lonesome for Mrs. Lydic. Possibly that can be altered as things shape themselves, so that she can be thrown with people that will nearer fill the needs for satisfying her desires; that is when we begin to have the people come in for their work in the institution—possibly at the university—it will change things for her. Dr. Brown was here in the latter part of the week—spent the weekend here—will be back in about ten days, I think. I don't know if there is anything definite that can be done [about the university] until we have the plans, and then can get the bids in on same—and then it looks like to me it is a great big burden, unless we can arrange to make the hospital come nearer paying—for its upkeep—and in doing that we seem to be becoming so mercenary that we partially, at least, lose sight of the intent and purpose of the whole thing—or possibly I've got a wrong angle on it . . .

All here send their kindest personal regards. Let us hear from you whenever you have the opportunity.

Ever the same,
Edgar Cayce

EC:GD

*   *   *

On March 30, 1930, Edgar was the guest of Edwin Blumenthal in New York, and reading 137-129 was given. Among the answers to many other questions about groups and individuals not associated with the Cayce Work, Edwin was warned of fraud. The warning was gently worded and advised him in a general sort of way to be more alert. This caused Edwin to question even more closely the motives of others, including those in the Cayce group. Edwin had become the more actively involved of the two brothers and seemed to become more and more of the opinion of other family members that Morton had no business being involved in the Work (see 900-406 reports).

The Work continued, however, and Atlantic University received its charter April 30, 1930, just a little more than a month before Hugh Lynn graduated from Washington and Lee. But within the ANI, the misunderstandings and misperceptions had begun to move beyond the private stages, becoming more public in nature. These sharp differences began at last to tear the already strained fabric of the board of governors. People stopped speaking to one another, and all communication among the various groups and individuals gradually ceased. Everyone was talking to Edgar Cayce. Edgar Cayce was talking to everyone. But the others weren't talking to each other, and one man could not do it all.

A happy note in the middle of the turmoil was Hugh Lynn's June 3 college graduation. The week before the great event, the twenty-three-year-old young man wrote to his father, reflecting on his college years and responding to his father's invitation to consider some role in the Work. The letter shows us an energetic, humorous, sincere, and already very dedicated young man, eagerly looking forward to his first job after graduation as Atlantic University librarian.

Apparent also throughout the letter is the great respect and affection with which he held his father, as well as Hugh Lynn's very clear understanding of the import of his father's Work and its contribution to the world. While Hugh Lynn may not yet have known that the Work was his destiny, he clearly felt his path lay somewhere in that direction. In this letter, he made it very clear what kind of role he saw for himself in relation to his father, the organization, and the Work. In the thirty-six years that followed,

Hugh Lynn's energetic pursuit of his vision for the Work—with this same dedicated clearsightedness—never wavered:

Sunday Nite
May 25, 1930

From Washington and Lee University
Lexington, Virginia

Dear Dad:

    This letter has been delayed a long time but this time it has not been entirely on account of my ever bothersome habit of procrastination. I have waited to answer several of your suggestions until I could say something definite. I have no doubt that you have kept up with the moves I have been making to bring those suggestions about and I certainly give myself enough credit for recognizing your handiwork in many places. I have tried to do it in the way that seemed best. I asked you for some very important advice. You gave it to me and I have acted on it. I am writing this to submit to you the results of my work on those suggestions. I know that you know all about it already and that you have planned it for a long time but just the same I want to tell you about it and I don't believe you have heard this angle before.

    You suggested that I become connected with the *work* in some capacity that I might study and live with it. I am answering Dr. Brown's letter which included an offer for the place of librarian for the coming year with an acceptance of that offer. You suggested and reminded me of that old statement of mine about the street cleaner. That as you well know is almost the same as saying the proverbial, "poor little fellow." I promise you that they will have no harder worker nor any one so interested in not only his own department but in the whole work. So far as it is possible for me, and you have heard me say that I have yet to see the impossible, I will become indispensable not only to just those I work under but to everyone I contact. I knew and you knew that it was not so much that I got such a place but just how I got it. I have tried very hard to apply the first twelve verses in that fifth chapter of Matt. I have tried to approach each one of the men on this subject as an individual. I have tried to make each one feel that I am depending on my self and appreciate and understand their position in the work. Time will tell how well I have succeeded. One of man's greatest mistakes is to underestimate the other individual particularly if you are matching wits with him. I learned a bit of this in Egypt and I shall not forget. At another time I learned humbleness to offset the self praise, that too I shall remember. Please don't think that I shall ever over look and forget the hand that has engineered this from a beginning that pre-dates any of the rest [of the folks'] thoughts on the subject. I refer of course, Dad, to yourself.

It is time though for us to approach the real reason that I am to become the librarian at the Atlantic University. You have possibly read the article of Bradley's in *The New Tomorrow* on just how a young man should obtain a real education. He suggested that one pick out a man whom they felt could lead them into the right channels and under whom they could rise to the highest point in the profession of their choice. I thought his idea was a pretty good one so I picked me out just such a man whose profession was the profession I wanted to enter and who I felt was the best in his line that I knew. The profession I wanted to enter was that old but much misused profession of "helping the other fellow." I found that this man had a pretty large business and that his peculiar situation was going to make it very hard for me to get in direct contact with him but on looking about I found that I had certain natural advantages. I contrived therefore to get into this man's business. Seemingly it was in a place a long way from the man himself but in other respects would be closer than appeared. I intend to stay very close to that man, to study him, to work with him, to become a part of him so far as it is possible. I know that through his development, through his intent and purpose this man has become the channel for a force that can do more good for humanity than anything I have ever contacted. I would learn from this man not only something of this power but more would I learn of that spirit, that purpose, that will that has made this man such a channel for good works to his fellow man. I shall come thoughtfully, prayerfully, humbly, considerately to this man asking that he only allow me the privilege of becoming a student at his feet. I got a long jump ahead when I picked that man as a Dad. I'll be there . . .

Good nite Dad
Hugh Lynn

*   *   *

Edwin Blumenthal was still waiting for Edgar to take a stand on the problems facing the organization and sent the following:

June 2, 1930

Dear Edgar,

"United we stand, divided we fall." These are not idle words and must be taken and studied, and the truth extracted from the words. Please understand that this letter is inspired in true friendship between you and myself and is not the result of any collusion, but is truly the result of my observation both as to relationship of material facts, and information given in your readings.

I do not intend to hide my thought from you by quibbling in words, and I am writing it long-hand so that it is between you and me. If when you finish reading this you feel resentment towards me it will be only because of misunderstanding by you, of what is meant from my heart, not my physical [words].

If you say to yourself "why does he so write me when I have sacrificed for so many years and now would have comfort," then remember you are trying to reward yourself, rather than receive the Father's reward when the at-one-ment comes. If you say to yourself have I not done my best and am I still not trying to do my best? Then stop, think hard from within and analyze what you are trying to do your best. Is it to achieve physical attainment for yourself, and kin, or are you trying your best to glorify our

Creator, our Father, the One for whom He of Nazareth gave his all, but received the universe for his giving?

In one of your recent God-given (not man) readings when I asked if my optimism regarding the financial standing of the Association of National Investigators was warranted, etc., etc., the answer was yes, so long as all concerned with the work have the rightful purpose in mind. Not in words but in mind. (or some similar answer.) Now the law of the Universal has told us this has not been fulfilled. For I must say now, due to absolute necessity our financial procedure must be changed. The budget cannot be sent to us just to be paid, for financial conditions necessitate a scheme of rigid economy even if necessary to let some employees go. Our monthly budget for the present will have to be maintained to around no more than approximately $3,000.00.

Now you well know this can only be changed in one way. That is faith in Him who provides all. If help financially is secured by prostitution of the work to some outsider's whims who may give for selfish motives, or by one not familiar with our deal, the pillars will be brought down on our head. Your readings will change in character, and eventually there will be no readings. For surely, Edgar, your power is of God and cannot be given by man. Are we to moan or are we to turn our head upward and ask the Master for his aid to do his work, to abide in his will, not our will.

Every penny that has been given by Morton and Tim and myself has been in a spirit of love and accomplishment of His work. When the Cayce Hospital was but a sand hill the money given to build it meant sacrifice to us all, but it was a pleasure and so it will always be.

But again in a reading we were told we must all fill our niche in the work. Together it would go on, alone it would fall. And here is the point, Edgar; unintentionally you have shut us all out of the work, you have not worked with us in developing the program. You have not consulted with us in expenditure of funds, and have not worked in harmony with us in endeavoring to get the greatest good out of the service to be rendered mankind by your readings. Your readings are the power of God, the voice of Jesus; not of any one of us as we stand physically.

Right here, Edgar, I would tear this letter up, but I am pushed on to write you more and mail it to you, knowing that one can thru a slip lose much spiritually although seeming to gain materially. So I must continue and I must send it to you.

God bless you for, who am I to pass judgement? As He said, "whosoever amongst you is without sin let him cast the first stone." So know, I am not casting stones or criticizing, I want merely to humbly help if I may.

In another reading you said there was a promise, "Be thou faithful until I come and thy fondest wish will be fulfilled." In God's name, Edgar, do be faithful, follow the hard but righteous path. Come to New York if you like and we will talk things over, but be faithful to thyself and Him.

Our heads are up, our hearts are true, His will, not ours, will be done. Let us do our work as He would have it. The University will be built but only when we are prepared to make it His house, as the ideal makes it.

Edgar, bear no hard feelings to us, for in God's name we love you. Let me hear from you either by mail or personally.

As ever, your friend,
Edwin

* * *

Management of the hospital was one of the unresolved issues and had been a continuing source of confusion from the beginning. One of the most serious issues was the lack of fiscal responsibility. The bills were mounting; expenditures were out of control. The Blumenthals seemed unwilling to appoint anyone in authority over Edgar Cayce, and yet Edgar lacked the business administration background or the ability to effectively deal with the day-to-day management. Conflict arose among the hospital staff over who was in charge—Dr. Lydic or Edgar Cayce? Edgar did his best to meet the conditions by turning to the Blumenthals for direction.

The following two letters crossed in the mail:

June 16, 1930

Dear Edwin:

Well, we have had our meeting and I am in hopes that we all feel we want to consecrate our lives, our endeavors, and our selves more and more to the service of our fellow man and our Master. I'm sure I do.

There was one thing that I spoke to you about in New York the other day, that I feel, Edwin, we're going to have to take some steps concerning. Just what is the right thing to do, I don't know as I am capable of judging. I can only tell you my impressions. I have not talked to anyone that it concerns, as yet—and while each one of these are seeking an audience, I felt it was best to write you before I had even let any one of them talk to me.

There are three patients—yes, four—leaving the hospital today. Feeling that they cannot endure the treatment they receive at the hands of some of the employees at the hospital.

Now, one of these—at least—so long as they were willing to go on parties, have plenty to drink around, and such things—they seemed to be very congenial conditions. The information in the reading, some two or three weeks ago, had a great deal to say to this individual about their conduct. When they altered same to conformity to the information, as they felt, seemingly this dissension has arisen. That all of these are afflicted people, and feel they are not being treated in accordance with the spirit of the information given—I don't mean the Doctor—it seems it's time for us to do something. The Doctor, of course, is not here for me to talk to him today. I understand he is to be back Friday. If this [is] to keep up, I'm afraid we won't have anyone in the Hospital as a patient, except those who possibly have their own nurses.

Think over the matter and let me hear what you feel is the proper thing for us to do.

Sincerely,
Edgar Cayce

EC:GD

June 16, 1930

Dear Edgar:

   ...Enclosed find check for $1000, which I trust will take care of the immediate necessities, such as groceries until we get the books in shape here in New York.

   In order to open these books, will you please have Shroyer send to me here in the office the complete set of books, both of the hospital and the Association. This will include the ledger, cash books, check books, canceled checks, and bank deposit books, and any other books pertaining to the ledger of both the hospital and the Association.

   During the time we have those books whatever entries are necessary at Virginia Beach can be held in memorandum form. We shall return the books just as quickly as possible.

   Judging from the report sent me, the Association has approximately $4000 in the bank. This, I believe, can be used towards current bills.

   Please impress upon Linden Shroyer and Mildred Davis the importance of their immediately sending these books, so as not to detain the payment of outstanding bills unnecessarily. I believe when this system is thoroughly inaugurated it will relieve a lot of pressure from the Virginia Beach end, and again a reason why prompt action is necessary.

   Nothing new here. We arrived home in good time to find the market worse than ever.

   Glad to have seen you all over the week-end. As ever,

Edwin

   Specific direction was not forthcoming, and Edgar found it very difficult to make a decision, especially one terminating an employee. His role was that of an understanding and forgiving counselor. The entire project suffered from lack of decisive action. No one was in charge; no one had the final authority to make a decision.

   The conflict between giving readings for individuals and readings scheduled through the hospital is illustrated through letters sent to Edgar as a private individual, seeking help "on the sidelines," as it were, and outside the framework of the organization. He complied whenever and wherever he was able, but problems in this area continued. The following letter illustrates the kinds of extrahospital requests for readings that he regularly received and which he found exceedingly difficult to refuse:

> **July 14, 1930**
> Dear Mr. Cayce:
>   ... I am a little disappointed that I cannot get a reading for our daughter sooner. She has been ill for a considerable time and I felt that in a case like this and in the name of humanity you would be able to give an emergency reading to help at the right time.
>   I expect to pay you a visit and see your institute and central office at Virginia Beach later on when our daughter's condition permits me to do so, and my intention is to give a donation to your institute, but at the present time I am unable to leave the town. I don't go out evenings therefore, I ask you again if you intend to give a reading please do it as soon as possible because just now is the time when we have to decide about the changing of treatments ...
> > Sincerely,
> > Mr. 5479
>
> P.S., As I have the application blank now I would like to get a life reading for myself, and I would appreciate it if you would kindly let me know the proper time to send in same ...

* * *

It is sometimes possible, in the course of human events, to identify a single act or set of circumstances that determined subsequent events. The following, so typical of the difficulties in communication, organization, and management of the hospital project from beginning to end, is one such event. In addition to the antagonisms that developed early on between David Kahn and Morton Blumenthal, a major disagreement developed over the purchase of furniture for the hospital.

The ANI Board reached consensus in the amount of money they could afford to spend to furnish the hospital and the manner in which they would proceed. They unanimously decided on a ceiling of $2,000 and that their order would be sent out for competitive bidding. David participated in this discussion and voted with the board in favor of both the amount and the need for bids in order to get the most value for the money. He then proceeded to try to sell the hospital $2,000 worth of furniture and to get Edgar to agree to be personally responsible for an additional $1,000 outside the ANI. The Blumenthals were able to dissuade Edgar from this plan, helping him to see that, since all the money he received came from the ANI, then the additional $1,000 was being paid by ANI as well. It is possible that this was the fraud Edwin was warned about on March 30.

Edgar did try to take a stand in the confusion, but his empathetic nature made it impossible for him to effectively move through the confusion or determine a stable course of action. Oddly enough, no one seemed to realize that he was constitutionally incapable of working in an environment in which friendship was not the highest priority. His very nature made it impossible for him not to place the relationship with each individual above all other considerations. He had also been raised in the South amidst the quiet fields of Christian County, Kentucky, and the gentle courtesy of the country remained with him throughout his life. He was, above all, a sincere man who did not fare well amidst conflict. In his makeup, there was no guile or deceit, no cynicism. From his most inner being, he wanted, he needed everyone to get along, to remain friends at any cost, and he made every possible effort to bring peace. In his mind, there could be no decision for or against any individual. There could only be misunderstandings to be resolved. Matters, on the other hand, required that decisions be made.

In the confusion that resulted from a lack of decisive action, antagonisms began to surface. No decisions meant no movement, no momentum. In the absence of action, resentments grew. No one could step in to make the decisions Edgar could not make, and he could not bring himself to let go of the daily detail and ask for someone to take those burdens from him. No one gave him the harmonious assurances he needed to be at his best at what he did. Anyone could have been the business manager of the hospital. No one but Edgar could give the readings. Yet everyone expected him to be all things to all people that the moment demanded. So he tried; he tried his best:

August 6, 1930

Dear Dave:

I received the wire that was sent you on the 24th. Don't get the wrong angle on this, Dave. I know how it must have made you feel, but *somebody*—**I don't know who—is getting things all balled up for everybody, and it's nothing more or less than conversation, as I can see, carried here and there and everywhere. People get the wrong perspective of what individuals are trying to do, and their purposes for same . . .**

Sincerely,
Edgar Cayce

EC:GD

In fact, Edgar knew who it was who was "getting things all balled up for everybody," but he would not confront anyone. A simple "Please don't," or "I respect you and value your friendship, but this has to stop," or "Please don't do this to *me*" might have been sufficient to turn the tide, but he simply could not be other than he was.

* * *

Health problems continued to plague Morton Blumenthal and, more and more, he fell back on his beloved brother Edwin to carry on in his place. Edwin, wishing to be aboveboard with Edgar Cayce in all things, tried to explain *their* position in an effort to keep things moving in a positive direction. David Kahn would not communicate with the Blumenthals. Frustrated at not being able to deal with David directly in order to keep the confusion, irritation, and interference to a minimum, Morton and Edwin spoke rather plainly to Edgar about his friend in the following two letters. These are perhaps the strongest letters the Blumenthals were ever to write:

July 25, 1930

Dear Edgar:

My reason for sending you the telegram regarding the furniture, was that we received a wire from Dave suggesting a means, as he called it, of buying all the furniture. I surmised from his telegram that he referred to the furniture entirely rather than that as accepted. I wired Dave in return, telling him that under no condition would we buy more than $2,000 worth of furniture and that if he personally meant to buy any stock, we would be glad to buy it for him if he supplied the funds. There are so many things now, that we are in no position to set aside any funds, for anything except paying back bills. Dave's suggestion of telling somebody else how to make the money rather than his helping us to make it, was most annoying to me. Not knowing what he had told you, I sent you the telegram, not wishing to bring up any old business that we completed at our meeting.

I am telling you this so that you will have a full understanding of what my intention was, for Dave acts as though he is determined to force us with all that furniture, which you will agree under no condition can be done. When we are ready to buy more furniture, we will all get together and do our own shopping and not be told by Dave what is good value and what is not. Again I say, it was a badly executed suggestion by Dave that prompted the telegram, and I did not know what he had told you.

Dave is very enthusiastic with our money and as you know his material suggestions have not apparently proven of great value. It might interest Dave to know that we have to date paid $11,000 worth of back bills and still find ourselves owing approximately $6,000 in back bills not including the furniture. So you can see there are plenty of places to use any money without having Dave add on to the expense.

. . . Regarding kitchen supplies for the nurses home, I believe it would be well to have all meals eaten at the hospital and not employ any more help in the home. The present force in the hospital should be able to care for the nurses home and thus incur no additional expense. When the new building becomes crowded then we can take necessary action.

I truly hope things are running more normally and that you find yourself in the best of health. Please give my regards to all and be assured I look forward to seeing you in the near future with the hope of again enjoying a friendly discussion and conversation regarding our various mutual interest.

As ever,
Edwin

August 18, 1930

Dear Edgar:

The following is a paragraph from a letter received by me from Dave:

"With reference to the furniture situation Mrs. Brown [David Kahn's secretary] arranged, as I understand it, that the hospital would only be responsible for about $2,000 worth of furniture. The additional amount, whatever it was, Edgar requested that it be left there, and that he would, through certain people who were offering from time to time to do things for him, to have them pay for this amount. He therefore, requested that the $1,000 be charged to him. I believe Mrs. Brown arranged that. However, the hospital will only be responsible for the amount agreed upon."

I truly believe that if you entered into such an agreement with Dave you did so in good faith. However, I also believe that it is a very ill advised move.

At the meeting of the Executive Committee, at which you and Dave were present, it was definitely decided what disposition should be made of the furniture proposition, and to all our understanding, the matter was closed, then purely by accident we find the decision is now to be entirely disregarded.

You must realize that if funds of any nature are to be donated to the Association, we surely have a voice in whether or not they should be accepted, and if accepted, for which purpose they shall be used. If Dave, for instance, did not agree to this, why should he be willing to expect $2,000.00 as part payment from us, rather than have you raise the entire amount of the bill. His suggestion apparently does not cover $500.00, as he seems to plan to bill you for $1,000.00 personally, and $2000.00 to the hospital, thus leaving $500.00 unaccounted for.

In your letter to me I was under the full impression that all but $2,000.00 worth of furniture was to be returned, and then later you stated that Dave would take care of all above that amount. Now Dave says you will take care personally of $1,000.00, so that after all our discussion and then our decision, I cannot help but feel that this is hardly a manifestation of the spirit of co-operation. If Dave has created this plan contrary to your knowledge, you must correct him at once. It appears to me the point is whether or not any Committee is to function, and if it is, surely decisions made cannot be disregarded, as apparently it was the intent to disregard the furniture decision.

I can only repeat what was decided at the meeting, and that is, that all but $2,000.00 worth of furniture must be returned, for truly that was the decision of the Board for the best good of all.

If there is any reason that this should not be done, it is unbeknown to any of us, and [we] feel that you should immediately take action, returning the furniture, or letting us know why not.

I assure you it is most distressing to me to have to insist on a point of this kind, it is a financial as well as a moral and ethical necessity. Let us not falter here and fail to work in harmony, for it has often been said: "It is the little things that count, as the big ones take care of themselves."

. . . It is unfortunate at the present time we do not see more of each other, for you know I surely and truthfully enjoy our visits. I look forward to seeing you at our next meeting, if not at an earlier time.

My best regard to all.

As ever,
Edwin

P.S. I am sending a duplicate copy of this letter, as much as it pertains to him to Dave so he will know the status of the affair.

Edgar and Edwin exchanged correspondence related to the above matter, with no resolution until August 27, when Edwin answered:

August 27, 1930

. . . You ask in your letter a very definite question, assuming deeds of wrongness in your own attitude. If you mean for me to answer that question, I am going to take the liberty of doing so. Without question, you have put your heart and soul into the work; but then you ask, where are you lacking? It is not for self glory, where am I little or small, and say you want to cooperate with Morton and myself. That sentence of cooperation brings a real pang in my heart, because I believe you do want to cooperate. I believe everything you say is said in true sincerity and desire of service, and the only answer to your question that I can see, or that I would write to you, rather than discuss personally, is that you have not permitted yourself to discriminate between the advice given by people to you, and when I say advice, I do not mean it in any childish manner,—I mean our discussion and council of friends.

You have not allowed yourself to discriminate between those who truly have the interest of His work at heart, and those who have other interests, including their own personal gain at heart.

We are all human, we are all far from perfect, we have much to gain, we have everything to be thankful for. Let us stop the feeling of any antagonism, any ill feeling, any lack of cooperation. Let's get together now and all join in one cause, those that can't, those that won't, are simply deferring their present opportunity.

Just one more word on this subject, and that is, whether you have done wrong regarding the furniture obligation, I think the wrong doing is only that you have made, and by this obligation are making, the cross of Morton and myself that much harder to bear, and for that reason is not fair or right, any more than it would be right for you to use funds received by you for readings; or for membership dues, or for hospital patients, in any fashion of your own choosing, and not deposit every cent to the Association or Hospital account.

We feel that no one man has the right to designate what contributions should be received, or what they should be used for, any more than, for example, you would have the right to use or appropriate as you see fit any funds received for readings, membership dues or hospital fees, regardless of any conditions or circumstances.

We shall have to call the next meeting some time the early part of September, and if you agree, I believe it would be well to have the Doctor present at that meeting, as he must know that expenses in the hospital must be reduced. Where there is a will, there is a way, and we simply must find the way to reduce those expenses . . .

As Ever,
Edwin

Events continued to move in the direction of dissolution of the group. Reading 254-51 was obtained on September 5, 1930. David and Lucille Kahn were present, as was L B. Cayce. The ANI Board was not notified that this reading was to be given:

. . . There are *many* conditions as must be considered. The attitude of each should be in keeping with the *ideal* as has been set, or is innately and manifestedly felt in the individuals as *respecting* the work as is being done by the association. First, let *this* be as a criterion of activity by each: He, or she, who would—through force—impel another as to way of thinking, or activity, is a tyrant.

. . . There being an indebtedness by the Association,

Faces from the
Edgar Cayce Letters

This 1903 photo shows the newlyweds, Edgar and Gertrude Evans Cayce, soon after their June wedding in Hopkinsville, Kentucky. Their wedding culminated a courtship of more than seven years.

L.B. Cayce, fondly known by his friends and family as "The Squire," and Carrie Elizabeth Major Cayce, were the most important influences on their son throughout his life. Edgar loved his mother without reserve, and turned to his father constantly for advice and guidance.

Gladys Davis was a young store clerk in Selma, Alabama, when she was asked in 1923 to take down and transcribe a Cayce reading for an acquaintance. Her performance was so sterling that she soon was hired by Edgar and Gertrude as their permanent readings stenographer.

Alfred D. "Alf" Butler, a young man Edgar knew from his Sunday school class in Selma, became one of Edgar's closest companions, a lifelong friend, and a valued sounding board.

David Kahn (below right) and his mother, Fannie Kahn (left), were longtime friends of the Cayces and supported Edgar and the Work over the decades.

Linden Shroyer, shown here with Edgar Cayce at a 1924 picnic in Ohio, was among the circle of friends who stood by Cayce during difficult times.

Morton Blumenthal (below left) and his brother, Edwin (right), provided the primary financial support for the Work for a time.

Hugh Lynn Cayce (standing) joined his former college roommate, author Tom Sugrue, at the dedication of the A.R.E. offices and vault at Arctic Crescent in 1940.

Another member of the Selma group of Cayce friends was W.L. Jones (right, shown here with Edgar), a charter member of Edgar's Selma Sunday school class.

This friendly get-together was held at the home of Lucille and David Kahn in Scarsdale in 1937. Clockwise from left, the diners were Lucille Kahn, Gertrude Cayce, Edgar Cayce, Mary Sugrue, David Kahn, S. David Kahn, Hugh Lynn Cayce, Gladys Davis, and Tom Sugrue.

Dr. Thomas B. House is shown here at his desk at the Cayce Hospital in 1929.

William Moseley Brown, Ph.D., a professor at Washington and Lee University, helped organize Atlantic University and became its president in 1930.

Ann Elizabeth Gray Holbein was the daughter of a longtime Cayce friend from Selma and a contemporary of the Cayce sons. She became an optometrist in Mobile, Ala.

Julia Yates Chandler was the manager of the Empire State Building and active in the Work in the New York City area.

This photo of the Cayce Hospital was used in promotional materials and gives one a good idea of the sweeping views it commanded from atop one of Virginia Beach's highest points.

This is the last photo taken of Edgar Cayce and his sisters. Shown together in 1942 were (sitting, left to right) Ola and Annie, and (standing) Mary, Edgar, and Sarah.

This photo of the Cayce family was taken sometime around 1940, not long before both sons were inducted into the Army during World War II. Left to right are Edgar Evans, Gertrude, Edgar, and Hugh Lynn.

This shot of Hugh Lynn in his military uniform shows us the man who was to take up his father's Work with a dedication that helped the fledgling A.R.E. survive and grow.

under the present conduct or conducting of the work . . .
same showing a deficiency, and as of an extravagance on
the part of those who have been in charge of same, it appears as the burden of the furnishing of capital is upon
the shoulders of a few; that it behooves the Association
and its trustees to so conduct or alter their charter, or their
numbers and activities of trustees, as to insure those furnishing such that the per capita, or the conditions in that
of real estate and holdings, be made in such a manner as
to prevent loss through the activities of those acting in
such a capacity, and that portions of real estate as held by
Association be transferred to those so furnishing such
capital, as to make same more of an even basis. That is the
condition to be met. Now meet it . . .

(Q) Should David E. Kahn direct the spending of the
funds that he contributes?

(A) He should direct as a voice *of* the Board that spends
same . . .

(Q) What has caused this present discord?

(A) That as has been outlined, of the extravagant expenditure by the one—or *felt* so—in charge.

(Q) Does this refer to Edgar Cayce?

(A) To Edgar Cayce.

(Q) In what way has he been extravagant, specifically?

(A) That is judged by individuals. Not from here.

254-51

1931

On February 28, 1931, the Cayce Hospital closed, ending a sad
and frustrating chapter in the long-held dream of a place where
the readings could be validated by medical science. Mr. Van
Patten, local Virginia Beach real estate broker and vice-president of the Cayce Hospital, paid off the last of the employees at
5:00 p.m.

A reading given during this same time also spoke rather
pointedly about what had happened to the hospital and the
ANI:

Many have lost sight of the purposes, the ideals, have presented strange fires upon the altars of truth . . .
In existent conditions, turmoils, strife—even harsh words that stireth [sic] up anger are in the minds and the hearts of many . . . proceed slowly . . . 254-52

It was a lesson Edgar Cayce—and his remaining supporters—would take to heart in eventually setting up the A.R.E.

As the hospital closed and the ANI disbanded, and despite the advice given in 254-51 the previous September, David Kahn brought suit against the Blumenthals for the hospital property. For a number of years afterward, he continued unsuccessfully to sue the Blumenthals in New York City, where the holding company for the hospital had been formed. Atlantic University, separately chartered from the ANI, survived the dissolution and, because it was free from ANI control, continued its struggle for existence.

Even as the hospital and the ANI were ending, however, the Work was moving ahead. In March 1931, Edgar Cayce wrote a letter to all the close friends of the Work, seeking guidance and support in creating a new organization. Tom Sugrue's response was insightful, supportive, and humorous:

March 20, 1931

Dear Mr. Cayce:
I've waited answering your kind letter in the hopes that a little reflection might assist me in making some helpful suggestions—but alas—all I seem to be able to conjure these days is day-dreams of digging up mummies in Egypt and writing such beautiful books that people cannot read them for weeping.

However, I've given the matter a lot of thought. Of course I'm tickled that a new organization will begin soon, feeling as I did that the old one would never get on its feet again. There was something unhealthy about the last days of the [ANI] which gave off a bad smell and made me believe it was past repair and near to desiccation.

Now for the new one. The readings [254-52, -53, -54] seem cognizant of all the mistakes of the past and caution against them for the future. Haste is one thing to be avoided—for in haste one is apt to take whatever is at hand and thus [make] form and foundation of inferior material. The belief that people who dislike each other will, through the work, begin to like each other is all right, except that it presupposes that these people will be idealistic enough to see all that. Experience has shown that they do not. It would seem the better part to begin with a harmonious group and let the irreconcilables come in when they can get over their conceit and ill-feeling. Other people are filled with enthusiasm on first contacting the work and then fade out and remain as deadwood. I think those who have proved that they have a consistent and lasting interest should be given a preference. I suppose it is necessary to get some men with money. I think in that case the people to solicit are those who have so much they do not want anymore, and those who have had it for so long that they do not place too much emphasis on it. You see what I mean by that . . .

A name for the new organization is a puzzle. It can't be one of those high-sounding but futile names. It can't be abstract or idealistic without leading the people to believe we are something which we aren't. Yet we sail under false colors if we claim to be exactly scientific. This reduces the range to such things as "American Institute of Psychic (or Modern, or Cosmic) Research," "American League of Independent Research (or Investigations)." I don't see how we can use such titles as "League of Olympus," "Association of the Agora," or such obscure names as "League of Universal Understanding," or such cognomens as "Cosmic Truth," or those involving "Single Essence," etc. Perhaps the Bible will furnish one—but there is sure to be misunderstanding of a "League of Gethsemene," "New Disciples," etc. So where are we at? The thing is so vast that a particular name is impossible, yet a general term leads to difficulties. So in the end I see only something like this as practical—"Society of Universal Service." After all, each one serves as he knows best, or is best suited, and we serve all and in all manners . . .

I do hope there will be less dissension. I don't believe I ever heard of a unanimous agreement in the old Association. It was a continual source of embarrassment. This time I'd like to see some co-operation. And when one of the workers who knows his business makes a suggestion don't let someone with no brains and a lot of money override him. Personally I'd like to have permission to throw a healthy punch at anyone who insists on being asinine . . .

I'm not being pessimistic—just saying what I think, as you asked me. Having an Alexandrian, or Caesarian makeup I suppose I have a tendency to fret at anyone being at the top except myself and friends—but so long as they'll let me work unhindered I'll be nice and stop biting their ears.

I'll pray for you on the 28th, and be with you in spirit. Add my vote to your own on everything, and call on me when you need me. My love to everyone, and the best of luck.

Always
Tom

On March 21, 1931, reading 254-55 volunteered the name Association *of* Research and Enlightenment as the name for the new organization. Tom Sugrue suggested that it be Association *for* Research and Enlightenment, and everyone agreed. On June 6, the application for the A.R.E. charter was made in that name, and the charter was granted July 7, 1931.

Timeline

1931—The Cayces leave the 35th Street house.
—The organizational meeting for the A.R.E. is held.
—The first study group reading is held, which develops into the Search for God program and results in the formation of Norfolk Study Group #1.
—November 7, Edgar, Gertrude, and Gladys are arrested in New York City for "fortunetelling." A magistrate eventually dismisses the charge.

1932—The first A.R.E. Congress is held.
—Atlantic University closes.

6

The A.R.E. Is Launched: April 1931-1932

As HE STRUGGLED to explain in his own mind why the hospital had closed, Edgar Cayce also struggled to explain it to others:

April 17, 1931

Mr. Alfred D. Butler
P.O. Box 1633
West Palm Beach, Fla.

Dear Alf:
   Yours of the 12th has been received. It's a long story to try

and tell you about the closing of the hospital, and still a longer one to try and tell you what caused it—for I don't know.

When you were here last summer, that meeting seemed to be the first rift—when one of the trustees asked to be relieved from his affiliation, if that was the way many of them felt. That was Mr. Bradley. In September Mr. Blumenthal, who had contributed the greater part of the money, asked that all the property be turned [back] to them (he and his brother and Mr. Brown) personally, so that they could continue to carry on with the work. I agreed to this, since it seemed that they had to have it in order to go ahead. In October Mr. Blumenthal decided to cut down expenses, so he put someone else in charge of the hospital as financial director, discharged the doctor, all of the nurses and the greater part of the help—and then proceeded to get all the patients to leave. Why, I don't know. We secured the services of another doctor—went along from bad to worse, as they refused to allow any more patients to come in. One of the patients already there decided to go home for Thanksgiving. When he wanted to return, they wouldn't let him come. When some of the others went home for Christmas, Mr. Blumenthal refused to let any of them come back. Then he called a meeting for the 28th of February, when they decided (he and his brother and Mr. Brown) to close the hospital, suspend operations, and legally dissolve the corporation.

None of these actions, of course, were legal—but whether anyone will take it up and fight it or not, I don't know.

Some say that it was caused by disinterestedness. Some say that he found another psychic that was closer to him, who possibly catered more to his individual whims. Some say it was purely selfishness, and my failure to conform to some of their ideas. All of these may be right, or all of them may be wrong. I refused to be dictated to as to when and on whom I was able to give a reading. That may be the whole case.

Now, since the hospital was closed, Sister [Annie Cayce]— who was in charge of the hospital—has opened a little home, where she is taking care of two or three patients. The physician who was at the hospital has established an office here on the Beach, and we have a physician in Norfolk who is on call whenever needed. So, should your friend desire to come to Virginia Beach to take advantage of the information that may be given, she could be taken care of here. You might explain the situation to her, and if she cares to make reservation we will try to accommodate her for the desired time. As we are so limited in space, it will be necessary to make reservations for the desired time.

As you will see from the enclosed sheet, we have had a meeting relative to the work being carried on. We haven't considered so much just how it is to be done, but why it should be carried on. We had a very enthusiastic meeting. There were over thirty local people here, with representatives—in person and by letter—from various parts of the country. We hope to have two or three more meetings preliminary to forming an organization for carrying on the work. I would like to have your opinion on the matter. If there are any suggestions you have to make, I would appreciate your doing so.

I certainly thank you for your interest, and I want to assure you of my sincerity in trying to be of service—and service alone. While the conditions have been a bit disturbing, if we are to believe the information the whole thing should not have been unexpected. Being forewarned, we had hoped to be forearmed—so as to guard against these conditions.

Thanking you for your letter, hoping to hear from you again soon, and with kindest personal regards to you both, I am

Ever the same,
Edgar Cayce

EC:GD

*   *   *

The new organization notwithstanding, members of the old ANI and Atlantic University met one another again in court, as all parties sought the recovery of their individual losses from the Blumenthal investment. Only a few received payment from the remaining funds.

During the reorganization period that followed, reading 5502-3 was given May 7 in New York. David Kahn asked how he should devote himself to the Work, and the answer came, in part:

> . . . As conditions of the material natures clarify themselves, as they will, do not mix material conditions with spiritual forces. Do not attempt to serve God and mammon. Do not serve thine neighbor with the one hand and draw from his pocket with the other. Rather let thy yeas be yeas and thy nay be nay, knowing that that as is given for the increase [is] from the Giver of all things.

When David ask from whom the message came, the response was:

> From self. Oft has this very condition confronted self, and as to whether to be able to put on again [as Nadab— See 257-5] those royal robes, and to prevent from offering the strange fires on the altars of the throne, has come to the self; and would the entity, the soul, be again associated in that love that makes for purity before the throne, the decisions in the flesh must be made. 5502-3

*　*　*

It was not only the hospital that the Cayces were to lose in the aftermath of the Blumenthals' withdrawal of support, but, just as painful, they had to move from the 35th Street house. Gardening was always one of Edgar's most beloved of hobbies, and in this letter, we see it is the garden he seems most concerned about losing as he anticipates having to leave the house, which was owned by the Blumenthals:

May 16, 1931

Dear Mamie:
     Just a line to let you hear from us . . .

Speaking of back yards, you should see this one. It is very much of a wilderness, but rather a pretty one I think. Since Christmas there have been blossoms of some kind. Violets—I never saw such violets outside of a greenhouse! Then the other flowers have come along from time to time. Several peach trees were just beautiful, and if they never have any fruit the blossoms were certainly very much worth while. Then the apples, pears, cherries, plums. The honeysuckle, the phlox and stocks, and the fleur de lis—or flags, all in bloom. The roses are just beginning to open. All in all, it's certainly very pretty, to think we may have to walk out and leave it any day. The chickens are coming along very nicely, too. Put off the last hen this morning—have something over a hundred little chicks, with about twenty-five of the older ones—still getting plenty of eggs to supply us, and in another two weeks I think we will be ready to begin on the fried chicken. Plenty of onions and considerable asparagus in the garden; beans, tomatoes, okra, beets, plenty of radishes—we are supplying the whole neighborhood, although they grow only in a little bed in the yard along the flower bed.

I was in New York last week. The organization meeting is called for the 6th of June in Virginia Beach. I don't know just what is going to be the outcome, but I feel that if things carry as outlined it will be really a very much better organization than before . . .

With love from all,
Ever the same,
Edgar

EC:GD

On Wednesday, July 1, the family had their last breakfast in the 35th Street house. They picked all the flowers, grapes, and beans, and dug up all the carrots and the beets from the garden. The move to Wright's Cottage on the oceanfront went on until midnight. The basement would flood four days later, but so many friends rallied around the family that even this inconvenience was taken in good spirits.

By July 7, some 115 members had signed up to be a part of the new organization. It had been only one short year ago that H.W. Leeke of the Cavalier Hotel had extended a membership in the country club to Cayce. This year, there would be no country club membership.

Atlantic University reopened in September under the leadership of Dr. William Moseley Brown, and Hugh Lynn continued in his duties as Atlantic University librarian:

September 19, 1931

Dear Mamie:

... The School here—Atlantic University—opened this week with a very, very, good attendance; in fact, I think there were very few people who thought it would ever open again. Somehow, I believe it's founded on a *living* principle and truth—and, if so, it *will live*, and I hope that Anne will have the opportunity to finish her education here ...

Ever the same,
Edgar

EC:GD

*   *   *

As had happened so often, however, bad news followed on the heels of good. On November 7, Cayce was arrested in New York City for fortunetelling. The few times he afterward referred to this devastating and humiliating event, his language was mild and he spoke of the need for forgiveness. His letters indicated he was struggling with the "why" of it all, which he called the "analysis." The following three letters illustrate his handling of the New York "unpleasantness":

November 23, 1931

Dear Mother Kahn:

We are home again, and after a few days of the reaction that I suppose generally comes from being under such a strain, we are feeling fairly well except colds. My father has a very bad cold, but is feeling some better this morning.

Mother Kahn, we just want to thank you for your kind words and your moral support, the prayers—that were so helpful and encouraging to us through the recent unpleasantness. We recognize that persecutions came to the prophets of old. Each and every one had their sorrows and crosses to bear. We hope that we may be able to show forth in our lives at all times that it is God's love we are trying to manifest before our fellowman. No exaltation of our own selves, but rather His grace, His mercy, that endureth forever. May those who have been misguided, misled, or who have wantonly tried to turn public opinion against us in any way, have His mercies. May the vengeance be in God's hands, not ours! . . .

Let us hear from you. Know how we all appreciate you. With love to you and yours, I am,

Always the same,
Edgar Cayce

EC:GD

William B. Cravis was a hotel manager in New Jersey and New York.

November 23, 1931

William B. Cravis
New York City
New York

Dear Bill:

Well, here we are! I'm sure it would have done your heart good to have seen how the people in this community received us, even after there were such scathing things said about us in the paper. They all say, except for Tom's paper [Sugrue], that the dismissal was on a technicality, rather than on the merits of the case. So, if you and Dave Levy and Dave Kahn can urge Mr. Hammerling to get a certified copy of the court proceedings, it will possibly enable us to get the local papers—with the public opinion—to correct this in the minds of many.

Bill, we don't know how to thank you for all the efforts

and love you exhibited in our behalf, during this unpleas-
ant situation. I just hope we will be able to repay you in a
small measure, and that we were not too great a burden
on you at any time. I believe our hearts are right. I know we
do not want to over-burden anybody. We do not want to
work on their sympathy even, in any way, as to become
burdensome to them. I know the strain you have been under, in so many ways, has made it rather hard for you. I'm
just hoping and praying that there has been a something
born of sincerity in individual purposes that has made
this at least easier for you under the circumstances. May
there come out of the associations and contacts you
made, that which will be a blessing to you and your
efforts ...

Sincerely yours,
Edgar Cayce

EC:GD

Dr. Fredoon C. Birdi was a naturopathic physician in Dansville,
New York.

December 1, 1931

Dear Dr. Birdie [sic] :
    We did indeed appreciate your letter in reply to our
wire, while we were in New York ... doubt you have seen
considerable in the papers regarding the little unpleasantness which occurred while we were there. I am more
than anxious to know your reaction to it. We have tried to
analyze the situations (but are asking for your opinion
also), and it seems it was one of the necessary things in
our experience that we might not only know who are our
friends in that city, but that we might have an opportunity
to stand justified before the man made laws as respecting
the work we are doing. Also, such persecutions are bound
to draw the line between those who are lukewarm and
those who have seen a vision, or who feel that through
such a channel they may gain help, aid and confidence in
their own well-being. What do you think of this for an
analysis? ...

Appreciating your letter, trusting you will let us hear from you from time to time, and with all good wishes, I am

Sincerely,
Edgar Cayce

EC:GD

Tom Sugrue had remarked, with concern, on Edgar's appearance in the courtroom even though Edgar had just been acquitted of the charge. Edgar later wrote to thank him for his concern and to assure him that, in spite of his expression, he had felt good about the verdict, at least until an incident shortly after, with a Delaware policeman who stopped him as he rushed to make a ferry. The officer, after asking if Edgar were going to his own funeral, spoke very kindly to him and dismissed him without a ticket, although he did follow Edgar for the next twenty-five miles.

December 3, 1931

Dear Tom:

We were very glad to have yours this morning. I certainly appreciate the nice way in which you put things, and express yourself.

Yes, I'm sure I must have looked tragic. I *felt* it when that road cop stopped me. Now I'm wondering when the third time will come. I certainly did feel good when I walked out of that court room, and I'm one of those mortals who cannot help but express in their faces just how they feel. I would make a very poor poker player . . .

We were all certainly received with open arms here by our friends, and I just hope we can live up to their faith and confidence in us . . .

Ever the same,
Edgar

* * *

While the Work was that which came through Edgar Cayce, it required more than one person to carry it out. However, it now had a much smaller group of people through which to express itself, as well as the benefit of some hard-won lessons. The Work reshaped and reformed itself into quite a different sort of undertaking. It began again, this time without big donors with dreams of institutions. This time, the Work sought a very different approach.

A small group was told in reading 5502-3 in May that:

> ... he that doeth the will of the Father, the same is respected by the Angels and the Powers that control those forces as man is lent in this earth's experience ...
>
> First, let each examine themselves and know within themselves whether they be about to drink of that cup necessary to be drained to the last dreg ...

In August 1931, Florence Edmonds asked Edgar if he would give readings for those interested, for the purpose of studying his work. Her sister Edith wrote him with a list of questions for the first reading. He agreed to the request and, in September, began what he later considered to be the most valuable work he had ever undertaken, second only to the readings themselves. This body of information came to be called the Search for God materials; the group that had requested and worked with these readings proved themselves, over the next eleven years and nine months, able to drink of the cup.

Working with the Search for God material in the informal setting in which the program was conceived kept spiritual growth strictly an individual matter. "Live it, apply it, and see for yourself what happens." This was the spiritual laboratory through which the Work could express itself—forever. Now, Edgar's Work was safe. As long as there were individuals who would try to live the lessons, the Work would continue. A jubilant Edgar described the study group's work in a letter to Robert N. Ladd, a sales engineer with a New York steel company:

> **January 28, 1932**
> **Dear Mr. Ladd:**
> **I really don't know how to tell you how glad I was to hear from you. We are in our studies considering the power of**

thought, concentration and kindred subjects, and to have you express just exactly the very thing seemed as near a physical application as anything could be . . .

Now for the Study Group: This group, in Norfolk and Virginia Beach, is comprised of about eighteen members, and is studying our information first hand. This, to be sure, makes it a very personal thing. We have readings at least twice a month, and meetings from once to twice a week. The lessons we are preparing are not just the readings, but each individual getting their own reaction from the information or subject given, prepares their experience of applying that information in their daily life; so the lesson—each lesson—would comprise the thought and experience of each member of the group, rather than the thought or experience of any one individual. It is an undertaking that is entirely different from anything that has ever been attempted in the world before (unless we have no record of it).

I am sure that you will see it is a movement quite worthy of a great deal of effort on the part of those interested in being helpful to their neighbor.

. . . This combined effort naturally makes our progress slow, as we all have to be in a perfect spirit of cooperation (Cooperation has been our first subject, or lesson) in order to accomplish anything worth while, but we feel the results will justify the time spent. We have been studying now for about four months and have only finished the one lesson on Cooperation . . .

. . . There is also a healing group of seven within this group of eighteen, as you will see from some of the readings given directly to the healing group . . .

Sincerely,
Edgar Cayce

EC:GD

Search for God and its sister program, the Glad Helpers prayer group, became the entire foundation for the Work of Edgar Cayce throughout the rest of his life. Edgar and those around him had learned a little something about the inability to serve both God and mammon and were dedicated to the necessity, the ideal, of each individual experiencing God directly.

When other activities took too much attention from or drew the focus away from Search for God, the readings would gently remind the group of its critical role, as in this reading in 1934:

> **Not that there is fault to be found, or any condition that could under the existent circumstances be altered. But those that function in the capacity of the Research and Enlightenment should set forth more the purposes and the place that each study group has in such a work.**
>
> **For, as is seen, unless there is a more definite outline, there will continue to be thought and expressed that the purpose of such is to propagate some kind of special cult or tenet or thought, that to some must eventually—or from the beginning—take the ideas of a cult. And this should be the farthest from the thought of any leader or teacher of such lessons. 262-61**

*   *   *

Perhaps Edgar's Work had finally found a home, but in 1931 the Cayce family had not. Gladys, increasingly aware of Edgar's state of mind, was to write a number of letters similar to the following one to all who remained in contact, to one degree or another, with Edgar.

The study group members also knew that all was not right with Edgar, despite his cheerful front. They began to organize a series of public lectures for him, both in Virginia Beach and Norfolk. The group underwrote the cost, giving Edgar Cayce any proceeds. Financial stability, after the years of security supplied by the Blumenthals, was slow to be regained.

While Edgar Cayce continued, as he always had, to counsel and comfort others, the loss of the hospital and the subsequent arrest in New York City affected him deeply. Outwardly, he continued to be the same kindly friend to all, but internally, events were taking their toll. Gladys knew that he had to have a home, a home of his own, a piece of ground where he could plant his beloved gardens and from which they would not be lost in the next move. Others in his life had provided for their families; they had automobiles and fine homes, all through using his readings for the guidance to make it possible. But the Cayces were thrown back on renting and were moved from place to place as landlords sold houses out from under them. Gladys recognized what was happening to Edgar and secretly wrote letters to a number of people she and Gertrude thought might help:

December 11, 1931

Dear Dave:

I just tried to get you over the phone, but was told you were in Chicago and wouldn't be back in New York until tomorrow morning. It is going to be very hard to write what I want to, and probably would be just as hard to say over the phone.

Gertrude has just taken Judge into Norfolk for a treatment. He is not feeling well at all. Yesterday we had this information to come at the end of a reading—a check physical for him [see reading 294-128 for exact wording]:

Unless there is sufficient material creation to hold this body, or those forces that are in the position of being changed, those in the spirit world would make such holds or demands as to make the separation from the body—See? Hence the necessities that there be made such activities, or such thoughts, as to *hold* for *material* activity—else the *spiritual* activity would begin.

We are calling here—there are things to be done! Conditions to be met! There is much need in the spirit world for the activities of the body. There are many that need those activities. There are those calling, desiring, wanting this entity's labors here. Many are calling and desirous of its entering—soon!

(Q) Are there not many more in the material world that need the activities of this body?

(A) Then there should be such physical or material

manifestations that would outweigh those calling.

(Q) How may this best be done?

(A) By their fruits ye shall know them!

Well, there's no use in our getting scared to death—because it won't help any—but we must get to work and *do* something! Just as it is necessary to counteract physical conditions by physical treatments, appliances, etc., it is now necessary to counteract that calling on the other side with material manifestations of our appreciation on this side.

Since Judge has been back from New York he has appeared rather listless and indifferent. I can see from this information that if we want to hold him here we've got to do something to make him *desire* to stay in the earth. Just to sit here in front of the hospital, a material failure, was bad enough for him—but to have that happen in New York was the last straw. If he had been appreciated in a material way, if we had protected him in a material way, as he is appreciated and protected in a spiritual way, it would never have happened—neither of the above conditions. We are letting the same thing happen that happened with Jesus, the Christ—there's not enough spiritual understanding manifested in a material way to hold him.

This has come as a test to us, and it is the strongest test we could possibly have. I'm just writing you the plain facts, and I *know* unless you and a few others there in New York get together and get some actual material results that he can see—both with the Association and with him personally—it's going to be just too bad for all of us!

While the hospital was going he had a material manifestation of his spiritual work, that he could see being exemplified every day. Now he has nothing. Only letters and letters from people, asking—always asking—for something more for themselves.

We've got to stop asking and looking to him for encouragement for a while, and give to him some instead. He needs more than anything else right now something to hold his interest, something to look forward to. He has nothing! It's alright to say he doesn't need money, and doesn't want money—that's very true that he doesn't particularly want it, but he's got to have it, because it's a material demonstration of what the work means in the hearts and souls of people, and unless he has some such material demonstration he will be called to the spiritual side.

We haven't realized just what we have asked of this man. He has given up his life as a material manifestation of God in this world, and what expression of appreciation do we give him—only a constant seeking from him for something more, something more—and usually that something being advice on material affairs that won't mean a blooming thing to any of us if he is taken from us.

Now Dave, I hope you see and understand this situation—it certainly is serious. I'm sitting right here in the house day and night, and I can see him gradually dying from the lack of interest in anything material. He needs outside interests, some material thing that represents the spiritual side. It's true his only desire is to help people, but if such people do not respond in a material way to help him, the natural thing would be for him to be drawn to the spiritual side where he *is* appreciated in a spiritual way. See what I mean?

Ever since I've known him he's wanted a home of his own, and there is a particular lot here that he has picked out and has said that some day he would build there. I think that if his friends would come forward now and do this for him, it would give him the greater impetus than anything else I can think of right now. It would only take about three thousand dollars to get the lot and arrange for the house to be built and paid for like rent. It's such a little, when we realize what he means to us. It would give him a new lease on life, something to look forward to, a sort of memorial to him from the people he has helped—who have put into material demonstration their appreciation of what he has done for them.

I had this idea a few months ago, you remember. Well, the time has come when it's got to be put in motion—or else! People build memorials to people after they are dead, and I can easily see why some of them die so early—it's because they haven't the memorial while they are living. We must build such a memorial for Judge, so he can *see* in *material form* that he *is* appreciated in this world and needed here!

Even if we haven't the money, we can get it—and we must! Won't you get together with Mr. Zentgraf and Mr. Levy, or anyone else you might think of, and see what you can do. Don't start off on some new proposition that may or may not bring something, but get something *now* in actual cash. This is a crude way to put it, but I'm hoping you will understand how very necessary it is.

It's not just the money that I think will create a new interest in him, but the fact that his friends—the ones he has given himself to—are cooperating to show him that they *do* appreciate him! Do you see. It is so tragic that he has to sit here and worry about this bill, that one and the other one, without any prospects at all of things getting better—and everyone saying, oh well, in a few months things will be better.

He shouldn't have a single material thing to worry about, yet he should have all the material expressions of appreciation and enjoyment that are on this earth. Otherwise, this isn't the place for him—he will go as the Master did, and another thousand years or so will roll around—maybe longer—until the world is ready to receive such a demonstration of God in material form in the manner that is due him. "Now is the accepted time—*Now!*" We *must* rise to the occasion!

I guess there isn't much else I can say. You should be able to see the situation at a balance, I think—and the seriousness of it. We've got to bring such a force to bear in this old material world that we can keep our beloved Judge here with us many, many years, to enjoy the material fruits of his years of labor for us.

Please hurry!
Gladys

P.S. Don't let him know that I have written, or that any such action has been forced—but just write him telling him that his friends are doing this as a material demonstration, in part, of what he has done for them. And *do* it as soon as possible!

Gladys and Gertrude were disappointed that there was no response from David Kahn to Gladys's letter.

By the end of 1931, Edgar also had to reconcile himself to the approaching end of Atlantic University.

December 19, 1931

Dear [779]:

Yes, the school has gotten in a bad way. When they finally fell out within their own ranks, it brought on the beginning of the end. I do not know yet just what disposition will be made, whether they will allow the school to go on for the rest of this semester so the students may have credits for their work or not. There's a great deal of jealousy, animosity, and a lot of pure undefiled cussedness—and it's such times as these that all such combined tends to make for very unsatisfactory, very unsavory conditions...

In 1932, Atlantic University closed its doors, too.

1932

Groups breaking up and leaving Edgar Cayce with financial responsibilities was by now an all-too-familiar theme, but 1932 was an especially bleak period for the Cayces. Those who had benefited from Edgar's advice would, from time to time, send token amounts of money (which usually arrived just in time to buy food), but the more serious and pressing issues were ignored or passed over. Each one was just at the moment hard up for cash, their businesses not doing well. Family obligations were pressing. Most promised to pay him later when they made good, if he would just give them a reading. There were few ex-

ceptions to these kinds of requests. The following letters typify
financial conditions for the Cayces in 1932:

May 2, 1932

Mr. A.C. Preston
5722 Georgia Avenue
Washington, D.C.

My Dear Mr. Preston:
    Your letter of April 27th, enclosing the note for renewal,
was received. I carried this to the bank, with the money
for the interest, and left it there—Mr. Parker not being in
at the time.
    The enclosed letter is self-explanatory.
    This morning I went in person to talk with Mr. Parker,
to see what might be done. He absolutely refuses to accept it on a flat renewal, and insists that it be paid. I understand what your situation is, Mr. Preston, and has
been—but something must be done right away. Of course,
I am here—and unless you do something will have to bear
the brunt of the whole thing. For the last two months I
have not been able even to meet my running expenses. As
you know, what little that has come in has been taken up
in attempting to get settled where we might have a place
to work—for a while, at least.
    Of course, they won't hold this open—but won't it be
possible for you to curtail it at least $25.00? I don't know
whether they will accept that or not, but I'll try—Of
course, $50. will be much better. I'm willing to do what-
ever I can, Mr. Preston, but please don't ask me to do more
than is humanly possible. I am enclosing another note
and am asking that you attend to this immediately, for
they will not hold it open longer than Wednesday or
Thursday at the very latest. Please let me hear at once
about it. You can no doubt well imagine the position in
which this places me, and the jeopardy of the credit I may
have had with these people and the well-wishing of the
public. Don't let me be called on this without some effort,
please!

Expecting to hear from you by return mail, and with kindest regards to you and yours, I am

Sincerely,
Edgar Cayce

EC:GD

Once again, the Cayces found themselves moving:

March 8, 1932

Dear Tom:

Yours of some days ago came just about the time we were packing kit and baggage preparatory to moving out from the Wright Cottage. Aren't you glad to hear that? We are at the other end of the Beach, almost, now, in fact have gone to Pinewood, if you know where that is. We have two little cottages on Lake Drive in Pinewood. We are gradually getting straightened out and I believe we are going to like it. It gives us one house for the work with some of the family quarters, the other home for living quarters and 'hash house' and when we get straight I would like for you to come down and take a look around and see what you think. Quite a change, however, from looking out your front door onto the ocean and sand and to looking out on a wooded place with mud and mire and sticks and stones; yet, you are almost a stone's throw of the briny deep.

Mr. Blumenthal though, I think, decided that he needed that house in his operations, so made a bid for it and we would have our rent raised or be forced to find another place, and then as we couldn't pay that very well, they already charging for it over a hundred bucks a month, why it was better to move, and we got both of these places for almost half that. Let us hope it is the best thing. What do you think?

I realize from your letter, Tom, you are getting hold of life in just about the proper shape. If all of us did take the time to take stock of ourselves, stand off, as it were, and watch ourselves pass by, see what sort of looking people we were, we would be in a great deal better fix. We would become quite a bit better acquainted with what our fellow man have to put up with when in our presence occasionally.

Yes, I am in hopes that all the affairs in the east will clear up. You have, no doubt, have and seen considerable anxiety shown in the last week over the Lindbergh baby. It has taken first place, I suppose in every paper in the world. That such a thing could be accomplished seems unaccountable. Here's hoping that it will be able to be cleared up in the very near future. What it must mean to a man to have been raised to the power, the position, fame, fortune, and everything, and then have that he loves most taken away. They can make fun of the old Book, Tom, but they can never get away from its lessons. Poor old Job had the same thing to deal with, didn't he? ...

There certainly is much to be thankful for in the interest the movie people [officials from Paramount and Warner, their families, and friends] have shown. I am wondering if we would be eating now if this hadn't developed. Whether this can be worked out in a satisfactory way and manner as to the adapting something from the work to the screen, I hardly know. I believe that it can. We may have a trial of same this summer if we live that long ...

Keep your chin up, you are going over big, Tom, you are bound to! It is in you, and if you put the trust in Him who is able rather than in your own self or someone else that might have a nice little pull today, you will make it.

We have all worked ourselves about fool crazy getting moved. I, as usually, tried to do all of it in a day or two and have been laid up in the bed for some time. Looking around, though, and am in hopes that I will recover.

Let us hear from you when convenient and possible, and take good care of yourself. With love from all,

Ever the same,
Edgar

EC:GD

A solution to the housing situation was slow in coming, but it was coming. It took still one more move, however:

May 6, 1932

Dear Mamie:

...We hope we have arrangements made for a place. If we move into this we will be across the street from the Catholic Church. We will at least be in spiritual surroundings, though outwardly individuals may be antagonistic. Yet the love of God is One, and I hope this will prove a most satisfactory move in every way and manner ...

Ever the same,
Edgar Cayce

EC:GD

Edgar's faith in the "love of God being One" was borne out as Father Brennan, the Catholic priest at the church, became a good friend. Over the years that Fr. Brennan was assigned to Star of the Sea Catholic Church, he and Edgar remained very close and regarded one another with affection and respect. The Cayces moved to Arctic Crescent on May 30, 1932. Edgar was ill and had to watch everyone else do all the work, but none of that mattered because, for the first time in their married lives, the Cayces had their own home. Edgar was fifty-five years old.

*   *   *

Tom Sugrue's letters were always a bright spot in Edgar's day. Edgar was very proud of Tom and treated him as if he were a son. The admiration Edgar had for Tom brought out the best in the young, aspiring writer. Tom responded by writing beautiful letters to Edgar:

May 9, 1932

My Dear Mr. Cayce:

...Your mention of the study group work and the fact that it is in some danger of bending toward a religion reminds me of my impression about all the people who ever came to the work and stayed with it seriously—I am afraid that all of them developed a myopia which kept them from getting the best from the readings—that is, they immediately lost their perspective of life as a reality. I see that more so in men like Bisey [Dr. Sunker A., who developed the formula for Atomidine] who is letting himself go now that his business worries are over. Of course unworldliness is necessary for spirituality, but that delicate balance between the two is so necessary. I think it is the secret of greatness—and I hope I shall be able to achieve it . . .

Now that spring has invaded even this dirty imperial old city I am feeling salt in my nostrils and an itch in my feet for cool grass wet with dew and all the pleasant things that come from earth in the early months of summer. I remember old smells and sensuous things that touched my body—water in brooks running over my nose and into my mouth—a cow rubbing her nose against my hand— wet roofs shining under a moon, the smell of wood smoke and the rough wool of a bathing suit. These, and old friends—the quiet streets of Lexington, the long boulevard at Virginia Beach blinding me with sunlight, the red plush of your chair in twilight and all those familiar faces washed and scrubbed for breakfast. These are things I shall always remember—thank God—not the pain and longing and disappointments—and as old Edwin Markham says—"the long, long patience of the plundered poor."

> For these as they taught me beauty,
> women and flowers and books;
> for things that are not my duty,
> ladies of lovely looks;
> for every star in the heavens
> and every wave in the sea,
> for every kiss that leavens
> and for eternity
> I make my songs and sell them
> for beggar's pence or none;
> and may your heart go with them
> toward the flaming sun.

And so goodbye for a little while—and I hope my guardian spirits will allow me the pleasure of a visit with you sometime in the summer—my love to everyone, and the best of luck and health—

Tom

Edgar wrote back about the toll that the move from the 35th Street house had taken on the whole family. Tom responded with the light-hearted humor and note of affectionate teasing that characterized the Cayce family and those fortunate enough to be a part of their lives. This glimpse into the college years of Hugh Lynn and Tom utterly dismisses the seriousness with which Tom actually approached his own education. We also are given another early glimpse of Tom's extraordinary gift with words with which he was later to so exquisitely craft Edgar Cayce's life story.

June 20, 1932

My Dear Mr. Cayce:

... Every now and then I get a sniff of sea air, or hear last year's music on the radio, and then I get a pain in my stomach for the beach, its moon and casino, the bowling alleys and little girls in white and yellow dresses, and all that pleasant life so conducive to thoughts that edify and cleanse and enervate.

And that reminds—do you think it right that a young man with whom I struggled and slaved for four years, with whom I actually lived and studied, should stop writing to me just because he has a touch of literary laziness? Your son I mean, who has not penned me a note these three months. Please remind him that he has ties that bind him to me irrevocably—I used his toothpaste, wore his ties, dirtied his towels, borrowed his money, his school-books, his automobiles and his clothes when they fit me. He can't let me down like that! I woke him up when he went to sleep in class, I sneered at him from my bed as he sat up pouring over those silly novels he insisted on reading, I listened to his recital of affaires d'amour, even sympathizing when I had the energy and was not too beset by my own heartaches; I even went so far as to try to keep him from buying green ties and purple socks, and this is what I get for it.

Tell him he can't get away with it. Tell him to remember the times he got me out of bed for classes, put me to bed after dances, goaded me into buying soap and razor blades, bore with me when I insisted on telling him what I thought of bridge and other silly pastimes. Tell him to re-member the dance tickets we shared at the casino, the girls we bored to tears and slumber, the hamburgers we ate with perfect knowledge of what they would do to us, and all those other foolish gestures of youth unbridled and pretty happy about it all.

I really hope I'll get down for the eventful [Congress] week-end, and since my destiny has a habit of spoiling me by granting what I want real badly perhaps I shall—any-how, here's wishing.

Tom

The first A.R.E. Congress was held June 29, 1932. Tom was not able to attend.

*   *   *

In addition to the positive way in which the A.R.E. was com-ing together, Edgar Cayce felt the Search for God groups were another bright light growing in the world.

October 21, 1932

Dear Alf:

... the study group is making progress. We have per-haps four or five small groups following the course; most of these are family groups, or one or two that meet once a week from home to home, as the original group does here in Norfolk. Last Monday our local group had their first full day of prayer and fasting. It is hard to tell another just how much such lends to the strength of an organization, how that it draws us closer together, enabling us to be better contributors that may aid our fellow man ...

Ever the same,
Edgar Cayce

Timeline

1935—Edgar Evans Cayce goes to Duke University in September.

7

The Calm Years:
1933-November 1935

1933

IN 1933, EDGAR Cayce was contacted by an astrologer he had known since 1927. While he addressed her here by her married name of Carmody, she was known professionally as Laurie Pratt. The following two letters authenticate some of the major events of Cayce's life from which his astrological chart was drawn:

February 28, 1933

My dear Mrs. Carmody:
Many thanks for yours of the 24th. I certainly appreci-

ate the privilege of being allowed to have a report from you on the astrological aspects of my life, as well as to what may be expected in the future . . .

I will give you in a very definite way some of the conditions that have arisen in my life, that have possibly been the periods when changes have taken place the more specifically. You will no doubt see these from the chart.

Yes, conception took place at or near the same place of my birth. I was a normal nine months' baby, arriving about the time the doctor and my mother expected me— and I was the second child my parents had. It was a perfectly normal birth. No unusual or surgical methods were used, or necessary.

As the readings have given, the first breath was taken into the body at 2:45 o'clock on Sunday afternoon, March 18, 1877.

Owing to the necessity for me to be weaned rather early, I was quite ill during my second nine or ten months—and undernourished. When they were able to obtain a wet nurse for me, I improved rapidly and grew normally.

My first accident (and about which I have wondered a great deal, though have never asked for information on this) happened on May 27, 1880, at 10:00 o'clock in the morning, when I fell from a fence and stuck a nail—protruding through a block—right in the top of my head. It pierced sufficient to enter the cavity. There was little trouble experienced from this. The doctor put a plate over the hole.

On June 8, 1881, at 1:30 o'clock in the afternoon, I witnessed the death of my grandfather by drowning (who was accredited with having most wonderful psychic abilities). I was the only individual present when this happened.

At 3:00 o'clock in the afternoon on May 22, 1885, I came very near to being drowned myself; in fact, it was reported that I had been. No one knew why or how I happened to be saved, as I slipped into a sink hole while wading in the water.

From 1880 to 1890 I continued to have days when I

played with unseen people, or fairies. I could give many of those experiences, if you see that they would fit into the chart anywhere.

In September 1886 I stared to school. I was rather dull or backward until I had my first experience in February, 1887, which you have seen related in the booklet. From then on no one could keep up with me in my classes.

At 7:00 o'clock in the evening, on January 9, 1888, I had a very painful and unusual accident. I fell on a stick which pierced the body, almost disemboweling me [see 294-79]. The medical profession tell me yet that they do not understand how or why it's ever been possible for me to have issue.

After this injury I was for several years rather sickly—had colds and fever, finally being cured by—what many would have considered—being hoodooed by a colored mammy, who gave me spider webs to take.

Any other incidents I suppose have been given in the little booklet, about the loss of my voice—which was from March 1900 to February 1901, and the operation for appendicitis on March 10, 1914.

On January 2, 1919 I first had an intimation of astrological influence. There were received between then and March 19th about fifteen or more reports from astrologers in almost every part of the world. Each agreed that on March 19th of that year, between 8:30 and 11:30 in the evening, I would be able to give the best report psychically that I would be able to give that year. They suggested that I make this demonstration public, though they altered widely—many declaring me to be as near a perfect Uranian as anyone for whom they had ever cast a chart. While the reading was not made public [and no records of it now exist], it was the first information we ever had respecting astrological influence in our lives, and the first intimation of reincarnation we had had . . .

A very interesting experience I had with Miss Adams [a Dayton astrologer]. I spent several very pleasant evenings with she and Mr. Jordan, before and after their marriage. The man [Arthur Lammers] for whom we gave the first horoscope reading (or Life Reading, as they have come to be called), went with me to Miss Adams and had her cast his horoscope. Outside of the reincarnation which came into the latter portion of our reading, the astrological influences were identical—except her phraseology, of course, was different.

Oh yes, you asked about my marriage. I was married on June 17, 1903, at 3:15 in the afternoon. My first extended trip began on January 1, 1920. Every commercial association that I have experienced, except one, began on August 1st. On August 1st, 1900 I went into the photographic business. My first business association away from home began on August 1, 1898. August 1, 1904 I went into the photographic business for myself. It was on October 6, 1923 that I quit commercial affairs and began giving my whole time to the psychic work.

If there are any other questions you would like to ask, don't hesitate to do so. I hope I haven't made this too long drawn out, nor bothered you. I don't mean to give the impression that there's something wonderful about it all, for I am sure—as you will see—I have had as many hard experiences in many ways as the next one. And, as some student told me a few years ago, "I don't know how you have fought off the women, but if you pass March '33—after that you should have smooth sailing."

Of course, I'll be very anxious to hear from you,

With kindest regards and thanks from all, I am,

Sincerely,

Edgar Cayce

EC:GD

August 22, 1933
Question Sheet, please return with answer

Dear Mr. Cayce:

I could not make out Key Cycles for the following events because you did not tell me the place where they occurred. Please write name of town after each date.

Loss of voice, started March 1900. What place? Do you know date?
A. March 29, 1900, Hopkinsville, Ky.

First extended trip, Jan. 1, 1920. Where were you on this date: Give town that you *left*.
A. While living in Selma, Alabama.

August 1, 1900, photographic business. Where?
A. Hopkinsville, Ky.

August 1, 1898, first business association away from home. Where?
A. Louisville, Ky.

August 1, 1904, photographic business for yourself. Where?
A. Bowling Green, Ky.

October 6, 1923, entered psychic work permanently. Where were you on this date:
A. Selma, we came to the decision that I would go into the psychic work permanently—and left for Dayton, Ohio.

Do you know date on which you first "relied on the promise" and exercised psychic ability to learn your spelling lesson?
A. Feb. 11, 1888, about 3 miles from the home in the county where I was born ...

Do you know the first date, or one of the dates, on which you attempted to give readings for gain, i.e., read the races, stock market, etc., which you said brought "fearful" results? Where?

A. Jan. 3, 1908, Bowling Green, Ky.

Date of your wife's illness, lung trouble, and date when
you gave the reading for her which resulted in her cure.
Where? Was this the illness that Miss Adams thought
would result in death?
A. First taken ill in March, 1910, Hopkinsville, Ky. The reading was given for her on October 10, 1910, at 3:00 P.M.,
Hopkinsville, Ky. [This was not the illness that Miss Adams
thought would result in death, for Miss Adams' horoscope
was cast for her many years afterward.]

*   *   *

Fishing and gardening remained throughout Cayce's life as
the two hobbies that gave him the greatest pleasure. He considered gardening more than simply growing food for the table, although the Cayce household was largely dependent on the
garden for much of their food and for beautiful flowers to deco-
rate the property. To Cayce, it was an activity of spiritual import.
For many years, he mourned the loss of the first garden he had
created on 35th Street, and no garden seemed to equal that first
one started in 1925. In February 1933, he was still making periodic visits to the old place, as the following excerpt to Mamie
Gray illustrates:

2/7/1933
Dear Mamie:
   ...A few days ago I was down on the 35th Street place.
The little trees there certainly looked beautiful, and they
really seemed quite glad to see me. It seems a shame to
have to leave things of the kind, but possibly they will be
of a service to someone. At least, if people appreciate them
in any way, I'm sure they will do their best to give their
expression of life, for God ...

In the following, he expresses both his personal philosophy
and that of his readings about finding God in nature. While the
letter is rather long and appears here out of order, it offers a rare

opportunity to catch a glimpse of the world through Edgar
Cayce's eyes:

October 21, 1932

Dear Mrs. Finlayson [Abigail, of Cleveland, Ohio]

As always, I was very glad to have yours of the 5th. I appreciate very much your telling me about your garden,
and troubles with it.

For so many years I had little opportunity to plant anything I have been at Virginia Beach all the time the family
tell me that I spend every spare nickel I can get hold of,
and a lot I shouldn't, on trying to have things like that
around me.

In the first place I lived here [315 35th St.] I had quite
an assortment on a very small lot, for though I only
had about 140 x 50 feet, including the house and garage, I
had fruit trees of every description almost—pear,
plum, cherry, peach, apple, grapes, as well as a little garden, though I had a very nice asparagus bed, onions,
beans and tomatoes, as well as a little bed here and
there of strawberries, raspberries, blackberries, and—of
course—an old-fashioned garden with roses, violets and
the like.

The last year I have been moving around considerable
and such things, you know, can't just be pulled up and set
down anywhere, and be expected to do anything; so practically the only thing I've saved out of all the beautiful assortment is my violets. They have been moved so often
that I suppose when they see anyone coming with a hoe
they wonder where they're going next. They are very
appreciative, and if given the opportunity they bloom
forth with all their might and main, and raise those beautiful heads with all the fragrance that is theirs alone to
give.

They are blooming beautifully now, and will no doubt
continue until next June, as they have done since I have
had them.

The place where we are now living doesn't just yet permit making much of a show for a garden, or trees, as we

are very close to a little fresh water lake. Can you imagine looking out one window and seeing the lake, while looking out another and seeing the ocean? The drain in the back of the place is rather low at present. If I can find such a thing as "the root of all evil" that you speak of, and cover up some of the reeds and rushes around the edge of the lake, I might have a very pretty little place. I love flowers, and some of these times when you are pulling up some of those that have gotten away from you, and you feel that you could send them, put them in a little bundle and send them down to us—I'll find a place for them, and assure you I'll take good care of them.

I love all nature, for there seems to be—as it did when I was a child—the attempt to speak to me very often of my Maker. Life in all its essence must be from that Creative Energy we have called God. Plants, animals and everything, including human beings, show their appreciation of every effort man makes towards setting forth that love that must have been expressed when God brought them all into existence.

Just as kindly thoughts and loving hands will enable your hibiscus to bring forth those beautiful petals, so do contention, selfishness, greed and avarice, bring forth those weeds that allow them to choke out life. The earth didn't bring forth the weeds and briars that were obnoxious until man erred, so they must be as much of man's making; for he is a co-creator with God, as no doubt you are learning more and more by reading and studying [Christian] Science.

Yes, no doubt we often fool ourselves and attribute things to ourselves that others looking on do not recognize as being just in accord with the actual conditions. Everything has been tamed, we remember, except man's tongue. As someone has said, we speak so loud that our neighbors can't hear what we say; or our actions speak louder than words.

For the last few days we have had some very stormy weather. It is rather our season for such, but today it is very beautiful outdoors. While the sun hasn't entirely bro-

ken through the fog and mist, we can hear the birds singing and it is warm enough not to have a fire, even with the
windows open. Shrubbery and trees in the forest and
about the house are all taking on all the golden tints of
autumn, and we are reminded that this is the time for nature—as represented in our flowers and shrubs—to prepare for rest, that men have called death; yet will bloom
forth again in the spring, if given any sort of opportunity,
to bring joy and gladness to those who love to see beauty
in any and all of its angles in their lives.

I'm sorry you didn't have as pleasant a visit as you had
anticipated. All these [disappointments] are necessary in
our experience, that we may more and more see the necessary things for becoming aware of what is good or bad.
While we are in the material world we only know by
comparisons. Man is prone to draw his comparisons consciously; hence we become more and more material-
minded. While we recognize there are spiritual truths, the
application to the material things of life must, to us, take
on such concrete examples as to force us to be more and
more material.

We still keep fairly busy with our work. There has been
the formation of some study groups in various parts of the
country, that are being fostered and supplied information
from a local group [Norfolk Study Group #1] studying the
information [readings] firsthand. I have been wondering
if at any time or another you would like to see or know
something about the spiritual application of the information that is seen or expressed in the lives of others, who
have been closer in contact with the information than
yourself. Don't understand, now, that I'm trying to sell you
anything, because you just said you didn't have any of this
world's means, or the "root of all evil". I think we often
misquote that, though. It is the *love* of money that is the
root of all evil, or the love of things that money brings, as
it is the medium of exchange. The love of having that
which will buy indulgences and pleasures for us is the
thing that brings the evil most in our lives, don't you
think? These [Search for God] lessons are only 25 cents a

month. I do not know whether they would be really of interest to you or not.

I will be glad to iterate to you what they are like, and what they are all about, if you are interested. I do not want to induce anyone to study or to take up the thought of such things, especially when I know they have such a wonderful course as you are studying, and—as you say—that is entirely free.

Know that we are always glad to hear from you. I have heard recently over the radio some of the great political overflows that you have had in your city [Cleveland, O.], and I enjoyed Mr. Hoover's address very much. I do not know, though, of any particular promise he made to those poor fellows that are out of a job now. I do not know that any promises any of the rest could make would be fulfilled. We all seem to be unbalanced. Those that would have more, and those that would like to see the other fellow divide with them—but what are either willing to give in exchange? We look on money as being the medium of exchange, and forget that the laborer is worthy of his hire. When we say that, we only think of so many dollars and cents. The laborer would be worthy of the hire of bringing contentment with whatever position or condition one finds self, knowing that *some* way is being provided for them to be taken care of; for, as He said, the birds of the air make no preparation whatsoever; very seldom is it, though, that they go hungry for any great period of time. Are we not much more than sparrows? The trouble is, we want to tell God what He should do for us.

Drop us a line whenever you find the opportunity.

Sincerely,
Edgar Cayce

EC:GD

1934

If any year could be considered uneventful for Edgar Cayce, perhaps 1934 was one of the rare periods of calm. The family finally was settled in their own home. Edgar could fish to his

heart's content, both in the ocean and in the lake in front of his
house. His two-year-old garden was underway. His beloved
Search for God work also had taken root. The country was still
in the grip of the Depression, however. The Cayces were accus-
tomed to "making do," but at this particular time conditions
were even more strained than usual. In addition, some of the
older members of the family were not in the best of health and
were often in Edgar's and Gertrude's thoughts, their worries
made larger by the financial constraints imposed on their ability to travel.

January 5, 1934

Dear Mamie:
   I was very glad to have yours written on New Year's Day ...
   We had for our Christmas a visit to Gertrude's mother.
Gertrude, the two boys and I, left on Saturday morning
before Christmas and arrived there Sunday afternoon.
Found all up, but Gertrude's mother is not well at all; has
been failing now for the last year or more. It is the first
time that her two children have been home on Christmas
for twenty-five years, but she had her two children and all
of her grandchildren. I don't know as she will ever see another one, but we can always hope for the best ...
   With love and regards from each and every one,
Ever the same,
Edgar Cayce

Ann Elizabeth Gray Holbein, Mamie Butler Gray's daughter,
was like a member of the Cayce family. She fell in age between
the two Cayce sons, and all her life, she referred to Edgar as
"Daddie." As an adult, she became an optometrist in Mobile,
Alabama. Edgar had no hesitation in talking freely in his letters
to her—and to any number of others—about the difficult times.

January 10, 1934

Dear Anne Elizabeth:
   I am just in receipt of yours of the 6th ...
   I assure you it is very gratifying to know that you stand
at the head of your class in school ...

We have been having, as I am sure everyone has through-out the country, quite a hard time making both ends meet. While I know that we have a great deal to be thankful for, the best of us at times become weary with the struggle, but we should all realize only those who endure unto the end wear the crown . . .

As you no doubt know, I spent most the entire month of November in New York, will probably go there again the latter part of this week or the first of next, to lecture be-fore a Society there. Can you imagine such? I don't know just how long we will be there this time. It will possibly depend upon many circumstances.

We did not have any Christmas here. I am sure from what they say that the young ladies here at the House, Miss Gladys and Mildred [Davis, Gladys's cousin] and my father felt they were very much left alone, for the rest of us went to Kentucky. It was the first time that Muddie's mother has had all of her children there (also her grand-children) at home on Christmas, or at any time, for that matter. Since Christmas she has been quite ill. In fact, we had a wire from them last Thursday and they did not think that she would live through the day. The information we got and suggestion for help seemed to have been of aid, and our last report is that she is getting along very well. Gertrude hasn't gone home yet, and possibly will not un-less she hears of her being worse again, so that may have, of course, something to do with our stay in New York. This time there are only three of us, Hugh Lynn, Miss Gladys and myself, as it was in November.

Hugh Lynn, as you remember, carried himself through the greater part of his university work by working in the library. It is not often they get in the first year unless you have some very good connections early, but afterwards, as it was with him, one usually gets along pretty well if they like that kind of work . . .

Edgar Evans is just starting out to his first party or two, and I think now he is beginning to want to learn to dance. So much for the young idea of being a woman hater! He is taller, though, than Hugh Lynn—lacks very little of being as tall as I am. He is getting along fine in school, but has one more year, could have finished this year if he had wanted to, but he decided that he would stretch it out another year and get all this school had to offer.

Let me hear from you.

Ever the same!
Edgar

EC:MD

May 16, 1934

My Dear Mrs. Smith:

Yours of the 13th came, enclosing your contribution, also the Group's, for which please accept our sincerest thanks.

I appreciate very much your writing me as to just how you feel about your reading. I'm glad indeed that the information means so much to you. I think you have the right idea exactly about the meditation and allowing yourself to go out to the inter-between land. If such experiences become a portion of the whole self, well and good; but as we have so often been told, there are times when we should "Stand still and see the glory of the Lord." It is indeed true that we sometimes try so hard that we become rather a stumblingblock to our own selves. We interpose ourselves. Let me use a little illustration:

You remember very well the story of Elijah being so anxious and zealous as to what he was able to do at the time there was a test between he and the sons of Belial, when the fire came down on the altar and consumed the sacrifice to Jehovah. But when he destroyed the priests of Belial and Jezebel spoke, Elijah got so scared that he ran away and cried unto the Lord, "I alone of all people am left to serve thee; everyone has turned against us." He saw the mighty tumult in nature, the fire, the storm, the lightning, the earth quaking and all the mighty forces in nature. He was fed by the ravens; the Lord told him to stand still, be quiet and listen at the still small voice from within. It is the promise to every individual, that we may be directed within ourselves. For, as Moses said, it isn't as to

who shall ascent into heaven or who will go over the sea,
but lo, we will find Him within our own selves. And, as the
Master said, "The kingdom is within." So, as we apply the
little kindnesses, the smile here and a kind word there,
we will be awakened oft to that peace which comes from
within.

I remember quite well an experience of Mr. D.L. Moody's
which he told me, when I asked him if God had ever spoke
to him. He said he was really having his first successful
meeting as an evangelist in Cleveland Ohio. As he prayed
earnestly one night, he had a vision and was told to close
his meeting at once and go to London, England. He did
that very thing, to the surprise of everyone and all his associates. In England, knowing no one, he wondered just
what it was all about. Then one day, walking through one
of the more unpretentious portions of the city, he heard a
child's voice singing. He looked up and saw a little box of
flowers on a ledge, the only one's anywhere in the quarter.
He went to the steps and something impelled him to go
up, and there he found a poor little lame girl that had been
trying to tend these flowers. When she saw him she ex-
claimed, "Oh, Mr. Moody, I have been praying that you would
come to London! God needs you so badly here!" The success of his meeting there is possibly still felt in London.
To him this was a speaking voice within, presented in vision first, and then the answer in the little lame girl in London.

We have no idea whom He will use, or by what means
we will be spoken to. We here have had a beautiful illustration to us this morning: Recently we have had requests
from very prominent and—worldly considered—very
philanthropic individuals in the larger centers; namely
Detroit and New York. And some very marvelous results
have been reported. Yet when our immediate needs had
to be supplied for our carrying on here, the funds came
from a lonely poor worker on the Alabama river.

What a lesson we have had every day! And yet I know
we do very little with all the glorious things that are shown
and told us. We feel very unworthy at times, but you do

not know how much good it does us for one like yourself
to tell us that the information you received is helpful to
you day by day.

Sincerely yours,
Edgar Cayce

EC:GD

*   *   *

Edgar Cayce was always open to talking with those whose interests took different paths than his. By mid-1934, he had met
Johannes Greber, a former Roman Catholic priest who had become a spiritualist medium and healer and who had received a
reading from Edgar. Greber wrote *Communications of the Spiritual World*. Edgar also had made the acquaintance by this time
of Eileen Garrett, a well-known British medium:

May 19, 1934

My dear Mrs. Finlayson:
... We seem to have a way of getting people in various
portions of the country acquainted with one another.
Have some people in Philadelphia now that we are getting together ...
I have a little patch of pinks—spice pinks, I suppose.
This is the first time they have bloomed since I have been
here. Not a great many on it as yet, but they are the most
fragrant things I have ever seen. Even days after they were
picked they give off a lovely odor. I certainly would love to
see, though, the flowers you describe in Oregon. I have
never been further west than Arizona.
The fox gloves and delphiniums are very beautiful when
we get farther back from the ocean that we are here at the
Beach. I have seen some very beautiful beds of them. I
would love to be able to have such. My nicotine hasn't
started as yet, but if it is anything like you describe it will
no doubt give us a great deal to think about as time goes
on ...
It makes me feel quite a bit like old times to know that
Mr. Finlayson had worked in Burrows Bros., as some years
ago I was associated with the firm also, though I was never

in Cleveland or in the wholesale house. I was on the road. But that has been so long ago that I wondered if they still maintained the wholesale department. In Kentucky, Tennessee and Alabama it was considered by most of the book and stationery people rather an event when the salesmen for Burrows Bros., opened their line for the fall trade, which of course, usually was early in the spring. I have always had a hankering to see the place, just as for many years before McClurg in Chicago changed hands, it was quite a marvelous store. Of course, my first venture in a book store gave me the back-ground, possibly, for the liking of this particular character of stores. The stamp department in such a store must be quite an interesting department. I know quite a number of people who have the hobby. In fact, the younger of the boys here has quite a collection, and I had the hobby myself a good many years ago, when I was the president of the Southern Stamp Association.

I hope you will be able to get that book by Dr. Greber. As I said, I know him fairly well, and I believe it is one of the best books on the subject that I have seen and possibly gives an individual the best approach to spiritualism than anything that I have seen. Most of the books of such nature are written as just experiences, but the basis for such an approach is not so often touched upon as well as it is in this book.

The experience with Mrs. Garrett was quite interesting, though our information does not agree altogether with the idea of individuals having controls that are not possibly much farther advanced than personalities that we may meet in the earth plane now, and it is very evident that there is not a great deal of change when one passes over except as comes in an actual spiritual growth.

I have quite a number of individuals in mind who were able to give an almost indeterminate number of readings in a day, but to have them in such a shape that you may study them and compare them from time to time to the experiences that arise in life is a different thing. I don't know whether such a use of one's self so often and so long

at a time takes from the strength of the body or not. When
I think of my own experiences and realize that I, indeed,
must live two or three lives at a time, it is rather appalling
when I think of it.

Christian Science has always had quite a fascination for
me, but it does not as you say at all times answer. People
are so inclined to want to fool themselves that much of it
is evidently just a condition of the mind and the body doesn't
always respond to everything that the mind dwells on . . .

Sincerely,
Edgar Cayce

*   *   *

While 1931 was three years in the past, the lessons of the New
York arrest remained fresh in Edgar Cayce's mind, particularly
the need to have recipients of readings take out a membership
in the A.R.E. The Reverend Dr. Horton Held, the Norfolk spiritual healer with whom Edgar had been in contact since his Ohio
days, had been working with a Mr. Hayes who had cancer, and
had asked Edgar to give a reading. Edgar had responded by asking that a membership application be completed. Dr. Held misunderstood, thinking that Edgar wanted payment before he
would give the reading:

4406 Locust Street
Philadelphia, Pennsylvania

June 9, 1934

Dear Mr. Cayce:

I must admit your recent letter hurt me a good deal.

I had written you as one practitioner asking the assistance of another in a very difficult case. Usually such requests come under the head of professional ethics and are
responded to . . . I would not under any circumstances ask
Mrs. Hayes at this time to assume the financial obligation
of a membership in the association, no matter how much
I may think it of value. She has all of the financial burdens
that she can possibly [be] carrying.

While not a blood relation of either Mr. or Mrs. Hayes, I
am always spoken of and looked upon as a member of the
family and whatever I would do in the interest of helping

Mr. Hayes towards recovery would have their gracious acceptance and cooperation.

All rules are more or less elastic. I hope that you will reconsider and assist me in this case.

With kindest personal regards, I am,

Faithfully yours,
Rev. Dr. Horton Held

June 14, 1934

Dr. Horton Held
4406 Locust St.,
Philadelphia, Penna.

Dear Dr. Held:

I have yours of the 9th, and am sorry indeed that you seem to have misunderstood my letter. I assure you I will be only too glad to try and be of help for Mr. Hayes. If you are willing to take the responsibility as a member of the family to request the reading, and to fill out and sign the enclosed membership application for yourself, we will be only too glad to comply with your request. For, as I said, it is not that we are asking Mrs. Hayes or anyone to take on financial obligations; it is simply that we are working under an organization which has certain rules and regulations that cannot be ignored. And, as you know, we are not doctors nor practitioners; but we are organized under the laws of this State to conduct our work along research lines. As you know, we do not give treatments; and unless one becomes a member, agreeing to become responsible for applying the suggestions which might be received through this channel, there would be no value in obtaining such information. It is not worth anything without the application ...

I know that many people who look at this organization see the dollar sign first, yet I'm sure there's no one doing a work of this kind that does as much gratis as we do.

Hoping to hear from you, and trusting that we may indeed be of some service, I am with all good wishes,

Sincerely,
Edgar Cayce

EC:GD

Mr. Hayes passed away before the reading could be given.
Edgar welcomed Dr. Held as a member of the Association with
the following words:

My Dear Dr. Held:
I have yours of the 18th and I am happy to number you
among the membership of our organization. We are hoping we may in some small measure contribute something
through our efforts that will make your life broader and
bigger. We believe we will have failed in our attempt if we
do not...
Someone has said, "No organization, no individual, can
be the same with the addition of another member or with
the meeting of another individual." The lives, the trend of
the whole affairs of the world are changed by each contact. If these are motivated or guided by the Spirit of Truth,
the world is made better. If not, there may be a large question mark...

He went on to speak of his experiences of visits from his
mother and others who had passed through death:

I have had the experience of meeting quite a number in
the astral. I have had the experience of having quite a
number of astral bodies attend meetings when I was attempting to talk, even in Sunday School, as well as in
larger groups. More recently I have had the blessed experience of having many conversations with my mother and
some experiences that to me are beyond the shadow of
any doubting. I don't ask others to believe them, only as
she seeks to aid do I seek her aid, and certainly not as any
means or activity towards even our work as an organization, but for personal meeting I am sure many of these
have been just as wonderful as when I had the privilege of
talking with her in the body last evening. Some of the
things that she told me were marvelous and make life
worth while and make our longing for spiritual things in
our lives and the experiences in our physical lives that we
are told are becoming so much more a part of us and not

merely passing fancies nor gratifying of physical things alone, but as the fulfillment of divine purposes that are within us with our relationships with others . . .

> Sincerely,
> Edgar Cayce

EC:GD

* * *

Agnes Wyrick was the widow of Madison Wyrick of the Cayce Institute of Psychic Research days in Dayton, Ohio. Madison died April 28, 1933, in Seminole, Oklahoma.

Mrs. Wyrick also received startling proof of life after death when her husband spoke through the sleeping Cayce in reading 583-8, given on June 12, 1934. She had been left with two young sons to support and raise. The following excerpt of her husband's words from 583-8 must have been a source of great comfort:

I know, [583], for I have seen—I have heard—that the way of life is ever the way that what thou metest to thy fellow man thou must meet in thine own spiritual and mental self. I keep the way, and will guide oft in the things that are in keeping with the better developments for thine self, for thine children. For, they are thine. He hath given them in thy keeping at this time. But know that I, in mine efforts, mine measures, will be nigh unto thee when thou needest me most. I, thy friend, thine husband in the flesh, speak with thee. [Mr. 953 who died 4/28/33, leaving her with two young sons.] Know that what we had oft considered as a way, a means for verification of the consciousness after life is before thee now. Ye *live*—I live! Life in its essence is as that which has been; for what is has been, and will be. In spirit the body suffers not, but there is the consciousness of all that has been before.

Prepare the manuscript that was partly gotten together. Have this used in a way that will help thee in thy financial straits in the present, and when this becomes necessary again for the distributions—seek; for this channel, [Edgar Cayce] thy friend, my friend, will aid thee. 583-8

* * *

Begun in September 1932, the *Bulletin* was the A.R.E.'s only membership publication at the time. Both Edgar and Hugh Lynn wrote articles for the *Bulletin*. The following, by Hugh Lynn, asks questions about the A.R.E.'s identity that are just as pertinent today as in 1934:

The process of building a consciousness of the existence of an organization, even in the minds of its members, is sometimes difficult. It is most desirable that the members of the Association for Research and Enlightenment, Incorporated, pause now and then to ask themselves a few pertinent questions.

What is the Association trying to accomplish? Are the purposes of the organization in accord with my highest ideal? What part am I playing in making the efforts of the Association a success?

Our Association is presenting the psychic work of Edgar Cayce. There are hundreds of psychics all over this country who can and do produce demonstrations of apparently a more sensational nature. There are few, if any, whose work is proving more consistently helpful to individuals in all walks of life. Our organization is daily recording proofs of an indisputable nature of the value of psychic information in alleviating human ills. There is open to the student a wonderful opportunity for studying laws governing psychical phenomena. The whole field of psychology is encompassed and verifiable evidence produced constantly of powers beyond the ken of present day understanding. More and more individuals are finding the information a mental stimulus to higher ideals and more spiritual thinking. Are we to be content that individuals here and there are being benefited, are being convinced of the value of psychic information? What can we accomplish beyond this?

There is a tremendous breadth and depth to this work that is too seldom realized by those who come seeking personal assistance. Where we are reaching dozens, thousands could be benefited, physically, mentally, and spiritually. With the open-minded cooperation of men in the medical world, we can evolve specific remedies for diseases so far beyond the control of science. If practical results may be obtained for an individual, then why not for many? Would it be possible to assist in finding a specific treatment for cancer, sleeping sickness, leprosy? The Association has for years carried on with limited facilities research work with a remedy for the dreaded disease known as pyorrhea, and has only recently turned over to a company the formula [for the product that came to be called Ipsab] for such a remedy that has proven effective in individual case after case. We need the cooperation of men trained in medical science, but men with open minds, intelligently seeking the cooperation of such psychic information—not as a revelation, but as the cooperation of a fellow research worker.

Turn to the little understood realm of the study of the mind. What new depths could be opened to the student willing to follow the path! We are not dealing with some indefinite collection of disjointed material, but with facts. Every day we may observe the demonstration of mental power unknown to the average man, yet time after time has come the explanation that such power is possessed by all and may be applied in their own surroundings to meet their individual problems.

Will we rest with our own conviction, our own realization that here is something truly touching the Infinite source of all knowledge? We are in a position of responsibility, for with knowledge comes responsibility. Is it not our work to give that which we have found good to the world?

Are we to be checked by criticism? Are we to be led astray by inaccurate estimates of the true values in life, by distant green fields? If such information is correct—and we can certainly prove that it is consistently accurate in physical readings—immense fields are open in the realms of scientific, psychological, archaeological, historical research.

So little is known of the values to be derived from psychical studies. At present, it is classed in the realm of hoaxes and frauds—tomorrow it will be the new science in our great universities. As members of the Association, a research organization, we have an opportunity of contributing to the growth and direction of this new science. There will ever be those who herald such research as a new cult, religion or philosophy of life. To understand the laws of the universe is to understand God—that is the kind of religion we need.

It is our privilege to present the work of a great psychic. What part are you playing in the presentation of the greater scope of the work? *What will we do with this man?*

Bulletin
October 1934

Timeline

1935—Edgar, Gertrude, Gladys, and Hugh Lynn are arrested in Detroit on November 30, on charges of practicing medicine without a license. Edgar enters a technical plea to free the others of charges. He is put on probation and returns home.

1937—L.B. Cayce, Edgar's father, dies.

1939—An ailing Tom Sugrue comes to live with the Cayces and begins work on *There Is a River.*

8

The Growing Years: November 1935-1940

AT THE END of 1935, a rather peaceful three-year interlude came to an end. On November 21, Edgar, Gertrude, Gladys, and Hugh Lynn were in Detroit, Michigan, guests of the Warshawsky family. Edgar had given a physical reading for a young girl. Her father went to the local police station and filed a complaint.

Nine days later, on November 30, a warrant was served for the arrest of all four. The charge was practicing medicine without a license. The four spent only a few hours in jail before friends were able to secure their release on bail. Edgar was very reluctant to plead guilty, but on the advice of attorney Douglas T. Johnson, he finally agreed. A plea of "technical guilt" was shifted to Edgar alone, and the charges against the others were dropped.

Three months after the Detroit arrests, in March 1936, Hugh Lynn wrote a report to the A.R.E. membership, telling them the story of the arrest and asking them help with the legal bills that threatened to sink the Cayces' financial ship.

March 16, 1936

Dear Member:

This letter will explain the delay in the regular issues of the *Bulletins* and the temporary disturbance in other phases of the Association's activities.

Our membership has been growing in Detroit, Michigan, due to the untiring efforts of our representative there. During the latter part of last year a small group of doctors there became interested in a few unusual cases for whom we had readings. At the invitation of our representative and other members Mr. and Mrs. Edgar Cayce, Miss Gladys Davis and I went to Detroit in November 1935, for a series of readings. We feel that much good was accomplished during our three week stay there. Only one incident, which led to considerable difficulties, marred an otherwise pleasant and helpful trip.

One of the individuals who sought a reading failed to comprehend the information and after taking a transcribed copy of the reading to doctors who laughed at him, he took the matter up with the local authorities. Little need be said regarding this person. We understood that his daughter, for whom the reading was given, was critically ill. The period was taken from others requesting readings because of our desire to be of help. A friend met the entire expenses of this man's membership. We were not advised of any attitude of unfriendliness or malice. Apparently there was some unwarranted feeling against the gentleman in whose home we were staying. It is best to put the matter down as misunderstanding.

On November 30, all four of us were arrested on the absurd charge of practicing medicine without a license. Through the kind assistance of friends we were released within a few hours on bail. It became necessary to employ attorneys and upon investigation of the law we discovered a broad statue under which the reading in a technical sense was classed. We returned to Virginia Beach. The case was postponed due to the illness of Mr. Edgar Cayce, resulting we feel from worry over the situation. In order to avoid undue publicity and close the matter as quickly as possible and acting upon the advice of Trustees of the Association and the lawyers in charge of the case we sought to have the case dismissed against three and a plea of technical guilty made for the fourth member of our party. The case was settled in this manner on March 3, 1936. Upon investigation by the probation department and the presiding Judge the charges were admitted as false and misrepresenting. The case was then quietly disposed of without fine or reprimand.

Unfortunately lawyers' fees, extra travel expenses and incidentals connected with the case entailed considerable expense not included in the Association's budget. It became necessary for us to borrow $475.00. This debt must now be met by the Association and I hope can be cleared before our regular annual [Congress] meeting in June.

As members of this Association carrying on pioneer work which is naturally severely criticized by the general public we must not be surprised at periodic persecutions. Work in any unexplored field is condemned, and it is well that this is so, for if it then contains true value it will grow stronger and stronger as it withstands the attacks of those who would ignorantly hinder its progress. It is unfortunate that the weight of such persecution must fall upon the individual who is giving so much time and effort to be of service to his fellow man. His concern over this debt resulting from the personal charges against him is natural.

I feel that this matter will be considered a personal responsibility by every member of the Association who is truly interested in the humanitarian aspects of the work. This is not merely a matter of a few hundred dollars. Fundamental principles are involved in your attitude toward this situation. Doubt, fear or shame certainly should not enter our considerations. This is not the first time in the history of the world that good has been attacked, that service has been sacrificed upon an altar of scorn. We should be glad that investigation by competent authorities proved the value and worth of the work, and perhaps, there should be a little pity for the ignorance which caused the difficulties.

Enclosed you will find a small envelope marked as a special contribution to this Detroit debt. Give as you are able, but however small or large, take part in helping to meet this emergency. It is not the amount but the spirit with which it is given which will count.

Very sincerely yours,
Hugh Lynn Cayce
Manager
Association for Research and Enlightenment

In the spring of 1935, Edgar Evans Cayce had graduated as valedictorian of his high school class and had been awarded a scholarship to Duke University, to which he went that fall. In the midst of the turmoil following the Detroit arrest, Edgar Cayce wrote to David Kahn asking for financial help so that Edgar, in turn, could send funds to Edgar Evans:

February 2, 1936

Judge:

. . . I wrote you asking how much you would have to have for Edgar Evans—you did not say. I thought I would get hold of Harry Goetz [Paramount Studios] or some of the old crowd and see how it can work out. It probably will not take so much—so let me know, so I can get busy and help you . . .

Dave

February 6, 1936

Dear Dave:

. . . just wish I was in shape physically and mentally to

answer [your letter of last Sunday] as would like to, but
have been entirely under the weather now for nearly 2
weeks. Part of the time all the way under—had to cancel
appointments and the like, and hardly feel like going as
yet but some of these [appointments] have been made
over and over and feel as if I just must try and make the
grade if possible. But am so tired, weary, worn, and all the
rest of the things one might say—feel if I don't rest some-
way, will break.

I haven't said anything Dave, for the simple reason I
have not wanted to be a burden anymore than I can
help—to one I think so much of, that I know is already
burdened unmercifully.

He is going now—just from week to week,—another
reason I know I have to go on, whether I feel like it or not—
am sure you can appreciate my position.

Sincerely,
Edgar Cayce

In March, Edgar Cayce had made his way by train from Detroit back to Norfolk, having been put on probation under the
watchful eye of a Norfolk probation officer. During the trip
home he had a dream for which he sought an interpretation on
June 30:

(Q) Interpret and explain the dream which Edgar Cayce
has on March 3, 1936 in which he was born again over two
hundred years in the future and traveled to various sec-
tions of this country where records of Edgar Cayce could
be found. [Detailed dream not read:]
[3/3/36 On train from Detroit to Va. Beach, following
end of court action in re his arrest in 11/35 for "practicing
medicine without a license." See 254-89 Reports of Court
Trial.]: I had been born again in 2158 A.D. in Nebraska.
The sea apparently covered all of the western part of the
country, as the city where I lived was on the coast. The
family name was a strange one. At an early age as a child I
declared myself to be Edgar Cayce who had lived 200 yrs.
before. Scientists, men with long beards, little hair, and

thick glasses, were called in to observe me. They decided to visit the places where I said I had been born, lived and worked, in Ky., Ala., N.Y., Mich., and Va. Taking me with them the group of scientists visited these places in a long, cigar-shaped, metal flying ship which moved at high speed. Water covered part of Ala. Norfolk, Va. had become an immense seaport. N.Y. had been destroyed either by war or an earthquake and was being rebuilt. Industries were scattered over the countryside. Most of the houses were of glass.

Many records of my work as Edgar Cayce were discovered and collected. The group ret'd to Nebraska taking the records with them to study.

(A) These experiences, as has oft been indicated, come to the body in those manners in which there may be help, strength, for periods when doubt or fear may have arisen. As in this experience, there were about the entity those influences which appeared to make for such a record of confusion as to appear to the material or mental-minded as a doubting or fearing of those sources that made for the periods through which the entity was passing in that particular period.

And the vision was that there might be strength, there might be an understanding that though the moment may appear as dark, though there may be periods of the misinterpreting of purposes, even *these* will be turned into that which will be the very proof itself in the experiences of the entity and those whom the entity might, whom the entity would in its experience through the earth plane, help; and those to whom the entity might give hope and understanding.

This then is the interpretation. As has been given, "Fear not." Keep the faith; for those that be with thee are greater than those that would hinder. Though the very heavens fall, though the earth shall be changed, though the heavens shall pass, the promises in Him are sure and will stand—as in that day—as the proof of thy activity in the lives and hearts of those of thy fellow man.

For indeed and in truth ye know, "As ye do it unto thy fellow man, ye do it unto thy God, to thyself." For, *self* effaced, God may indeed glorify thee and make thee *stand* as one that is called for a purpose in the dealings, the relationships with thy fellow man.

Be not unmindful that He is nigh unto thee in every trial, in every temptation, and hath not willed that thou shouldest perish.

Make thy will then one with His. Be not afraid.

That is the interpretation. That the periods from the material angle as visioned are to come to pass matters not to the soul, but do thy duty *today! Tomorrow* will care for itself.

These changes in the earth will come to pass, for the time and times and half times are at an end, and there begin those periods for the readjustments. For how hath He given? "The righteous shall inherit the earth."

Hast thou, my brethren, a heritage in the earth? 294-185

It was not a prophecy, not a prediction, but a message of reassurance, comfort, and hope.

1936

Edgar Cayce's relationship with his fellow man was his relationship with God. In the following lines, he explained why each individual was so important to him throughout his life and why it was impossible for him to place even the dream of his hospital above his living ideal that people were more important than buildings, budgets, possessions, or plans, more important than organizations, and that his Work—as a reflection of humanity's relationship to God—was to be a Work of and through people:

January 23, 1936

Dear [1035]

It was very lovely of you to write me as you did on Jan 5th, and want to assure you I appreciate every word of it, and feel very much complemented that you wanted even to ask me the questions as you did. A very lovely letter from a very lovely person and deserves a very direct answer to many of your questions and I only trust I may in some small way be of a help to you at this time. First am sorry to hear you had a burn, hope there is no bad after effect either from the burn or from your illness, you make me a bit ashamed tho not to want me to at least try and help, but hope you are all OK and feeling just fine.

Now about your reading that it has made you dissatisfied with your self or about the way you have been trying to convince your self, well that is a great big help. For there are to me, [1035], a few very trite sayings to some that is the crux of the whole matter, "They that seek shall find" is among them and am sure you will [agree] and have found it true. "Even tho the gold we seek be in her hair" guess you have read the little book of mine where I tried very humbly to tell of some of the experiences that had brought about my beliefs, for can't say I have any Philosophy, or any pet ones at least, for to me God is *one* and any religion or Philosophy I may have must be just that in any language any sect and clime and just as understandable to a child as to any grown up. Yet, I do believe every one should have a reason, not just an excuse for their beliefs.

For my self I had a very unusual experience [as] I grew up, and believe can appreciate your experience until you were 13, well I was 19 when I came to the same cross road as you no doubt find your self just now, and looked every where for the answer, but you can only find it within.

For from my first premise God is *one* then I, body, mind, soul must be included in that one, and only that that is the Image of him may reflect *God*, and I can only see it in the flesh in myself, isn't that good reasoning? Then life or that we call life is *God*, then we can't prove God we may only experience *Him.*

Experience Him by and through the manner we treat our fellow man, for they too have in them that which may reflect him and we catch that reflection, and there by become aware of his presence, his love, his mercy, why, for to be loved we must be lovely, to have mercy shown us we must be merciful, and as He is all these in that we see and know *Him*. But when we attempt to give goodness a name and with all its diversification we see about us. We confuse ourselves and declare there is no God. Then what is the Law of one? The whole gospel the whole being is sum[m]ed up in this:

Love the Lord thy God with all thy heart thy soul thy body, and thy neighbor as thy self. All the fandangles we may add in any way is just trying to explain that. Why should we love God, The first law is self presivation [sic] and if for none other that is a wonderful reason, for when we apply the law as above it becomes proof to us in That He has said, and application of it proves it "Thy Spirit beareth witness with my spirit whether ye be the children of God or not."

Now I don't want to tire you with all this when no doubt you have gone over all these and many more many many times, but that you are thinking and do think, shows and is proof of the Love of God, for as has been said, and we may prove that also by applying same, "*In* Him we live and move and have our being" and it is very hard to put a real answer in cold type for each line may need its own interpretation, But look within and you will surely find him there, try out the fruits of the spirit on others and you will see and know him as your very own companion, and these fruits are as you know. Be patient, be kind, be just, long suffering, gentle, forgiving, merciful, loving, for against such there is no law, but do show forth the love of God, and the still small voice speaks within.

Write me again and again, do want to help if possible and none of your problems are ever ridiculous, but every one worth while and I thank you for writing me, and May His blessings keep you always.

All here send love to you and your Father, are expecting 'Ax-tell' [Edgar Evans] home for few days after examinations, write me again.

Sincerely yours,
Edgar Cayce

*   *   *

1937

In April 1937, Edgar Cayce's father, L.B. Cayce, passed away. This rugged individual of strong religious conviction and opinion had shaped his son's early years. His optimism contributed greatly to his son's ability to remain optimistic in the face of setback and hardship:

April 19, 1937

Dear Anne:

. . . Just returned from a sad mission last Saturday. My father, Mr. L.B.—perhaps you remember him—was buried last Tuesday in Kentucky. He was a great sufferer toward the last, but the fire which destroyed the home where Sister (or the two sisters, Annie and Sara) lived and Dad with them, hastened his death am sure as he got a burn about the face and head getting out of same.

Know I will miss him as he had been with me practically all the time have lived here at the Beach; but Life, Death, good and evil comes in the experience of us all. Guess it is what we do about them all that makes the difference with us and what we feel . . .

Ever the same,
Edgar Cayce

EC:GD

Selma, Alabama
May 2, 1937

Dear Edgar:

. . . I had a dream about Mr. L.B. It was something like this. For some reason I was at a Railroad Station and a train came to a stop and to my happy surprise who did I see getting off the train (I was not expecting him), and I rushed up to take his two suit cases and invited him home with me. His answer was "am sorry W.L., but I don't have time. I'm just passing through and changing trains." Then I awoke. I never thought anymore about it, but after I got this sad news then I thought there must be some connection . . .

Sincerely,
William Lamar Jones

May 8, 1937

Dear W.L.

... Thanks for yours of the 2nd. Yes, have felt like giving up sure enough. You see we were to come by Nashville and bring Mr. L.B. back home on our way from Selma. When he was ill we were waiting until he was able to travel before starting out. He got much better and we had made the plans to go, and he was taken worse, then got better again, and was getting along fine, until the fire. He was scared, and right badly burned about neck, ears and face. Am sure it was the inhaling of the flames and smoke that hastened his death, not burned bad enough to have caused it perhaps, but all the excitement and the rest.

So, well, we have just not been able to do anything since, and now it is time to make arrangements for the Congress next month, so we just can't make it [to Selma] this spring. We do not know how much we have relied on someone until we haven't them to go to with the problems of the day. But know he is free from suffering and he has suffered am sure during his last illness. Yes, he thought the world and all of you and Mrs. Jones, and often spoke of you. He was not able to answer your card, tho he spoke of it to the others. Miss him, well, more than can ever say. He was in the fire on the 7th of April, died on the 11th, buried on the 13th. Funny your dream, and very emblematical of what happened...

Sincerely,
Edgar Cayce

EC:GD

Lucille Kahn was the wife of David Kahn. Lucille's first reading from Edgar Cayce was taken on December 13, 1924, when she was in the Severn Hotel in Indianapolis, Indiana, where she was performing with a theatre group. Lucille was from Oklahoma; her father was a successful rancher with oil wells in production on his property. She, too, wrote to Cayce about his father's death:

May 6, 1937

Dear Lucille:

Yours of a few days ago is the most beautiful letter I ever received, thank you. It is impossible for me to say how my Father's death has affected me, did not realize how much I had depended on him for advice and council until cannot have it, very nice of you to say how I had been toward him thanks, he thought so much of you and Dave, there was a letter he had started to me the afternoon before his death and it is mostly about Dave. The fire am sure, well, nature, accident, providence, mishap or any of the names one might call it, showed us we may go too far. Am only sorry was not with him, or didn't go to him when he asked so repeatedly for me, but couldn't . . .

Thanks for writing Sister [Annie], do wish she could come there and rest, poor child she needs it, she has spent her whole life ministering to her Mother and then her Father, now she will miss Dad more than us all, for as you say the rest have home interests she has none now, but guess she will expend it on Sara and Lou and is well if that is what she wishes to do . . .

With love from all here

Sincerely,
Edgar Cayce

1938

In 1938, Hugh Lynn was, of necessity, taking a more active role in his father's Work. He wrote the following for the upcoming annual A.R.E. Congress, and it also was also published in the July *Bulletin* for that year:

Seven years ago we held our first Congress [6/29/32]. The suggestion for such a series of meetings came through a reading on the work of the Association.

Our new Association was just beginning to take its first faltering steps when a small group of individuals from Norfolk met for the first open Congress reading. Norfolk was still humming with the talk of the closing of our hospital and the Atlantic University in which we were interested. It was not easy to start over, but those first steps were made easier by the faith, courage and cooperation of the small Norfolk group who came to the first Congress meetings.

Through the past seven years the Association has brought many well known speakers on psychic subjects to Congress meetings. There has never been any effort to give publicity to the work of the Association other than through individuals who have found its study and presentation of the psychic work of Edgar Cayce proving helpful in their lives. Neither has there been any effort at holding pretentious Congress meetings.

It is our desire to give a picture of the work of the Association during the past year. We know that in bringing people from all parts of the country together, people of varying social interests, economic standards and religious points of view, all interested in the one subject of Edgar Cayce's psychic readings there may come a renewing of thought and effort in making it possible for the greatest good to come from this work.

Our problem is not to go out into the highways and byways and gather in a crowd. It is to bring together those few individuals who have been moved by the tremendous possibilities for accomplishing good which are opened through this work.

Hugh Lynn was also spending time in New York, appearing on the radio program, *Mysteries of the Mind,* taken from a phrase in the readings. The program had been developed through Tom Sugrue. Hugh Lynn, who was staying with the Kahns in Scarsdale, was in his element and wrote home frequently, including two letters to his father that highlight the sense of humor that marked their relationship:

Dear Family ...
Dad, I do wish you many happy returns of the day. Of all the people I know, I know of no one who has a better right to be happy about a birthday ... There are plenty of people

in this world who in their hearts are glad you are celebrating another birthday. Being a son to you is not an easy job, though a very pleasant one. Here's hoping I have many more birthdays to celebrate for you in my heart, and with you in carrying on our ideal . . .

Love,
Hugh Lynn

Dear Family:
    I would not write again so soon but . . .
    Dad, I am sure that some time in your career you must have had the experience of having to explain to a lady why she shouldn't give you two or three hundred for a trip and introduce you to all of her well-to-do friends. But I had my first try at it this afternoon late . . .

Love,
Hugh Lynn

*   *   *

On his birthday, March 18, 1938, Edgar Cayce decided to start a day-to-day diary. It lasted until May 21, with the entries becoming shorter and shorter as time passed. As Gladys was to remark years later, Edgar's diary was written in the letters he wrote to people, sometimes as many as thirty a day. Like his letters, his diary entries were a mixture of his family life and the Work. He closed his first entry, for March 18, by saying, "May I live as God would have me live."

On March 30, after skipping some entries, he wrote: "Oh God, make me thankful for all the nice things people have written—let me so live that my life before men will be in keeping that they feel has and does develop in their experience—keep me humble yet, glory in being a child of God."

The diary continued:

April 5th: Edgar Evans went back to school—Duke University—this afternoon, saw picture alone tonight. Caught the big fish—bass—weighed 7¼. Life—and all its ramifications are but the attempt of something to give expression—thus it behooves none of us to speak ill of the other fellow.

April 27th: Unusual experience this afternoon in a way—each time am able to go into the unconscious have to wait for the Light—without it cannot lose consciousness—usually it is a shaft of light—blue white light—or streaks of light—but this afternoon it appeared as buttons of light—or rosettes—with their shading in the form of a rosette—caught a nice big Ling [a fish related to the cod] this afternoon.

May the 2nd: An unusual stress, financially—H.L. left for N.Y. again last evening, Mrs. Ellington and Jane [a member of SFG #1 and her sister] brought us the material for upholstering furniture, is to help fix same today—

May 3,4,5,6 1938: Left blank—not because of nothing doing—wrather lack of the incentive to record same—but what a lovely job Mrs. Ellington has done on the furniture this week, all but one piece finished and is better than had there been a professional doing it lovely—what friends mean to every one—surely we should know better than most—for am sure we have the loveliest ever, thanks—all thanks to Him who is the giver of all good and perfect gifts—ours is friends, lovely ones. Ecken came home Wed, evening will stay until Sunday afternoon.

Saturday the 7th of May 1938: Ecken and I went fishing this morning—fair luck—in the canoe on the Lake—some casting brought mediocre results, had lines a bit better. Well really put in the afternoon—alone—on the Lake, some very good meditations—must go to Sunday school and Church oftener—losing something that am sure need—if nothing else the touch with our fellow man.

May 10th, 1938: Memories—what tricks our minds play us at times, recall the 10th of May 1890 Circus and all—no didn't go—that is why recall so well, worked in corn on the

Seay place, in the field where there used to be the meeting of the little folk that played with me some time before—seems so long ago—yet—as but yesterday . . .

May 20th, 1938: Last evening or early this morning dreamed again—for possibly the 51st or more time of walking with the veiled lady—only this time almost saw over the cliff am always trying to climb, never known or had the idea of who the lady is.

May 21st, 1938: This morning—after three and before five—Dreamed of being with the Master and receiving a blessing from Him, for my poor undertakings—he telling me—soon would be better—when I fully understood.

And the time was coming when it "soon would be better," when, accompanied by the veiled lady, he would indeed see over the cliff.

* * *

Agnes Wyrick, widow of Edgar's friend Madison, maintained a very close relationship with Edgar Cayce until his death, and he aided her at every turn, including the following example of his advice and counsel concerning her son. There had been talk of Mrs. Wyrick's son coming to Virginia Beach for the summer and finding a job during the tourist season. Edgar felt that Virginia Beach in the summer (even in 1939) was not a wholesome environment for a young boy.

February 10, 1939

Dear Miss Agnes:

Thanks for yours of the 7th—hope you will be able to get Hugh Lynn's programme, it is very good and is receiving a good deal of favorable comment—you should be able to get it over WGN your city, or if they do not carry it regularly, they may if you ask them to . . .

Hugh Lynn is home this week as it is Scout week and he is Scout Master here, is having quite a time with his boys and their meetings, he is very fond of the work and in working with the boys, several of his troupe were up for Eagle scout last evening.

Time has a way of flying by—yesterday our youngest was 21 and will graduate from the University in June. He is at Duke University.

Think it will be fine for [your son] to go back to farm, if he likes that sort of a thing. There are many things open here in the Summer Miss Agnes, but do not know that would ever suggest them for a boy of mine unless we were right here with him each day, for there are so many pit falls in a place of this kind that it is seldom very good environment, possibly not speaking well for our place—but am being honest with you about it, but will be glad to look about if he would like, would require that he be here early in season for very soon all places are taken up.

Have been looking forward to seeing you and the boys down this way and hope you have the opportunity before the summer is over . . .

Had a funny dream about Mr. Wyrick night before last dreamed he was leading a great procession, couldn't make out what it was for some time, then realized or was told it was the Pope crossing over to the other land and you don't know how curious it made me feel when was awaked out of sleep early this morning to hear announced the Pope was dead [Pope Pius XI, who died February 10, 1939].

With love and regards from all,

Sincerely,
Edgar Cayce

Apparently, Mrs. Wyrick heeded Edgar's advice about her son working at the beach.

December 2, 1939

Dear Miss Agnes:

Thanks for yours of the 30th—and as we wish some cards am writing at once . . .

Glad the boys are coming along nicely and am sure both of them enjoy trying to help out—just hope everything will be better soon—we have been quite anxious about Gertrude (Mrs. Cayce) while we lived in Dayton—she got a bad fall injuring the side of her face—or nearly severing the 5th nerve didn't leave any scar to speak of but recently has given her good deal of trouble with the sight of that eye—information sent her to Ky to a Dr there she has been away a month now, hoping for her to get home today— not so much better as yet that is from the information but helped and is to continue another treatment here— doesn't promise the full recovery of sight however ...

We had thanks giving on the 23rd here—but Mrs. C. away was a very poor one and besides since she has been away the maid had to get sick—and am not the best of cooks—but between H.L., Miss Gladys and I we have made out and haven't made any of us sick—besides we have a school mate of Hugh Lynn's here [Tom Sugrue]—he is helpless, the Dr's just about ruined him—and he has come trying to get some help—better but still very helpless as yet—has to be moved whenever he gets about paralyzed in lower limbs altogether.

Let us hear from you Miss Agnes—often think of you— and never a day don't offer a silent prayer for you.

With love to you and the boys,

Sincerely,
Edgar Cayce

1940

The Work continued to grow, necessitating a comparable expansion of the Cayce home in the summer of 1940.

October 30th, 1940

Dear Miss Agnes:

Glad to have yours of the 25th ...

There seems to be plenty of campaigning going on— personally feel it will be bad if they do not return Mr. R. [President Franklin D. Roosevelt] to the Whitehouse—tho am not for a 3rd term but under the circumstances seems we need him if I understand anything about it.

Have been building offices this summer and fall—join onto the house but had gotten so we couldn't carry on in the home—the files especially were getting so heavy they injured the safety of the Bldg., are just getting fixed up— by degrees—as it is a gift from those we have tried to help—but will be a great help when in order.

Both our boys are in the draft—one [Edgar Evans] has already been called—guess he will have to go about Dec. 15th or there about tho don't know of course, he was on the 168 list . . .

With love and best wishes from all,
Edgar Cayce

Timeline

1941—Edgar Evans Cayce is called to active military duty in April.
—Hugh Lynn Cayce marries Sally Taylor.

1942—*There Is a River* is published.
—October 7, 1942. Charles Thomas Cayce, Edgar's first grandchild, is born.

1943—Hugh Lynn Cayce is called to active military duty in April.
—Margueritte Bro's article in *Coronet* magazine is published, resulting in a deluge of requests for information and for readings.

1944—An exhausted Cayce's health begins failing visibly. He collapses, and his symptoms prompt Gertrude to take him to the Virginia mountains to recuperate from what his doctors diagnose as a stroke. They return in late November.

9

There Is a River: 1941-1944

1941-1942

EDGAR EVANS WAS called to active duty in the army in April 1941. Both Edgar and Gertrude knew that at any time the letters they wrote might be the last communication to their beloved younger son. This letter illustrates how real and present the awareness was of the possibility of loss:

February 19, 1942

Dear Ecken:

Well have such a bad cold and feel so punk don't know as should try and write when feel so bad, was abed day before yesterday, got up but this morning feel like going back to bed again if didn't have a meeting for tonight would.

But feel as if my race is about run, have done nothing to brag or boast of, haven't done so very many things am ashamed of, have tried to set for you and Bubber [Hugh Lynn] a fair example, advise you as best as have known how, tried to give each of you a fair education and to assist you to live in this world, that seems suddenly gone mad, but is really an outgrowth of man's seeking the gratification of selfish desires wrather than the Will of *God*, Christian Love and Christian Grace is after all an individual thing, and is very true, so long as to our own selves we are true we will not be false to any, but that is not from the material angle of life at all, from the Spiritual. Does the individual so live that He as a man is working with God among his fellow man there is a place for that man. For the Earth and the Fullness there of is the Lords. And His will His purpose with man will not be placated, many alone wishes to hurry—and oft man has to do that to meet the evil as is abroad, but deep down in side there is the *peace* as is of His making and is his promise to man—"*My peace I give you? Not as the world knows peace but peace as comes from God.*" And that Peace may be the pleasure of every man who keeps his heart his purpose wright with God.

So my message to you during these trying hours is—So live as not to be ashamed ever to meet thy Maker. There will be much to be done when this war is over, more of those who have *His* purpose in mind will be saved than others—for this is a purging, that we as individuals and as a Nation may better bear fruit in the work of the Lord.

Mother am sure writes you all the news, so there is little for me to say, all seem pretty fair but me, I am wrather tired and world weary, haven't fought so well, but have tried to keep at it even when all seemed against me save *His* promise.

Give thanks each day for His Blessings, pray for the safety of *His* people, then live just that in relation to those about you ever, Judge no man, God alone is our Appreciator—only poor weak miserable man would deign to judge his fellow man, keep physically fit, mentally alert, Spiritually purposed, always.

Love,
Dad

EC:GD

The following year, Hugh Lynn also was called to active duty.

*   *   *

In 1942, Thomas Sugrue's story of Edgar Cayce's life, *There Is a River,* was published. With the publication of the book, whatever peace and tranquillity Edgar and Gertrude had found was over. The book went into non-English translation, carrying Edgar's name and news of his work around the world. The book had been in the making since 1927, when Hugh Lynn had written to his father:

I have met one fellow [Tom Sugrue], at least, who will some day be well known as a writer ... He wants to get a Life Reading ... He is very interested and I am anxious to get him placed. We get along miserably together, both too sarcastic and disagree on many big ideas, yet must have had some attraction somewhere else ... He wants me to go to Columbia with him next year, work part time and school...

5/16/1927 HLC to Edgar Cayce

Tom had his first reading June 7, 1927, and immediately began telling Edgar, as often as possible, that he was going to write Edgar's biography. Fifteen years later, the book was a reality. For almost three of those years—1939 to 1941—Tom had lived with the Cayces, writing *Such Is the Kingdom* and working on *There Is a River.*

There Is a River was published by Henry Holt and Company

in New York in March 1942. On the day the author's copies were finally delivered to the Cayce household, everyone was excited to see this dream become a reality and to hold a copy in their hands. Hugh Lynn proudly made telephone calls alerting friends, and the household on Arctic Crescent was soon filled with friends who came to get their copy.

The books were delivered in sturdy wooden crates. After they had been unpacked and before he even looked at a copy, Cayce took the wooden crates to the backyard, where he chopped them up for firewood, neatly stacking the pieces before returning to the house. He smiled at Gladys as he entered and, by way of explaining where he had been in all the excitement, said, "First things first." Then he picked up his copy from his desk. Holding it in his hands for a few moments, he then put it down, saying, "Well, well." He never did read the book cover to cover.

1943

The publication of *There Is a River* introduced a host of individuals to Edgar Cayce throughout 1943 and 1944. Among the thousands was Margueritte Harmon Bro, mother of Harmon Hartzell, Kenneth Arthur, Alice K., and Andrew H. Bro. Margueritte Harmon Bro was born in David City, Nebraska, in 1894. She had her first reading from Edgar on March 31, 1943. One of the founders of Spiritual Frontiers Fellowship, she authored more than twenty books on subjects ranging from the Far East to drama, religion to psychology, and counted among her closest friends such leaders of spiritual thought as Sherwood Eddy, Louise Munnecke, Olive Hoit, and Arthur Ford.

The daughter of Transylvania College president Andrew D. Harmon, this brilliant and dynamic lady entered the Work somewhat late in Cayce's career, their relationship spanning only the last twenty-one months of his life. The legacy of her son and daughter-in-law, Harmon and June Bro, in their association with the A.R.E., however, was to endure for more than fifty years.

Margueritte Bro had learned of Edgar Cayce by being given a copy of *There Is a River* to review. She immediately wrote Tom Sugrue.

March 8, 1943

Mr. Thomas Sugrue
Henry Holt & Company
257 Fourth Avenue
New York, New York

Dear Mr. Sugrue:

I have a hunch your mail box is about to pop with letters from book reviewers who have had a whale of a good time with your biography of Mr. Cayce. It was given me to review, rather at length, for the *Christian Century*. If you know the magazine you may know also that it is the weekly bible of the bulk of the liberal Protestant ministers in this country and in England. If you do not know, you might take a look in *Readers' Guide* for the sort of thing it publishes. Maybe a short-cut would be for me to send you a copy.

Anyhow, I want to do as good a review as possible because I think the book has significance for Protestantism at the present time. It happens that each year I talk to several hundred ministers, in various sorts of ministers' meetings, and I am keenly aware of their longing to feel that prayer and all other outreaches into the resources of the universe have an authentic "scientific" underpinning. These adventures in the subconscious which Mr. Cayce has carried on are certainly a move in that direction.

But even more important than that, perhaps, is the responsibility to see that Mr. Cayce gets financial undergirding for his work and that reputable scientists pay more attention to him. He would be "meat and drink" for Dr. William Sheldon of Harvard University but Dr. Sheldon is in the armed forces at the moment. (You may know Sheldon's *Psychology and the Promethian Will,* also his *Varieties of Human Physique* and *Varieties of Temperament*). Other men come to my mind who are equally authentic and could surely be interested.

I just wrote to Dr. Garrison of the *Christian Century* asking if I might postpone my review until I come back from the East, on a chance that I might see you or Mr. Cayce.

The end of this week I am leaving for Massachusetts and New York, and could be reached at the home of a friend whose address is 211 Chestnut Street, Westfield, New Jersey. I shall be returning by way of Washington. Virginia Beach sounds as if it must be in that vicinity.

In the hope of locating you rather quickly, I am going to send one letter to you in care of your publisher, another to Virginia Beach, and enclose a carbon in a note to Mr. Cayce. I scarcely need to add that I would surely appreciate a prompt answer and that I hope—wherever you are— you are moving toward complete recovery. I also hope that in their interest in the subject matter of your book the 4 reviewers will not overlook the fact that you did an exceptionally good job in handling difficult material objectively and interestingly.

Sincerely yours,
Margueritte Harmon Bro

MHB G

It was clear that Margueritte had been strongly affected by Cayce's story and that she intuitively understood the need for a strong financial foundation for the work:

March 10, 1943

Frances Shimer College
Mount Carroll, Illinois

Mr. Edgar Cayce
Virginia Beach
Virginia

Dear Mr. Cayce,

I have just finished reading Mr. Sugrue's book about you—which I have been asked to review for *The Christian Century*. I was much moved by the book, particularly by your sincerity and by the integrity of personality which has kept you from exploiting a gift. I was moved, too, by the stupidity of all of us who refuse to accept the thing we cannot explain. The more we know the dumber we seem to become. Lao-tze had the right idea when he said that learning seems to close as many doors as it opens.

It sounds mildly cockeyed for me to announce that I might be useful in getting some more scientific recognition and maybe some financial underpinning for your work but stranger things have happened. Oddly enough I am just starting east to make a few talks to minister's groups and churches in Massachusetts and Vermont. I had planned to come home by way of New York for the sake of seeing the new plays. Now my husband wants me to do an errand in Washington. So—adding two and two to make six as can be done—it seems to me I might also go to Virginia Beach (which I cannot locate but the postmaster assures me is on the map) and see you. I would like so very much to meet you before I review the book. No doubt you know that a good many thousand ministers read the *Christian Century.*

Let me hasten to say that I would not be coming critically. Anything but. I have had enough experience with answered prayer to know that we have only touched the fringes of our resources in this universe. If you have an open date, I would like to get a reading, too.

I wish I had a long and impressive pedigree with which to reassure you but I am just a nobody-special from the Middle West. Our family has belonged to the Christian Church since our friend A. Campbell started same. My father—A.D. Harmon—my brother—H.G. Harmon—and my husband—Albin C. Bro—are in *Who's Who* since they are all three college presidents. For several years we were missionaries in China under the United Foreign Missionary Society; my husband was the living link of the Richmond Church. By way of occupation, aside from rearing five youngsters, I write articles and books. No, I am not after an article. I'm after the main thing we are all after—deepening of my own spiritual life.

If I am not delayed I should reach New York about March 21st and can be reached in care of Mrs. Ruth Nichols, 211 Chestnut Street, Westfield, New Jersey. If you are willing for me to come to see you, would you drop me a line. March 29th, 30th or 31st would be the best time for me. I have to be back in Chicago by April 3rd.

Enclosed is a carbon of the letter I wrote to Mr. Sugrue yesterday. I hope some enterprising angel gets one of these letters to its destination. I'm reminded of the old song, "If you don't receive this letter, write and let me know."

Cordially yours,
Margueritte H. Bro

P.S. I don't want to burden you with letter writing—you could wire me collect at Westfield.

Edgar's response was welcoming:

March 12, 1943

Dear Mrs. Bro:

Have yours of the 10th—do hope you will arrange to come by Virginia Beach, and if you will let me know at once will try and reserve a period for you that you may have a reading while here.

Forwarded the letter to Mr. Sugrue that came here, he is in Lexington VA for the winter, and seems to be getting on very nicely, however the difference in the altitude and the severe weather I do not believe has been as good for him as it might else where, but like many of us circumstances alters cases.

Will be very happy to meet you and talk with you, am particularly interested in the family connection with A. Campbell and the Christian Church. As a child I was sexton of Old Liberty in Christian Co. Ky. Where it is I believe said that Campbell and Stone first met. And working in that Church the 1st Christian in Selma, Ala. As well as 1st Christian in Louisville, while there and other places, Bowling Green and others, makes a something with in one, that is not easily eliminated, tho I at present teach S.S. in the Presbyterian Church here.

Possibly I am not personally as much interested in individuals with a pedigree as should be, have been often

told that at least, for to me each Soul is as precious in the
sight of God as another, and to be the means of telling and
manifesting the Love of God through Jesus the Christ to
each soul I hope is my purpose, possibly why the work as
has manifested through me hasn't received as much recognition as it might is because I haven't been allowed to
identify myself with any particular group, will possibly be
of interest to you to tell you more of this when see you.

The best trip from N.Y. to the Beach is through Washington, but the train comes direct to Norfolk from New
York, possibly can come here and then go to Washington,
but you will have your own plans, but let me know what
day 29th-30th or 31st will be most convenient for you to
be at the Beach for as you have possibly noted can only
work twice each day—with one days rest each week.

Just hope may be the means of being of a service to
you—thanking you for your letter.

With every good wish,

Sincerely,
Edgar Cayce

Margueritte Bro wrote the now famous article entitled
"Miracle Man of Virginia Beach," which was published in *Coronet* magazine in the September 1943 issue. She did not expect
this "little squib," as she called the article, to be published. The
response to this article was so overwhelming, when added to
the increase of inquiries from the publication of *There Is a River*,
that the fledgling A.R.E. threatened to crack under the strain. In
an effort to keep pace with demand, Edgar gave a record fifteen
readings in one day on April 22, 1944.

Meanwhile, Hugh Lynn continued to stay connected with the
Work through his letters home and his family's letters back to
him. Hugh Lynn's letters seemed written as if he knew his time
with his parents was coming to an end, that the partnership of
Edgar, Gertrude, Gladys, and himself was to undergo a radical
and permanent change. It was as if Hugh Lynn was sharing on
one level how the Work would be carried on without his father,
while at the same time trying to elicit from his father a closer
adherence to a regimen that would allow Edgar's work to con-

tinue just a little longer. Hugh Lynn seemed to try to coax his father back to life, distracting him with a new project, encouraging him to make the necessary effort to let go of the pressure of the office, requests, and needs of others, and to think of only himself in order to live.

By this time in his life, Edgar was as sensitively organized— physically, emotionally, and spiritually—as the finest of crystal and was at great and permanent risk of shattering from the discordant voices, some of which only he could hear. Empathetic to a painful degree, he was haunted by the needs of those who sought help through him, pulled in many directions by the sincere and concerned advice of many friends who could not hear those voices or feel the needs as he could. He had no escape. Edgar was faced with the daily management of his own work in addition to carrying on the affairs of the Association. Giving readings, handling correspondence, counseling with friends and visitors, speaking, publishing *The Bulletin*—all now rested on his shoulders. He had not been so burdened since the days of the hospital, and he was now sixty-seven and in ill health instead of forty-nine and healthy.

Added to those heavy responsibilities was the fact that the Association for Research and Enlightenment was also the Cayce home. The office door could not be locked, nor could a journey of several minutes be undertaken to separate the Cayces from the business of the day. The telephone rang, as it always had, at all hours of the day and night. Telegrams were delivered. An extra plate had to be found at the lunch or dinner table for the unexpected visitor. There was no assurance of privacy. A knock on the door could come at any moment. People would leave their cars parked on the street and join Edgar unannounced on his fishing pier or in his garden to talk with him, seeking his advice and counsel.

There Is a River and the *Coronet* magazine article made Edgar Cayce a household name. Thousands began writing for readings. Up to six secretaries were engaged to handle correspondence. Edgar weakly tried to handle each letter himself, dictating responses well into the night when he should have been seated by his beloved radio or escaping into the world of make-believe at the movie theater.

Without Hugh Lynn's youth and energy and with Edgar Evans also absent, both Edgar and Gertrude began to fail. Attention, as always, was focused on Edgar, and yet quiet, invisible Gertrude, always in the background, always working just a little beyond her strength, was very ill. She was always delicate, and the strain of having her two boys in the war, the crush of work and constant visitors, the lack of money to have the help she needed in the earlier years to manage the large and extraordinarily busy household, all combined at last, and she broke under the pressure. It was not a dramatic collapse, and no one really took notice until much later. Just some little thing within her finally gave way, and for nearly a year before her husband died, Gertrude quietly lost a little ground each day.

Many friends from Virginia Beach and Norfolk were writing overseas to Hugh Lynn, hoping he could, from the great distance that separated them, influence his father to take better care of himself. Most who wrote to Hugh Lynn hoped that he could distract his father from the maelstrom of requests and demands, even to leave Virginia Beach, if necessary, to rest.

Hugh Lynn's response was to plan a series of letters which were designed to turn his father's attention away from the turmoil of the day, structure the routine, and encourage him to look to the future, to a time when the turmoil would be at an end.

In the May 11 and May 13 letters that follow, the now-thirty-six-year-old Hugh Lynn demonstrated a remarkable vision for his father's Work, a vision both sufficient and necessary to guide it carefully through the uncertainties of an as yet unseen future. Hugh Lynn, Edgar, and Gertrude had always struggled with each decision, every move, every project, and every activity, carefully considering the long-term effects on the Work, measuring each step taken against their long-held spiritual ideal.

Shaping an organization, creating a structure to provide a continuing and permanent vehicle for the Work that did not imitate other organizational models was a continuing challenge. It had to be unique. One thing they knew: There would be no putting the bottom line first again. The material mindset would not, could not, be the determining factor. As radical as that stance sounded then—and sounds even now—expediency, decisions driven from "the without," compromise for the sake of the moment, had—for Hugh Lynn at least—no part in the spiritual leadership of his father's Work.

The long-range effects of decisions made and steps taken that resulted in consequences to be dealt with in the future were very much on everyone's mind. Edgar and Gertrude, looking back on a long list of organizations that had come and gone, were especially sensitive to placing the long-term spiritual goal first. Sometimes it seemed easier to say what the Work should *not* be rather than what it should be, but clearly, those with the "eyes to see and the ears to hear" should recognize it when something was a "not." It was this invisible central corridor through which Hugh Lynn sought to travel so that those "in the Work" would recognize and respond to its call. His letters to his father sought desperately to show an ailing Edgar how to find the central way as well.

England
May 11, 1944

Dear Dad:

This is the first of a series of letters which I am planning to write you. In a previous letter, I outlined them and since that time have tried to think through the various topics carefully.

Naturally, this is only an expression of opinion, a basis for further thought, correction and additions. A long time ago I learned that it is not a subject which belongs to any one person or to any small group of persons. We need—and must have, if it is to be successful—the prayer and thought of many people. If I am a bit heroic or bombastic you may attribute it to a youthful imagination which has never been curbed. (Thanks to you and mother.)

Perhaps more than any other question which has been asked me about the work is, "What will happen when your father dies?" Curious business men and nice ladies have put it differently, more objectively, but always as that one $68.00 question. During the early days I hedged, later I quickly dashed off a thousand unrelated words of explanation, and later still—I just didn't answer. This was not due to the fact that I did not have an answer but because the answer was harder to explain than silence.

I am not kidding myself about this matter. It is not wishful thinking; for, as you will see it is the result of a long study of the readings—and of you. It is an important question, for upon it depends all of the planning which will be the subject of the rest of my letters on the work.

For a long time now, I have known that you *knew* that it is possible, in this life, for you to live as long as you believe it necessary. There isn't any magic in this. The price you paid for it and the price you pay daily is high, much higher than most people are prepared to pay. It has amused me, in an odd sort of way, that most of the people who asked me that question will not themselves live to see it answered.

There isn't anything new or startling that I can bring to your attention about this matter. I would like to discuss a few relative facts which are pertinent.

"The work" is demanding, not on physical or nervous energy, but in requiring obedience to physical and spiritual laws which govern all life. You are inherently (this word is used advisedly) a person of extremes. At one end of the pole *you are the law:* at the other end you break all law as easily and gracefully as anyone I have ever known.

Your age, the tension of increased work, the responsibility of an expanding influence on your work, all are at a point where you can no longer "get away with anything."

Once upon a time, you could get mad without it hurting several hundred people. There was a time when you could eat what you pleased. There was a time when you could go without sleep for days, without rest or relaxation for days, and get away with it. Today, the tension is too great, the responsibility has passed beyond the understanding of a finite mind. The balance is a very fine one.

If you persist in unbalancing this complicated set of laws which are active through you, there will come a time when you grow too tired to continue.

There will never be any ailment of mind or body which can destroy you, until you stop renewing the vital energy and power which is your very life in the service you render thousands who come seeking help.

I do not believe that this idea—this fact, for I have witnessed it work more than once—should be proclaimed as any basis of future planning. It is the kind of idea which builds isms, cults and fanatical, wild-eyed followers. But, I do feel that it should be a part of the understanding which exists between you and me, and among those who are helping to map the plan through which your life and work [are] to become an inspiration to many more thousands of men and women who are going to need the kind of understanding you can give them.

There must be set up within you and in the minds of those around you a definite plan which will make possible this complete mental and spiritual and physical renewal on a constant basis. When the real job has been completed—then there will be time to rest on another plane.

Is there any need for me to mention the value or importance of the work ahead? If there is then my letters which will follow will gradually unfold to you just one set of dreams—and God's dreams are unlimited.

In this plan I speak of there must be a place for many things. You will know the inner needs much better than I. All that is suggested here can not be achieved in a moment, but all of these points, as simple as some of them seem, must be considered.

1. Daily prayer and meditation Personal and others for you. Your idea of having all who will hold the period of the readings with you should be emphasized. There is no need for me to emphasize or mention your own periods.

2. You must get rid of details and petty responsibilities brought on by the expansion of the work. This, I know, is hard with me away, but it is essential, Dad. Even if others make mistakes or bad decisions. You can not continue to be worried, upset and kept disturbed by answering every question, making every plan. I wish I could explain to all those who are working with you there now what I found out a long time ago as a little boy. It is useless to try and keep anything away from you. You know things that are going to happen before they happen sometimes; you

know what people around you are thinking most of the time; and how people feel all the time. Questions regarding petty decision, indecisive statements only upset you. Arguments get nowhere. People working with you should accept responsibilities of the whole phases of the work; *tell you about decisions and go on.* In line with this point of the suggestions, please ask Harmon to outline the full jobs and responsibilities of each person in the office now. Make them full. I would like to see the set up. Please, Dad, this is important. You must turn loose all the odds and ends. Dozens of people can handle details, there isn't but one that can handle *your* end of it.

3. More frequent rest periods, relaxation, time for travel, quiet, talks with people, etc.

The actual reading periods do not hurt you I am sure but the tension resulting from continued strain and rush will gradually take away all the beauty and life of the whole pattern. Dad, this is a subject that I have spoken with you about before, unsuccessfully. There is nothing like trying again with a new angle. Do you honestly feel that several readings given at one period are complete and satisfactory, as helpful as they should be? Is it fair to the people for whom you are working to try and stretch yourself too far? Is it not taxing the delicate balance of your own inner life to endanger the future of the work by "squeezing the goose that lays the golden egg?" I know how you feel about it and I know the promises you have received, but these very promises are based upon your keeping a fine balance of observance of all mental, spiritual and physical laws. Considering outside tension, others' influence and mistakes, etc., this is most difficult. More frequent periods of rest and relaxation will help. You have had to take periods of rest lately, resulting in cancellations and confusions in schedule, disappointments, etc. It would be better to have planned rest periods and then— if you must fill them up, not have to cut out whole periods. Let's put it more strongly. You just do not have the right to overtax yourself. Even *He* rested frequently.

4. Very shortly now there is going to be a need for re-

cording what you have to say while awake on various subjects. Please take ten or fifteen minutes each day—hold to a short regular period—and dictate your thoughts on some definite subject. Believe me this is more important than anything else anyone is doing there beyond actually taking the readings. Don't try and write it yourself—dictate it—you talk easily and pretty soon will be having trouble holding yourself to the actual short period set—hold yourself to the time though, and it will help you condense. Dictate just as if you were giving short daily inspirational talks for thousands of people to hear. Thoughts about everyday subjects, common problems. Please think yourself about some subjects. I will send you others from time to time in v-mails. Please begin this right away, Dad. It will do you good now and later. Don't let anything else get in the way of this period. Use all the Bible references you wish but don't use a verse as a text.

All of this is much too long, perhaps, Dad, but I am deeply interested in trying to set down in black and white certain major plans. You are the first consideration and the center around which these plans must be constructed. As I complete the series of letters, one by one, you will see, I believe, just why I have begun with these items related to you.

First, to the individual; next, to the groups; then, to masses. That is the way it goes in substance; and, there is that other question which has perplexed so many, 'What will ye do with this man?'

Today, you could go to sleep and move on to newer and more active fields of service. Your life would be far more complete than anyone else's that I know. You would leave behind you a host of those who through your work will have an opportunity to serve *Him* in the light you have given to the most important of all paths, that which leads back to *Him*. We need you, this mad, crazy world, needs you, Dad.

You cannot give them all readings—you will not be able to give one thousandth of them readings—don't try. But there are ways of reaching into the lives and hearts of many more thousands. Take your time—that little bit which is left to us in this century can be fixed by you almost to the moment if you so will it. Stop for a moment and visualize the tremendous sweep, the full import, of the work ahead. Slow down, get rid of messy details, rest, relax—prepare yourself for work ahead in the next five, ten, fifteen, twenty years of serving the masses who are going to so need help. You must not be just a legend, but a living force, an example of that which you know yourself to be—His servant, through whom He is touching lives with new hope, new power, new vision.

> Good night, Dad,
> Hugh Lynn

Hugh Lynn tried valiantly to shoulder the organizational responsibility from England. Despite the conditions under which he existed during World War II, his total attention could be devoted to the smallest detail of his father's everyday life. Every influence possible through the written word was exerted to relieve his father and to distract him from the things that fretted and distressed him.

> England
> May 13, 1944

Dear Dad:

Frankly, I had not intended writing another letter of this series so soon, but I find myself with a free evening, the typewriter and a mind crowded with thought of all the plans conjured up by the last letter. My thoughts are not in an orderly arrangement, so I will probably have to rewrite this.

There is one basic principle which I have discussed with you many times. Let us restate it now as a premise upon which to construct an outline of the expanding Association's work. The greatest contribution which you and the work you do can make is *a spiritual one.* The physical readings—bodies, minds cured—the Life Readings—mental and spiritual tangles straightened out, these are only part of a plan; just as Jesus' healings were part of the plan to focus attention upon Him and insure the acceptance of the truths which He taught. Whatever you do, whatever is done to tell people about your work should be done with the one purpose of stimulating men to a greater consciousness of the Father.

The fact that you can do something that appears miraculous attracts attention, stirs the imagination. In the form of a personal physical reading, a Life Reading, the book, a talk with you, a pamphlet, this may turn into a lasting awakening to a new understanding, a new life.

Most dangerous of the mistakes which may be made is the interpretation of some phase of the work in terms of religion, a dogma, a cult or ism. The readings have consistently warned us, but it is easy to grow set, trapped in a few pet systems of theory which we have worked out, and which, if we stop and think deeply, only go just so far.

It would be just as fatal, I believe, to become entirely cold and systematic, pushing the whole work into so called scientific channels; or, to turn it into a commercial enterprise, turning out scads of booklets, books etc., for mass consumption.

There is a narrow middle path which is hard to work, hard to understand, seldom seen clearly. Oddly enough walking along this path means different things to different people: greater spiritual understanding and vision; freedom from karmic debts; greater powers of expression; joy; opportunity to serve others; ways of giving of self. Unless the work does not give an individual these inner realizations there should be a careful introspective survey made immediately.

There is another great fundamental principle regarding the work which we should review briefly. All the information given in the readings is relative. By this I mean that it is limited only by the mental and spiritual development of those who are seeking help, who are working with it. This means also that it must grow step by step, bit by bit. There is no great revelation to be made, no final goal in the sense that an end is to be reached which can be measured in any physical sense. As the readings frequently put it, it is not enough just to get well, not enough just to acquire knowledge.

Too, in being relative, we must consider each phase of the work involving the use of information as important within itself but related to every other phase of the work. There must be a unity and coherence in our thinking and planning, not a pushing and surging here and there, like a cat, trying to get out of a paper bag.

There is another general principle which perhaps causes more difficulty and misunderstanding than any other; yet, at the same time is responsible for all the progress which we make. This is not easily stated for it concerns the laws of karmic relations governing those who are drawn to the work. It is intricately involved in the tangled lives of those close to the work. Herein lies the explanation for the strong attraction of some to the healing phases, of others to the philosophy. This explains the conflicts which have in the past torn asunder the progress which had been made—and at one time brought you personally close to giving the whole thing up for this life. A great part of the personal responsibility assumed by those who take part in the work is in working out this intricate personal problem of past associations. It is a known fact that individuals become more sensitive and acutely attuned to these karmic problems, hence the tension which frequently results.

You deserve in this regard a separate discussion about book length. The thing that you forget and most people around you forget at times is that being an extremist of the first water (that is almost a literal statement, though I meant it as quib), you can instantly reflect these involved past emotional crises and in the next second bathe them in a purity of expression which dries them up. Other people cannot follow you in these extremes and confusion frequently results. This is not only true of you but of all those involved in the work, in a lesser degree.

Any plan of program must take these past relationships into consideration, and be so arranged as to take care that the greatest possible advantage is derived from the urges which surge (that is a mild term for it at times) through all the personal connections.

Trying to keep these general principles in mind, I would like to outline the general pattern of the Association which is studying and presenting your work. This has been done, of course, in our booklets about the work. Some of this will be rehashing, there will be some revisions, and there will be some expansions. Parts of this outline must receive attention in later letters.

I   The Readings
   A. Physical
   B. Life Readings
   C. Others

Under this heading I want to add a few more ideas regarding taking, recording, readings, reports, filing, following up readings. These steps are pretty fixed. They involve a given number of people. The work of each of the persons concerned with this work should be carefully studied and thoroughly understood in relation to its importance in the whole scheme of the work.

1. There isn't much to be said at this point regarding mother's manner of taking the readings. She has perfected a technique all her own. I want to write her about this a bit later.

2. Gladys' taking of the readings is perfect. I regret to hear that she is not keeping up with them. I wonder about getting someone else and I predict that there will be many difficulties. I would certainly have a life reading and ask the specific question. Under no circumstances should anyone be hired to be so close to so important a phase of the work without such a reading. The readings require understanding to be written successfully. I doubt if you will find anyone too quickly. I would strongly recommend that Gladys be allowed to direct, plan and entirely control the full plans for this recording. I know that you trust her ideas and opinions in this direction. You should not have to (and in this instance you do not have to) worry about it. This should be a first step in relieving yourself of a lot of

the both of details. I know how it upsets you when things get behind, but this is a phase of the work which should be completely detached.

3. I would like to write Gladys about the other items involved in the reports, filing, follow-up, etc.

The above matters involving the readings represent the first steps in the work which are, of course, most important. It is essential that considerable planning be done in securing an adequate staff for this part of the office work, that a division of the work be made so as to allow the perfection of a system that will meet the expanding needs.

As an eventual set-up:

You

Mother taking readings

(Someone trained to take them to replace her in cases of emergency.) This training should include reading back readings on the work, and explanations from mother, observations, etc. For the best interest of all concerned I think it should be mother, except in extreme emergencies.

Gladys (to handle all staff involved in taking, recording, filing, handling reports, follow-up, etc.)

Secretary

Girl for filing, reports, follow-up letters (Ultimately, if not now 3 people, two besides Gladys, one in training to take readings, but both under her direction.)

Here arises one of the important and perhaps for you most difficult parts. Beginning as soon as you can—let Gladys have entire responsibility for the work of these two or one (if it is that now) persons. You are going to be entirely too busy to involve yourself with the details of this work. In insisting that you keep a hand in it, you will only wear yourself out and them into states of nervous prostration. Working with you is like working with electricity. You must realize this by now. For your own sake, theirs and the work, don't mess with details of the work in this direction. Check it, comment, if you like but leave the responsibility of handling the plan and the people up to Gladys.

II   Office Work

1. You need a secretary to whom you can dictate letters, who handles the mailing of form letters, mailing of publications, books of Assoc. This may be too much work even now, or it may be differently divided. To it could be added handling mimeograph machine.

Naturally, the amount of this work will govern the number of people involved.

This person or persons should be under the manager but free to handle your correspondence, unless it takes one person all his time to do this.

Note: Please break down the present office force as to their specific work. As soon as I have your outline of them. I will write you again. Please indicate just what each one does.

III   Indexing and Extracting

I wish to devote a full letter to this phase of the work. I want to discuss the long range objectives and their importance and set up on paper, at least, a plan which may permit work towards that long-range program in the efforts put forth now.

IV   Publication Program
I will devote a letter to this giving a full outline.

V   Research Program
Letter

VI   Building Program
Letter

VII Membership, Study Group, Lecture, etc.
(I've broken this up a bit for better reference later.)
Letter

Dad, I realize that I have leaped about in this letter from theory to details. I told you I might do that. Please think this through just as hard as the first one.

Love,
Hugh Lynn

England
June 4, 1944

Dear Dad:

This isn't an Association letter. It is just one from me to you, a poor attempt to span three thousand miles and talk with you as I would very much like to do today.

It is a bright sunny day, a good chicken dinner is under my belt. John Charles Thomas is singing, via a recording. I woke early this morning and lay quietly in bed for a long time going over your letters in my mind . . . It will not be possible for me to put on paper what I think or feel about you. I am going to try someday, but just now—Well, let's talk . . .

I am not too sorry to hear about the Sunday School class [Edgar was not asked to teach Sunday school following a "reorganization" of the church's programs]. I do not like to see you get hurt. You know that, and the situation there at the church is not an easy one to move through without getting hurt. Remember I sent you an extract from *A Time for Greatness*, on principles. It applies in this case. Your direct approach is based on a consideration of principles. People like those who make up the new class, I know them, are not concerned over principles. They do not like to be upset. They do not understand you. They did not understand Him. If you can continue to go to the class it will be wonderful. Odd enough, as I have told you before, one of the most wonderful experiences of my life was being with you at a time when you were (strange as it looks on paper) in jail. The difference is only in degree. You arouse a sense of uneasiness, you make people look at themselves. That is why people like Minishesky (or whatever his name was) are nasty to cover up themselves. That is why men, most of them, in that group can't listen to you. You are a symbol of principles which are not lived. In all of this I am not trying to be critical. This is not a condemnation. It is an estimate of the situation. I can understand such people, so can you, and if you can continue to smile, like you did at the man who found the prayer in your pocket—well—you live what you talk about . . .

I hope you can turn loose a lot of the details in the office. Let me try to organize the office force on paper. Turn it over to them and let it work out. You can do the best job of withdrawing of any body I know when you decide to do so . . .

Try to keep from getting upset with people, Dad. I'll be home before too long and try to take all the tension off you—you and I can have our personal disagreements over details without getting upset—too much.

That trip I suggested for home—Nashville, and Hopkinsville. It would be a good rest, if you got reservations long enough ahead of time to be sure of good ones. You could start setting the time now. If notified ahead of time it is not so bad for people—"Due to circumstances, etc. . . . "

Kiss that monkey of mine for me [Charles Thomas Cayce]. Yes, he is going to be a very fortunate little boy. As a doctor he will have an opportunity few people ever had. I know you must be having some interesting experiences with him Dad—don't forget them. You know I am interested in every one of them.

Love,
Hugh Lynn

But Edgar Cayce could no more listen to his own son in 1944 than he had listened to Morton and Edwin Blumenthal during the hospital days. A simple man, childlike in his love of and trust in the goodness of his fellow man, profound in his faith in God and his relationship to his Master Jesus, Edgar could only do what he knew to do. No one was there to take charge and make him comfortable with leaving Virginia Beach and the office details far behind. The trip to Nashville and Hopkinsville, which might have renewed and refreshed him, did not happen.

He continued to put himself under for readings when he could, giving as many as nine readings at a time. But it was the waking world with which he no longer had the strength to cope.

He grew more tired, thin, bone-weary, unable to deal with the thousands of letters, telegrams, endless telephone calls, and visitors. Unable to turn a deaf ear to the pleas for help, he could not still the voices, voices only he could hear. Gertrude and Gladys would often hear him sigh as he moved slowly from one task to another. He could not find relaxation during the day, and often at night he could not sleep. The peace he had brought to thousands was denied him.

Weakened by overwork, thin to the point of transparency, Edgar's flame was flickering now, and that bright and shining light within him through which the information passed grew fainter, becoming dimmer with each passing day. His last letter to Margueritte Bro touched lightly on the price he was paying:

August 29, 1944

Mrs. Margueritte Bro
Shimer College

Dear Mrs. Bro:

Thanks for yours of the 22nd. It doesn't take much in the way of stories, it seems, to double our mail. This last little skit you put in Coronet just doubled our mail again, so the mail is running about two hundred or more each day. Well, I suppose that is what one pays for being "infamous!"

I wish it were possible for us to take a vacation in your neighborhood, but there is not much rest for the wicked. But Gertrude and I are leaving tomorrow, going where I hope nobody knows us, where I will be close to the doctor—in the same building, in fact—and where [Gertrude] can have a little rest, in a hotel. Maybe I ought to be out in the open, I don't know. I have to do something. The reading was very sassy. You know it sometimes says too much. When asked how long to stay, the information said "until well—or dead, one."

Tell Mrs. Walgreen [of the Walgreen Drug Stores family] that I certainly appreciate her offer, and hope that we may some day have the opportunity of accepting, if she keeps that offer open.

Yes, we have had quite a number of suggestions as to how to start the Building Fund. In fact, we have someone with us at present—we have been sort of overshadowed in the last few weeks with people who have ideas and want to do something on the Building Fund pretty soon, now, and possible you will hear from it. The reading o.k.'d it, so possibly it will be all right. I like the idea of name plates, and maybe we can put that in when we start to furnish the building. It ought to be all right.

I think Tom is going to work, and that will be real good. Tom can write, if he wants to. I hope your book is coming along just the way you want it. October ought to be a good time for it, if it tells what these boys who are coming back want—for they will be back, not so long off.

I think Miss Gladys is getting that data together for you. I had a nice long letter from Harmon, and I hope that his stay here will prove a helpful experience in his life, one way or another. Sorry to hear Kenneth is not so good. I hope he will soon be all right again.

Let us hear from you. With love from all,

Sincerely,
Edgar Cayce

EC/GD

* * *

Edgar Cayce gave the last three readings for others on August 29—readings 5389-1, 5391-1, and 5402-1. On Wednesday, August 30, he and Gertrude left for Roanoke, where he put himself under the care of Dr. Henry Semones. In his absence, the Association struggled with how to handle matters, including categories of membership. The following renewal form letter was sent:

**Association for Research and Enlightenment
Incorporated
Virginia Beach, Virginia**

Dear _____

Your Associate Membership will expire _____. We pre-
fer not to make future appointments for readings with
these renewals on account of being booked for readings a
year or more in advance, however, we want to retain you
as a member of the Association, if you are interested.

If check physical readings are desired, your membership must be renewed in order to secure these readings.

Our Active Membership will enable you to receive the
weekly letter and our publications for the year for $25.00,
with $10.00 for the reading during the year; making the
membership with the reading $35.00 a year.

If you do not wish an Active Membership you may become a Sponsor for the Research Fund and receive our
weekly letter for $6.00 a year, or the Bulletin with extra
articles for $12.00 a year, or both.

Thanking you for your past cooperation and interest
and we hope to give you a year of inspirational and helpful information.

Let us hear from you within thirty days as to your preference for membership or Sponsorship, as the Bulletin
will cease with the expiration of your membership.

Cordially,
Mary Wirsing
Membership Secretary

MW/gm

Feeble, sometimes irritable because of his inability to "get
under" in order to do the readings, Edgar's last sad reading for
himself was given in September. With the first words, those
present—Gertrude, Gladys, Dr. and Mrs. Harry Semones, and
Dr. Henry George II—knew that this time there was to be no
miracle:

Let not your hearts be troubled, neither let it be afraid,

for, "Lo, it is I, and I have promised to be with thee, even unto the end of the world." 294-212

Margueritte Harmon Bro stayed in touch with Edgar during his convalescent trip, voicing her concern about his health and echoing the advice given him in the readings:

Frances Shimer College
Mount Carroll, Illinois

October 11, 1944

Dear Mr. Cayce:

Although I promised myself that I would not write a word to you until I heard that you were back at home and feeling like yourself, I just *hafta* break down and find out how you are doing—as your old lady-friend put it. You are on my mind, which means of course in our prayers, many times a day and I feel sure that strength must have ebbed into your heart again. But I surely do wish there could be a bulletin about you.

The first day after I got your letter saying you were going away to stay until you clicked again, I meditated for a long time about you. Many people must have been doing the same thing. Finally I seemed to get a clear picture of what the difficulty was. You have to live simply and in almost constant contact with the Life Force; to maintain the spiritual energy necessary for your kind of work would require three or four hours of meditation daily and a quiet, unperturbed spirit at all times. And here we have been driving you with routine office work and all sorts of management problems. My deep desire is that in your enforced absence Gladys will be able to work out a system of office management which will not necessitate your direction. She is a highly intelligent woman and—like most of us—can probably carry a larger load than she ever dreamed of carrying when it is laid at her door. Probably you have to find your own refilling a good deal as springs must rise again in a fresh-water pool which has been dipped away. I hope these weeks have already brought that sort of refilling to you and that silence only means you are busy with more important matters than letters.

If you began to gain at once then perhaps this has been a real vacation for your sweet wife. I just love that gal with an affection which is much too warm to be the product of two year's friendship; we must have our roots in former experiences. I hope she has had not only a rest but a gay time. And while I'm hoping aloud, I will add the hope which lies along-side my hope for Kenneth's return [from the war]—the wish that Hugh Lynn and Edgar Evans may be home for Christmas. I declare, I think I'd be out to celebrate with you if that should happen!

Your letter was the first I knew that squib had been published in *Coronet* and it surely bowled me over. I told you, I think, about quoting it to Mr. Shevelson when I was writing him a letter on another matter. He wrote back that they were much interested and wished they could print it but feared it would sound too much like tooting their own horn; he wondered what I thought. I never answered his letter; just didn't get around to it. Of course I had never meant the squib for publication but if he had asked me face to face I don't think I would have seen any reason he shouldn't print it. It simply never occurred to me such a little squib could stir up all that reaction. In the summer he wrote he was using it but still it did not occur to me that it made any difference. The odd thing is that I had a September *Coronet* while still at Cable and I read it but I never saw that bit. Your letter was my first knowledge of it. And last Sunday is the first time I've seen it.

Well—when I think of the way Hugh Lynn wished more people know about your work I almost have to laugh. When I think of the help you bring to many of those hundreds to write to you I could fall on my knees in gratitude. But when I think of the work it causes you—and at a time when you cannot handle more work—then I could chew up my pencil.

One big thing I have learned is that we cannot afford to let a printed word go out about you until it has cleared your office. I'm asked right along to write something about you but haven't touched my pen to paper since the original *Coronet* article. Sometimes I itch to gather up some of the reincarnation stuff. But I'm sure you are very wise to put the publications and all published materials into Tom Sugrue's hands. He seems to have judgment and balance. I know I shall like him personally and look forward to his being at the next Congress. It goes without saying that I'm ready whenever you or he can use me to write anything for your use.

I'm simply delighted that Mr. Sugrue is going to get out some more pamphlets. It would be "sumpthin'" if he could be right there in the office or at the Beach; maybe a few more turns of the wheel will bring him back to you again. He and Hugh Lynn would be an unbeatable combination...

I'm having fun with my little building fund bank. Wonder how long before we can start building. Wouldn't it surprise the collar and tie right off you if we had a building next summer? Well, I guess that would be a little speedy even if there were no restrictions. Couldn't you build the second-story first so that us visitors would have some place to stay??? Sometime this fall we are going to have a Shimer tea in Washington, D.C. and I'm busting to get Albin to go down to the Beach with me for a few days. He has never heard a reading.

Did I write you that my book was held up on account of paper shortage? In my last reading you said that March would be a better publication date. The editor, however, was determined to have it out in October and the thing was in page proof all ready for the presses when this paper cut hit Doubleday. I just laughed aloud when the letter came. I must live right to have the readings send a paper shortage.

A great deal of affection is tucked into this letter—and a lot more concern than appears in the written words. I shall be mighty happy to hear you are back at work. Love to you all,

Margueritte Bro

* * *

In a letter to W.L. Jones, Gladys gave a name to what was wrong with his ailing friend:

October 16, 1944
Mon. afternoon

Dear Mr. Jones:

Thanks so much for your proxy made out to me. I will do the best I can at the meeting on Sat., and advise you the outcome.

I talked to Mrs. Cayce this morning long distance. Mrs. Hesson (his sister) has come up from Nashville to help nurse Mr. Cayce. They say he has had a slight stroke, but he is steadily improving. For quite a while he had daily tremors which were quite nerve wracking, but now they have stopped. They moved Sat. from the hotel to the doctor's home—about 10 miles out of Roanoke. The doctor's wife runs an Inn; in fact, their home and the Inn is one and the same—a perfectly lovely place—I went out there with them the Sunday I was in Roanoke when we got the reading. The address is:

c/o Meadow View Inn
Cloverdale, Virginia

It is a little village, but mail is delivered twice a day. I know he would be delighted to hear from you. I am sending all mail on to him after I read it to see if there is nothing in it to worry him. You can write to him direct to the Inn but tell him I'll keep you posted from here, so that he doesn't have to answer until he is well enough. Mrs. Cayce is practically exhausted—just hope she doesn't break down now. He is very weak, but everything is being done that the reading called for. He is so much better—they feel now that he is out of actual danger—it will just take time, and plenty of rest. Mrs. Cayce says he may be able in three or four weeks to come home, if he improves as fast in the next month as he has in the last . . .

. . . We are hard hit financially, due to the fact that all the money coming in for all those readings was paid out for office help as it came in—which was the wrong set-up but we never could convince Mr. Cayce that it wasn't necessary or a wise thing to do. It will take time to build up the Association program based on information already received through the readings.

Sincerely,
Gladys

*   *   *

Finally, Edgar's family and his doctors felt it was time for him to return to Virginia Beach. In December 1944, both the Cayce sons were still in the army. Edgar Evans had managed some leave time to go home and made arrangements to bring his father home by ambulance. Hugh Lynn, however, was stationed in England, and his repeated requests for a hardship discharge went unanswered. Hugh Lynn's contact with his father continued to be limited to letters.

December 2, 1944

Dear Hugh Lynn

I have been wanting to write you for a long time but I guess you can surmise from what others have told you it hasn't been an easy thing. As you doubtless know from letters you have received from Sally, Mother and Ecken, I have been home a little more than a week now.

I really think I have improved more since I have been home than in all of the time since I have been sick, and I can tell you I have been pretty sick. I suppose the readings were right in sending me to Roanoke but they certainly are doctoring or working from a different viewpoint here than they did up there.

The Colloidal Chemistry Theory is by some man in England and all of the medicine had to come from there. Most of it is given hypodermically and you are not given any meat or animal protein or milk in your diet at all. What they are doing now is just the opposite, so I don't know which way I'm going—up or down. I just hope it is for the best and I can come out of it alright.

I want to thank you for your letter and your faith and confidence in me personally. When you are the same age as I your boy can and will say as nice things about you as you do about me. I am not deserving of it and I feel mighty weak and insignificant and if it weren't for one or two little things that have happened lately, I think I would give up.

Someone brought me a beautiful picture of the Master. I don't remember which one it is but I thought as I looked at it there must have been some time when He must have looked like that—just where and when I don't remember. I looked at it in the middle of the night. He began to speak right out from the picture. It was as He said at the time of the Transfiguration. So I had the experience of seeing the Transfiguration and He told me if I would be rejuvenated that I must be transfigurated and that I should begin to try to work to that—choosing the witnesses and going to work on it.

Our own Prayer Group in Norfolk—Florence, Miss Wynne, Mrs. Barrett, Mrs. Eggleston and the rest of the group—I think you will recall are working with me. We daily have a meeting and it seems to be going nicely. They were here yesterday for the meeting, but nothing in particular has happened yet. The doctors all say (Dr. Irvin and Dr. Woodhouse) who have been here, say I'm better and I'm getting along alright. What I have to have is just rest and more rest. My great trouble is I can't sleep. For the last two days it seems to be a little bit better, as I have been able to get a little sleep without having to take too much dope. But I haven't taken any dope now for more than week. I guess Ecken will write you the details. It certainly was good to see him. I don't know whether I will be able to go to Florida or not. Mother certainly has been through a lot and is so true and faithful. How she stood up under it I don't know. Just hope she doesn't break down. Kathryn [Patterson, a friend from Ohio] came to our aid when Sarah had to go home. Sister Annie is with us. I know she makes sure that I get something mighty good to eat. She is just bringing my lunch now so will just send my love and will write soon again.

Love, Dad

Edgar Cayce wrote his last letter to Hugh Lynn on December 12, 1944, dictated to Gladys from his sickbed because he could not get downstairs to his typewriter:

December 12, 1944

Dear Hugh Lynn,

I have been wanting to write you something about your boy for some time. He is such a cute kid. I was talking to him yesterday and he said, "I am daddy's boy." I said, "Who is your daddy?" He said, "Hugh Lynn Cayce." You know there is something about his growing up in the atmosphere of the phenomena; for of course, for years he has had a personality—but it surely is cute to hear him say, "Hugh Lynn Cayce" when you ask him his daddy's name. I want to get Tommy some fishing poles for Christmas—I think he will enjoy them.

I think I must be a little better as I am figuring, if the Lord is willing, to have dinner with Tommy and Sally, Christmas Day; if I can figure out some way to get downstairs. I think we will work it out some way or manner. I haven't been down the steps and back up again as yet. I think I will feel better if I can keep that promise to myself to eat Christmas dinner with Sally and Tommy.

Have been looking for Dr. George and Dave for a week now, but they haven't shown up yet.

Take real care of yourself and let us hear from you.

Lots of love,
Dad

* * *

Margueritte Bro understood what a toll Edgar's illness was taking—not just physically but emotionally—on those closest to him.

December 13, 1944
3:15 A.M.

Dear Gladys:

I've been lying here brightly awake for hours thinking

about you. You're an amazing person and the Lord's confidence in you is more precious than a crown. He wouldn't give large burdens to any but a large soul. I feel stronger in my own life whenever I think of you—which is often.

I was surprised and pleased and worried, all at once, to hear that the Cayce's are home. Oh, I wish I could help Mrs. Cayce during these days. I feel sure that he will come through and that he will be an even more sensitive instruments in the hands of God. But the days of being tempered are terribly hard. My heart turns to you all many times a day.

It's simply swell that Edgar Evans could come home. How I wish he could get a bad case of dandruff or hives and have to stay!

Here is my subscription to the letter—*This Weeks' Readings*. How swell that it is being kept up. And how well. I was touched indeed that you had copied so much for me. I meant only a paragraph but this is helpful and I'm greateful [sic].

Take care of yourself, Lamb, and give my love to all. I hesitate to write when he needs all his energy.

Love to you,
Margueritte

Her last letter to Edgar Cayce was written fourteen days before he died:

December 21, 1944

Dear Mr. Cayce,

Today right in the midst of a prayer I had an amusing thought and laughed right out. I was wondering if you can tell when people are praying for you and I thought how interesting it would be if every effective prayer literally rang a bell. The thing which made me laugh was thinking what a riot of sound you would live in! I just wonder if any man in America has more heartfelt prayer arising in his behalf. No doubt more people *say* a prayer for the president of the United States but those who pray for you do so with all their heart.

We have treasured every word from Gladys about you. It is good to know you are home. The trip was difficult I'm sure and the going will be slow. But it's a higher hill to climb than any you've ever climbed before and from the height you will be able to see a long way across the path of the stars. To be a seer—a literal see-er—is a great calling. I have a deep thrill thinking of you and of the insight which must be rising within you these hard days.

For two weeks I've combed the town to find some little thing which would give you and Mrs. Cayce joy. A book is always my first choice but I wonder where you would get time to read. A good apple comes a close second—especially along with the book—but goodness knows what kind of diet you may be on. Finally today I gave up and am enclosing a very small check which I hope you will spend for some little thing you will both enjoy . . . But you may want a few fish hooks. We shall be thinking of you on Christmas Day. It is hard to make merry but a high and holy joy is possible for us all. I just have to think what the darkness would now be if Jesus had never come and shown us his Father's will made manifest among us, to know how great our Light really is.

As the newscasts pour in with their tale of carnage and disaster it sometimes seems as if we cannot stand one more night of it. And then again I feel that we have to go on—a good deal as a poor little chick has to go on straining his way out of the shell which shuts him from a larger measure of reality. Isn't it Buddha who says, "I bring you sorrow and the ending of sorrow"? Through sorrow to peace and understanding. I hope the star's own message will fill your heart during these next days.

We wonder if either of your boys is with you. At least you will have the grandbabies and their mothers. You are really blessed in your daughters-in-law. Alice and Andy are home with us and Alice is having quite a bit of company, including some homeless soldiers but then she says one doesn't have to be very big-hearted to lug in some good looking men. Mollie is homesick a-plenty but cannot leave her job with *Time* in New York. Harmon and June are busy and broke and having their own Christmas; the dog still does not write.

Kenneth, of course, is in camp. But we are all together in spirit and will be gathering you around our fireside of specially beloved friends.

A great deal of love to you all,
Margueritte Bro

Timeline

January 3, 1945—Edgar Cayce dies of the effects of the stroke.

April 1, 1945—Gertrude Cayce dies of liver cancer.

December 1945—Hugh Lynn Cayce finally is released from the army and returns home to take over his father's Work.

10

Family Farewells: 1945

THE NIGHT BEFORE Edgar Cayce died, Gladys witnessed the following:

> On the evening of January 2, 1945, Gertrude, standing
> by the hospital bed, was getting ready to tell Edgar
> goodnight and get some rest while Gladys took over until
> the nurse arrived for the midnight shift. Gertrude reached
> over and kissed her husband. He said, "You know I love you,
> don't you?" She nodded, and he asked, "*How* do you know?"

"Oh, I just know," she said, with her dear little smile.

"I don't see how you can tell—but I do love you," he answered. Reflecting he continued, "You know, when you love someone you sacrifice for 'em, and what have I ever sacrificed because I love you?"

Gladys reflected on how much they each had suffered through the years, and how hard it was for them because of their different manners of expression. But the readings had indicated that love knows no barriers, that when there is the same spiritual ideal in marriage, all material obstacles can become steppingstones.

The next evening, January 3, 1945, at about the same time, Edgar Cayce died. There must have been a most beautiful sunset that evening, because the golden glow out of Cayce's southeast bedroom window made it appear that the sun was setting in that direction instead of on the west side of the house. At 5:50 p.m., Dr. Woodhouse said all had been done that could be done. Gertrude was seated at the dining room table, crying softly. Cayce's sister Annie brought him up some oyster stew, which he had known beforehand that she was making for him. He took two or three sips of it. At 7:15 P.M. he stopped breathing. 254-116 R27 and 294-212 R34

Tom Sugrue wrote the following *Bulletin* article to the A.R.E. membership about Edgar's death:

Edgar Cayce passed from this life on Wednesday, January third at 7:15 o'clock in the evening, at his home on Arctic Crescent, Virginia Beach, Virginia. Funeral services were conducted at the residence on Friday morning, January 5th, by the Reverend B. Clower, former pastor of the local Presbyterian Church, and in his native town of Hopkinsville, Kentucky, on Monday morning, January 8th by the Reverend Monroe G. Schuster, pastor of the First Christian Church.

He had been ill since August 1944, when the strain of overwork pressed him down to a sick bed. For more than a year he had worked under unbelievable handicaps. His son, the manager of the Association for Research and En-lightenment, Hugh Lynn Cayce, entered the Armed Ser-vices. At the same time an unprecedented number of requests for readings came to Virginia Beach. Often there were more than 500 letters in the daily mail. The library, which had seemed so large when first built, was jammed with stenographers working at correspondence. Mr. Cayce himself examined every letter, and worked late into the night dictating answers.

During the morning and afternoon periods he gave not two but from eight to twelve readings. Still he could fulfill but a small portion of the applications. The others, with their tales of misfortune and suffering weighed heavily on him. For the first time in his long life of service he could not help everyone of his fellows who asked for aid. He worked harder and harder, but the appointments ran on and on, until they were more than a year ahead of him.

His own diagnosis, given in a reading last September was that he had reached a point of complete nervous ex-haustion. From this he did not recover.

As this is written the shock of his passing is so deep that even the most glib tongues are stilled. Once a person came to know Edgar Cayce, he thereafter could not imagine a world without him, without his readings, without his per-sonality, his friendliness, his simple and complete Chris-tianity. The roll of those he served is long. How many he reached through his readings, through his sixty years of Bible teaching, is incalculable. His only ambition was that after his death even more people be reached and given whatever in the readings was good and helpful.

That is the first reaction to his death—that faith must be kept with him, and his work continued. It is symbolic that his own passing was brought about largely by the change in his work; that is, he could no longer give all the readings which were requested of him, and the necessity for giving to people the information of general use in the readings was growing each day.

Now that he is gone this will become the whole of the work, and as it proceeds the real stature of Edgar Cayce will be revealed. Truly he fulfilled the Christian ideal; he laid down his life for his friends. He was a great man. We shall not see his like again.

Thomas Sugrue
A.R.E. Bulletin, January 1945

*   *   *

Hugh Lynn, unaware of his father's passing and not knowing that the last letter he would ever receive from his father was making its way to him, continued to write as often as he was able. His heart and mind were always in Virginia Beach. He tried so hard to lift his father above the concerns of the day, to get his father to think only of the good he did through the readings, and to allay both his parents' fears and anxieties about his safety in the midst of war.

January 7, 1945

Dear Mother and Dad:

This Sunday has seemed so much like other days in the week that it has passed without even a thought of the usual Sunday events. While I am not going to church over here, I haven't forgotten all of the other personal thoughts and acts that go to make up religion in an individual sense. But I do not think that you would ever doubt that this was true. In fact, for sometime now I have been reading the Bible more regularly than I have for years. Without the quiet few minutes early in the morning and late at night, it would be hard to keep any semblance of balance.

Mickey Rooney sat just across the table from me tonight at supper. He is doing a fine job in his work of entertaining in small units. He doesn't look much like his pictures. Only a few weeks out of the states—I imagine he is having real trouble adjusting himself to this new type of living.

Our lights are "acting up" again, so this will have to be cut a bit. The French system of lighting is pretty good, everything considered.

Mail is still bottled up somewhere, and I am not getting much these days. One whole week seems to be out in one spot, and I feel sure that Sally wrote me several times during that week. Boats are still being sunk so we are losing mail now and then.

Don't worry about the news. Everyone over here feels that this particular activity is a good sign.

Nice box of candy from Mrs. LeNoir. I'll write her. It was one of those pecan rolls. We are eating more from boxes than in the mess hall these days until the Christmas boxes are gone.

Love to all,
Hugh Lynn

Eventually, however, he did receive word of his father's death.

France
January 29, 1945

My Dear Muddie:

There are many things which must be said, but now is not the time to put them into words. I will try to write often until I am able to catch up.

First, by the time this reaches you I hope that you will have rested and recovered from the shock, though you must have gradually prepared yourself for the possibility. Please try to rest, my dear, and take care of yourself. When you have rested, and there is time (do not feel compelled to write) let me hear from you about the service and what you did about Dad's burial.

This is a strange kind of suffering which I have passed through here. Strange as it may seem to some people my greatest problem has been trying to crush the resentment of the futile, wasteful, events and circumstances that have made it necessary for me to be separated from all of you there during this period.

You know, perhaps better than anyone else, how I feel about death. I know that it is only selfish of me to think of Dad's death as something out of key with movement of events relating to a much larger plan than we can see, and understand. I know of no one who was better prepared by faith and works to "step through the other door." We must simply gather up the threads and continue to weave the pattern of which his life was so much a part. We know that because Dad has changed forms does not mean that he has in any way ceased to work for the ideals and principles on which his life was built and to which his every thought and act were dedicated.

Our problems (and I always remember what the reading said to me about using that term—only in my mind) can be resolved into a few general classifications. In order to help my own thinking let me put them down, though you and others will have to approach them differently.

Dad's great development will make it possible for him to do a great deal to advance the basic ideals of the work. We must make ourselves proper channels for the inspiration which can flow from him, or I should say through him. The difficulties will be in eliminating, so far as we are able, all selfish desires, all personal desires, and working on fundamental and universal principles. We must realize that his new vision and plane of consciousness will give him an understanding and points of view far beyond those we can see, not because he has passed on but because he was prepared to pass on. Naturally, we are going to miss him, we have all depended on him so long, but he has directed us carefully and we cannot let him down by failing to apply and live the truths which his work exemplified. He would want us to be brave, he would want us to be joyous, he would want our love to grow more universal, freeing him to work in wider fields. How many times have you heard me say, "Dad has finished his work—over and over again. Ours is the job of giving to others the good which we have known and enjoyed so long."

So, Muddie, I do not ask you not to feel lonely, I do not ask you not to miss him, but I do say turn the power of your love for him into praying, and wishing and believing that he is now free to labor in other realms for the Master whom he served so well here. Know that he is able to help us now, even more than before, in achieving the greater expression of the truths we know so well.

We are confronted with the practical ways of carrying

on. Naturally, I have given this thought each time anyone has asked me the question, "What will become of the work when your father passes on?" The answer is not one that you or I or even those close to the work can give alone. Let me state my own position simply. I intend to do everything in my power, give everything that I have found good in the work, to others. I feel that we must develop a plan that will allow anyone who so desires to help in the way he or she is best fitted. There are many ways. We must find the best. First, for us all, we must live the principles we believe in. You have been a great inspiration to me, and I feel that you can help me give my son an understanding of the "lighted path."

I expect to talk with Dad as soon as I have prepared for it and he is ready. It is possible, I will not know until I have talked with him, that he may use a channel for a continuation of his work here. You had thought of this possibility, I am sure, and it would present some new angles. Do not feel disturbed about not hearing from him immediately—he was a busy man here and I am sure he was needed badly over there, so he must be busy. It won't take him long to get rid of the body ties. We must not let our minds hinder him—I have no fear in your case, for your love has always been stronger than your mind.

Gladys will let me know about the Association affairs when she has time, I am sure. It will be hard to make definite plans until I talk with all of you and many of the members of the Association. There are many possibilities, this will certainly be a time for the dividing of the sheep and the goats.

Now for a moment for personal things. I have made application for discharge on dependency basis. So far I have heard nothing from it. My CO and Higher Hq. approved, but anything can happen. I will let you know as soon as I hear anything. In the meantime an allotment will be coming to you. It will help a little to tide things over until I can get home. If I find that I will not be discharged now, then we must take steps immediately on the Association program. If I am coming home, perhaps it can wait for action, beyond clearing things up, until I arrive.

I am enclosing Joe's letter to me about the service. Please keep it in my file for I will use it later. I also had a letter from Mrs. Brown about attending the services. Ecken's letter of the 15th and those from Mrs. Brown and Joe are the only word I have had so far. One of the boys did get a newspaper clipping from a Penn. Paper. The mail will come through in time.

Please, Muddie, take care of yourself. Perhaps, I can come home now, and be with you before too long.

Goodnight, my dear
Hugh Lynn

*   *   *

No longer needed by her husband, Gertrude now gave way. She became very ill while in Hopkinsville for her husband's funeral, suffering a great deal from the cold and fatigue of the long train journey.

Management of the Association and the Cayce household and the care of the now-stricken Gertrude fell on Gladys. She would write the most detailed letters to Tom Sugrue, and to Hugh Lynn and Edgar Evans, on an almost daily basis. Hugh Lynn's letters to Gladys and earlier letters to his parents indicate he was thinking of the business at home nearly every waking moment of each day.

These were perilous times for the fledgling association. The transition from a group of people associated because of their personal relationship to Edgar Cayce the man into a group of people who would carry on the next phase of the Work, based on the information alone, was in delicate balance. Amidst the strongly clashing personalities more concerned with the "who" than the "what," the collaboration and accord between Gladys and Hugh Lynn emerged as one of the greatest factors in the survival of the A.R.E. On the state of the association, Gladys wrote the following to Hugh Lynn:

March 6, 1945

Dear Hugh Lynn:

How shall I begin? Both you and Tom are clamoring for news of the Association. I haven't written before because I have been completely confused by the various meetings we have had. At the meeting of the entire Board (I mean official, the semi-annual meeting using the proxies, etc.,) nothing at all was accomplished, in the way of deciding upon a definite program. Everybody went around in circles and each person had a different idea as to how to proceed. Outside of wrangling over petty details concerning the office work, there was very little done. All could agree better on what we were *not* to do than on what we *were* to do. They *all* agreed that we should *not* advertise the fact that we would investigate other psychics—at least not right away, since this would open us to all the crackpots in the country who are looking for a sponsor.

Also we are *not* looking for a psychic to take Dad's place, since no one *could* take his place, and our main job in the Association is to study the records he has left and present that which has been found helpful to mankind. These are thoughts and expressions which have come from that meeting and the subsequent meetings of the Executive Committee. All agreed that the Ass'n pamphlet should be available soon, presenting the program of the Ass'n, but all had different ideas as to the channel the work should take.

Riley [Simmons, a member of the A.R.E. Board] said he'd like to see a school for the study of metaphysics. Miss Wynne gave a lecture on the Study Group work and how it was the only answer. Florence wanted everybody to meet around an altar to meditate. Mr. Miller was very passive as Chairman (probably because he had flown the coop back at the meeting in October when such a fuss was raised). Hillery Poole was sick with a cold, in bed, and couldn't come; otherwise the meeting might have had a little more order to it. Actually all we did was read over the minutes of the last Executive Meeting (a copy of which I sent you) and pass on the moves already made by the Executive

Committee in relation to office details and management.

So, I felt so discouraged over the whole business I didn't know which way to turn, and in the meantime I was deluged with letters from all over the country—people saying they had been to this or that medium and had heard from Mr. Cayce, wanting to know who we had found to take his place, and a million and one unrelated questions like that which should be answered generally and not necessitate an individual letter to each person.

Dave was telling people all over the country about hearing from "judge" through Buddie's [one of David's relatives] automatic writing. I began getting letters from people saying they felt if Mr. Cayce was coming through a channel like that the members should be acquainted with it and have the advantage of his messages; not a word about the authenticity of such a source.

The Diary-Letter came to me as a solution from my standpoint, a way to answer all these people and give them a standard, a way to hold the interest of the members until we could gradually wean them away from Dad's personality toward basic principles of the Association. The Association should, I feel, be "all things to all people" and thus help them all. Each member of the Board is right but there needs to be a correlation and a presentation which will cover all phases of the work and at the same time put the stress where it should be, on the *ideal.*

After my trip to N.Y. (which I will tell you about later in detail) I'm inclined to think that all this confusion has been a good thing, for it has prevented the Board from coming to a definite decision as to which phase to present first. If such a decision had been reached, it would no doubt have been suicide for the Ass'n. Our whole future as an organization depends on how the program is presented in the new booklet entitled *The Association for Research and Enlightenment, Incorporated.* We've got to have everything in that booklet. It is as important as *There Is a River* was. I've talked to the Trustees in N.Y. (including Mrs. Emmet [Beulah H., of New York] who just "happened" to be there for the week-end), and they all feel that we should go slow about branching out into any one direction—that we should take the next year or two to get the index completed and to "round up" those who are to work with and promote each phase.

After the Board Meeting was such a "flop" I thought we would have to depend on the Executive Committee entirely to come to conclusions as to practical working plans. The Committee meets twice a month. It consists of Mr. Miller, Florence Edmonds and Riley Simmons. Hillery Poole [a Norfolk railroad employee who became very active in the A.R.E.], as President of the Ass'n, is automatically Chairman of the Executive Committee. This makes everything hunky-dory. But I found after a few meetings that unless I had everything pretty well outlined so they could say Yes or No, we still floundered around and accomplished nothing. I also found that the way I presented the problem made all the difference in whether their reaction was favorable or unfavorable. This scared me stiff. Then I began to read over the readings on the *work* and I began to see a light.

After beginning the research on the *work* file I evolved some plans which I presented to the Executive Committee and which they agreed on. I'll send you a copy of each of these. Your letters to Dad have been invaluable to me in putting into words the step by step to be considered. I wrote Dr. George, at the advice of the Committee, asking if he would be Chairman of the Advisory Research Board. Also I wrote to three Active Members in Los Angeles who offered their services, asking if they would be Regional Representatives. Because Judy [Chandler] had seemed to take her job seriously as N.Y. Representative, I suggested that she be appointed Chairman of Regional Representatives throughout the country. They agreed to this and I wrote her accordingly. After I talked with her in N.Y. and she realized the amount of work it would involve she would not accept, and I think it is a very good thing. Judy can never be of much help to us in the Ass'n—she is too involved with Judy and cannot straighten out her own personal problems, much less the Ass'n's.

Meantime financial help had come each month to Muddie from the N.Y. group, and they had started to work on copying the A.M.A. card index system for us to use with the Physical Readings. Now and then I would hear tales from this, that or the other one, about what the N.Y. group was doing. Dave would phone every now and then and give me a lot of stuff he had received through Buddie. When I asked him about the N.Y group (I knew he had visited it) he said, "Oh well, you know they have their own psychic." Judy had written all that stuff about although she was the N.Y. Representative, she had been insulted by Lane Mellinger, Sec'ty to the Group, I think I sent you a copy of that letter.

Mrs. Harrison [Irene, of New York City] had asked me to come to N.Y. to visit them and rest, whenever I could get away. I decided to go—I felt if I could get away from everything here I might be able to get a perspective. Judy insisted that I spend the week-end with her first, as she was too busy to see me any other time. I think I'll give you a diary of my N.Y. trip, otherwise I'll probably forget something that might be important. More later,

Love,
Gladys

Before Hugh Lynn could even respond, Gladys had to write him the following report on his mother's condition:

March 15, 1945

Dear Hugh Lynn:

Muddie says she wrote you yesterday that Dr. Taylor is taking her in to the hospital tomorrow to have X-Rays made of her stomach. Lydia and I have been worried sick about her but she wouldn't let us write you, as she kept hoping that she would get better.

About a week after she got back here from Hopkinsville this trouble became apparent. She thought at first it was an impaction in the caecum area, so she started using the Castor Oil Packs and taking the Olive oil internally. It seemed to get better at first. She kept up the Packs religiously and is still using them—it's about two months now.

Since I returned from N.Y. two weeks ago she has steadily gotten worse, and weaker each day, because she hasn't been able to keep anything much on her stomach. The whole abdominal area is as hard as a board, all over, and at times we could feel hard knots in places, but now the entire area feels like it is encased with a thick, hard substance. Ever since I got back and found she wasn't responding Lydia and I have been urging her to go to a doctor. Now she is worried about the X-Rays, thinking she may have to have an operation, etc., (not having been told the true condition or the probability).

Well, I've just had a talk with Dr. Taylor and the Red Cross. They're wiring this afternoon asking that you be allowed to come home immediately! I certainly hope you will be on the way home and not even have to read this letter. He thinks Muddie has cirrhosis of the liver, and that there is nothing to be done. At the most he thinks she won't last three months, and if she doesn't gain any strength and keeps losing ground as she has done in the last three weeks she won't last that long.

I feel like I'm going through a nightmare just writing this, so I can't imagine how awful it must be for you reading it.

Right after she came back from Hopkinsville she told Lydia and me that she felt like, since Dad's passing, that one of her vital organs had been bodily removed; that she felt that way physically, it had nothing to do with her mind.

I must admit that mentally she has been the bravest thing I ever saw—she has made herself take an interest in others and not mope or feel sorry for herself. It is purely a physical condition which has perhaps been slowly developing until lately and the strain she has been under during the last few months has weakened her so that she couldn't throw it off.

Thank goodness Sally is getting on fine from her operation—I'm sure you are already getting letters from her.

They found it was not a tumor but a cyst on one ovary—they just removed the ovary and it was a clean, clear-cut thing, no involvement. She is planning to come home the first of the week. Dr. Taylor hasn't told her yet about the seriousness of Muddie's condition, thinking the grief over having to write you about it would put a stop to her splendid progress.

Kathryn is doing a fine job taking care of Tommy, and he is the one bright spot in the picture now.

I'm sending a copy of this letter, of course, to Ecken and Aunt Carrie. I'm sure that Aunt Carrie or Lillian Katherine will want to come at once. Muddie wrote Lillian Katherine this morning, I believe, suggesting that she'd like one of them to come if they could, and telling her about having to have the X-Rays, etc., but of course she didn't have the news to give them that I have here. We have persuaded her to stay in bed to gain strength (presumably) and, of course, will not tell her what the doctor says. I'll write again tomorrow.

Love,
Gladys

March 15, 1945

Dear Hugh Lynn and Ecken:

Muddie wanted me to write you this morning giving you these details as to what she has done, though she is also writing you a note separately. She wanted to get financial matters straight so that if she has to stay in the hospital or have a long drawn-out illness her money won't be tied up so it can't be got *at* without her signature. So, I've just come from the bank and have gotten all these things done . . .

Muddie says that Kathryn Patterson has offered to come over and stay with her as soon as Sally doesn't need her, in case she can be of help (and how!). (Of course, Kathryn knows the whole story but Muddie thinks she is offering to stay on because she wants to remain at the Beach and get a job.) So Muddie was explaining to me this morning that since she can depend on Kathryn, she

doesn't want to ask Miss Carrie to come, knowing it will
mean giving up her job which she has had such a long
time trying to keep, and besides she doesn't feel Miss Carrie is strong enough to wait on her if she should get down
hard and fast in bed. Anyway, I sent Miss Carrie a copy of
the letter I wrote you yesterday, for I knew she should be
prepared. It is better to know the worse and then be hap-
pily surprised than to have such a shock all of a sudden.
Dr. Taylor was going to try to get a room in the hospital
today—maybe the worse by the first of the week ... She is
not in any pain but very uncomfortable ... I'll write again
tomorrow. Please know she'll get all the care and attention it is possible for her to have. Just remember that I love
her, too. Her greatest concern, of course, is that this is worrying "her boys."

Love and tears for you,
Gladys

P.S. Muddie said yesterday, "This is Edgar's birthday."
Lydia said, "Yes, and you ought to ask him to help you—
looks like to me he's trying to pull you over to him—guess
he wants you to be with him." She said, "Yes, but he ought
to think of our boys."

 ... It grieves me to write you like this but I know you'd
rather have the details. I keep trying to think what I would
like to know if I couldn't be on hand. It is indeed a cruel
thing for you, especially; you will truly be a wonderful soul
if you can live through this experience without bitterness.
We keep hoping that you'll be flying home any day and
calling up from N.Y. to say your on the way.
 Muddie is so patient, so little trouble; such a difference
from Dad's illness—he wanted somebody doing something all the time, and he had it, from beginning to end.
Lydia hovers over her like a hen with one chicken, fixing
and bringing her a bite of this or that she feels she might
be able to eat. Dr. T. said give her something often rather
than much at the time; no special diet except no fats or
greases of any kind. She seems to keep down canned to-

matoes better than anything else and has a sort of craving for them. We're giving her beef juice regularly (Mr. Brothers [a local businessman and farm owner] got it for us— quite a job here nowadays). Canned tomatoes are also hard to get on account of high ration point value, but fortunately Shay [Chapin Wilson, Gladys's brother-in-law] raised a lot of tomatoes last summer and Mama canned them. We don't have to worry on that score, though I'm sure we could also get points if we needed them. Her room is filled with beautiful spring flowers. I told her I never knew anyone to have so many flowers with so few people knowing about her illness; it has come on so quickly.

Sally is to come home tomorrow. Dr. Taylor is bringing her out himself. Muddie keeps saying she knows Sally was expecting her to come in and get her, but she just can't now. I've never seen anything like her determination and will power. Evidently she just kept on going for months when an ordinary person would have gone to bed. She hasn't been well for several years, you know, and has continued to doctor according to the readings. I feel that the strong emotional reaction of Dad's death and trying to hold on to herself has caused the condition to settle in the liver, or rather the spleen which registers all emotions, or is affected greatly by them. Tommy always says when he leaves, "Goodbye, Money,—I come see you tomorrow." Bye now. I'll keep on writing from day to day, just in case you don't get leave.

Love,
Gladys

Monday noon,
March 19, 1945

Dear Hugh Lynn:

. . . Dr. Taylor says he told Sally the exact situation, so I'm sure you have heard from her about it. He came by to see Muddie yesterday afternoon and told her he is arranging for her to go to the hospital just as soon as he can get a private room. Sally had to wait a week before she could get in. When going out to the car with him he said, "Gladys, it's no use—it's cancer of the liver—she won't last six weeks—she'll just get weaker and weaker—the liver keeps growing by leaps and bounds. Yes, it's bad—too bad—very sad."

I don't think he has any feeling at all about the X-ray except as something to divert her mind, to keep stalling . . . Muddie is so weak that we'll have to carry her downstairs and in and out of the car, using pillows on the back seat, with me sitting on the floor by her. He thought an ambulance would be best but Sally convinced him that the effect of her going away in an ambulance would be just too devastating. He tells her she'll only need to be there a couple of days for the X-rays, and not even that long except that she's so weak and will have to rest between times.

I just can't realize it. Just think, last Monday she and Lydia went to the hospital to see Sally. Lydia drove, because she felt it was too much of an exertion on Muddie, but otherwise she walked and did everything Lydia did.

Ecken phoned from Fresno Saturday night—he has just gotten Muddie's letter saying she had been to Dr. Taylor and he had suggested the X-rays. He hadn't gotten my letter which was written the next day. I wanted to talk with him so badly but of course couldn't since the phone was right outside Muddie's door. She got up out of bed and went to the phone and her voice sounded good and strong, so that Ecken remarked on it, but when she got back in bed she was completely exhausted. Mrs. Banes, Betty and Dot [Edgar Evans Cayce's mother-in-law and sisters-in-law] came by yesterday afternoon and they're writing Ecken in detail, thinking maybe he can get emergency leave and tell Muddie in such a way that she'll think it natural.

I wired Miss Carrie this morning asking her to phone me tonight after eight, collect, to phone 954 (the office). She will have gotten my letter and I know she'll be wanting to ask questions and plan to come. I don't know what we'd do without Lydia. I'm sleeping in the sun room, with the door open, so I can hear every move Muddie makes.

She gets so nauseated and can't retain her food—she tries
so hard to keep down the medicine Dr. T. is giving her.

Love,
Gladys

Gertrude was confined to her bed, no longer able to be up
and about. Edgar Evans managed a two-week leave from the
army and had come home. Gertrude had her beloved younger
son with her at last:

March 26, 1945

Dear Hugh Lynn:

   Thank goodness Ecken is here. He came by plane, arriving last night around 10 o'clock. He has two weeks
leave. Muddie perked up considerably yesterday knowing
he was coming—that is, as much as she could, poor thing.
Altho the Banes had tried to prepare Ecken (they drove in
to meet him) he was still terribly shocked to see her so
wasted away. It is the most pitiful thing I ever witnessed
because it has happened so quickly that we notice it more
than we did with Dad. While he looked perfectly awful at
the last, we did not notice it as much because we had seen
him change so gradually. Ecken says he does not know but
what it is worse on him to be here and see her like this
than on you to be away and remember her as you saw her
last. Still, one thing we're so grateful for is that she doesn't
actually suffer. As Dr. T. said, she is just getting weaker and
weaker each day. She is so glad to be with Ecken yet it is
such an effort to open her eyes long at the time or to talk.
He sits by the bed and holds her hand. Miss Carrie is so
relieved to have Ecken here—it makes it so much easier
on all of us. I'm still keeping the "night watch" as I sleep in
the little sun room with the door open. She doesn't require
much attention, just three or four times during the night
she has to have a sip of grapefruit juice or a piece of ice in
her mouth to help the nausea and to prevent the feeling
of dryness she has in her throat. If I didn't "take over" very
positively each night like that, Miss Carrie would never
budge one inch toward resting. It is pitiful to watch how

she hovers over Muddie trying to do something for her when there is nothing to do. Ecken is sleeping in the reading room.

A special delivery came yesterday from Mrs. Smillie [Natalia, a New York interior decorator] sending $300 for Muddie. With all our troubles we certainly haven't lacked friends. At least we don't have to worry about the finances. She also sent $50 to the Ass'n for renewal of Active Membership for herself and husband.

Sally sends Kathryn over each day with Tommy. He is so precious. Miss Carrie says (as does everyone else), "My! Isn't he the spittin' image of Hugh Lynn?" Poor Sally, it is so hard on her—Muddie was up and around when Sally went to the hospital, and now—Well, maybe I shouldn't write this way from day to day but if I don't we'll never be able later to go back and tell you how it was. Ecken is going to the Red Cross this morning, after talking with Dr. Taylor, and is going to try to get another wire through asking that you be allowed to have emergency leave. If you could just come home on a bomber right away you might get here in time. We keep telling her that you'll probably show up any time now. When Dr. T. came yesterday, as he went out the bedroom door she motioned to me to ask him what her trouble is. Later when I told her he said it was her liver and we had to get a reaction from it, she said, "Does he think it's serious?"

Love,
Gladys

Letters passed furiously between Hugh Lynn and his mother and between Hugh Lynn and Gladys, but there were frustrating gaps in communications. Mail was agonizingly slow; cables were prohibitively expensive and were used only under the most urgent conditions. When ships were sunk, mail was lost forever, and months could pass before this was even known to the writers. V-mail was a method of microfilming correspondence to reduce the bulk for shipping; in the U.S., the letters were printed and remailed. It severely limited the size of letters; what could be said often had to be spread over a number of small mailings, which then would be put together like chapters in a book. Each V-mail had to be a complete message for as Hugh Lynn said, "at least *some* of them will arrive."

This series of three V-mail letters did not arrive at the Cayce home until April 10. Edgar Evans was with his mother when she died April 1, 1945. Hugh Lynn's letters were written at nearly the same time that Gertrude was passing through "God's other door":

March 30, 1945

#1 My Dear Muddie:

This is a hard letter to write, my dear. Let me explain why. First, I cannot put what I want to say into a letter. I can't get what I am going to *try* and write on one V-mail. You may not get all of them together, for I'll use two or three. They are faster than air mail and at least some of them will arrive. Too, Gladys has written me how critically ill you were on March 18th. Several days ago, as you will know from my letters, I received a cablegram from Dr. Taylor. Since that time you have not been out of my heart and mind for one second. As you know, that heart and mind have been pretty full, but your place has been reserved for a long time. I know that by the time this reaches you a month will have passed, a month that may have seemed like ages to you. It will not be easy for me to express in words the time lapse, or to comprehend the changes that this time may have wrought. More than all this, I cannot tell you tonight that I am on my way home. There is still no word on the last of my applications. It is being checked on now, but I cannot wait to write later, for the Army red tape unwinds slowly. I may hear in a matter of hours or days, or weeks and it may then be no. So, let's face it. It is an old story to you, but let me say it again, knowing that however sick you are or wherever you are you will hear and see and know and understand. My thoughts, my love, my prayers are trying hard to span the time and space.

Love, Hugh Lynn

#2 Dear Muddie:

We left France yesterday and tonight I am sitting in a small German home in a little agricultural village. Out of the window, I can look down a small deserted street. The people have moved out. They are subdued, resigned, unhappy. Even the children do not smile. It is a beautiful country, rolling fields and small patches of woodland, all carefully cultivated and well kept. No one moves out of any of the village houses after dark, except our men.

So, this letter is being written from a very appropriate setting.

I don't want to tell you about the trouble or sorrow of these people, or of my own suffering, but of the beauty of the country which is lasting, like the beauty in my heart and mind when I think about you. The gold of our sunset tonight and the lovely green of these fields and woodland are lasting. When these people have buried the pain, and hate and turmoil in their hearts, the beautiful things will remain. Just so, when the hurt in my heart has passed, all that is beautiful in my memory about you will be there, on and on and on. It is this I want to tell you about. This you must remember.

You must not worry about Ecken and me. For many long years, we have lived and worked together in joyous, happy days and through hard times. Always you have given us wise guidance, and an example which we will always try to live up to. Love, Hugh Lynn

#3 Dear Muddie:

It is important for you to realize how much fun it has been being your son. So many times, I have seen you faced with problems, conditions that I have known to crumple up so many people, and you have risen above them—and (the important thing) carried others with you. These things we will not forget. To few people has there been entrusted the guidance of so many lives—not in the outward way to be seen by men, but in the background where the going was tough. These things I know, and will not forget. Never have I known of such unselfish love for two human beings as you have always shown towards Ecken and me. This, too, I will never forget. It would be easy to go on and on.

It makes me proud to think of you. It makes me deeply happy to know how ready you are to pass through that other door. There is so much beauty in your living, my dear, that I cannot be sad at the possibility of you joining Dad. You held up his right hand—sometimes both hands here, so it does not surprise me that he may need you now.

We have come, Muddie, to an understanding of karma in a way that we have for a long time been explaining to others, and I find that your life represents so much that is fine and beautiful that I cannot allow my selfish desires to mar this period of waiting and wondering.

My prayers are that you will not suffer, my dear. I know that you must realize how much love has been, is and always will be yours. Hugh Lynn

Once again, the sad task of informing the A.R.E. membership of a Cayce death fell to Tom Sugrue:

On Easter Sunday morning at 7:15 o'clock, in her home on Arctic Crescent, Virginia Beach, Virginia, Gertrude Evans Cayce passed away. She was buried at Hopkinsville, Kentucky, in the family plot which three months before had been opened to receive her husband.

Thus ended the love story of Gertrude Evans and Edgar Cayce. It began on a hot summer day in the early eighteen-nineties, in Hopkinsville, where the Cayce family had come to live from their farm in south Christian County. Edgar was working at the local book store. One day a family friend, Miss Ethel Duke, drove up in a horse and buggy and called him outside. In the carriage with her was a pretty young girl. "I want you to meet a cousin of mine," Ethel said to Edgar. "This is Miss Gertrude Evans. Gertrude this is Edgar Cayce."

That was the beginning. He went to a lawn party at Gertrude's home the next week. Soon he was visiting at the

Hill regularly. They became engaged, and on Wednesday, June 17th, 1903, they were married. Through the years they worked together, and it was Mrs. Cayce who sat beside her husband, acting as conductor, during most of the 15,000 readings which he gave during his long career as one of the world's great psychics.

Everyone who knew Mr. Cayce was amazed by his strange power, but those who were privileged to know the man personally, and to observe the family life which surrounded him, came eventually to be as equally impressed by the phenomenon of a home which seemed to achieve the ideal which every person cherishes for this sacred institution. There is no doubt that the Cayce family life was unique and inspiring. Not only was there complete harmony between the four members of the family—Gertrude, Edgar and their two sons, Hugh Lynn and Edgar Evans—but they had a genius for absorbing friends and visitors into the group in such a way that a stranger felt at home almost instantly. Many families are closely knit, but usually in such cases the members present a united front against outsiders. The opposite was true of the Cayce's. A friend of any one of them was a friend of all four. Their home was always big enough for one more friend, one more visitor.

Probably this is explained by the fact that individually and collectively they tried to live Christianity. They never gave lip service to an ideal; they carried it out in deed. But the guiding genius of the organized friendliness was Mrs. Cayce. She loved her home above all things, but she conceived it to be a place of rest and comfort and refuge for not only her family, but for anyone who needed these precious blessings.

Her youngest son, Captain Edgar Evans Cayce, was with her when she passed. Her oldest son, Sergeant Hugh Lynn Cayce, was at his post of duty with General Patton's Army in Germany.

Thomas Sugrue
A.R.E. Bulletin, April 1945

*   *   *

Hugh Lynn wrote to Gladys in May explaining that his application for return to the States had been refused and that she should explain to the board "that I am like a man trying to move around in a dark room. I know the shape and size, but the furniture has been moved around a bit." Efforts to obtain a release for Hugh Lynn continued until his discharge was granted December 12, 1945. He returned home eleven months after the death of his father and nearly nine months after the loss of his mother.

Beginning in December 1945, and continuing for the next thirty-seven years, Hugh Lynn ran the race that had been set before him, traveling along that invisible corridor between materiality and spirituality he had seen so long before.

If it is true that a spiritual leader is one who sees that which no one else can see and who holds out against the current until land forms around them, then the evidence of the thirty-seven years of Hugh Lynn's career, following his father's death in 1945, distinguishes him as a member of that elite and timeless group.

It is now more than fifty years since the death of Edgar Cayce. No longer the sole prerogative of a single family, his Work has grown and spread until its mark is indelibly impressed upon nearly every country of the world: Edgar Cayce, Psychic Diagnostician; Cayce Petroleum; Edgar Cayce Psychic Research Institute; Cayce Institute of Psychic Research; Edgar Cayce Publishing Company; Association of National Investigators; Atlantic University; Association for Research and Enlightenment; the Edgar Cayce Foundation; the Cayce/Reilly School of Massotherapy. The roll call of names represents many efforts throughout the years by groups of people trying to create a vehicle for this remarkable body of information and the continuing changes it brought and still brings in the lives of all those touched by its transformative qualities.

Why am I trying to serve my fellow man through such an organization—The Association for Research and Enlightenment?

First, let me ask you a question, and you decide it in your own mind: Is it the words one says that convinces

you, or the spirit with which they are said?

I can't say any word that all of you have not heard before. Consequently, you know all of these things. They may
be put together in a little different way because they've
been a part of my individual experience. But unless they
can carry some conviction to you, and answer something
within you, they don't mean anything.

Edgar Cayce Lecture
February 28, 1938
Norfolk, Virginia

Epilogue

I AM CERTAIN that my grandfather himself did not have a clear idea of how to carry out the Work. I think all he was ever truly certain of was that, if he followed his simple mandate of using his gift to try to help one person at a time, God would take care of the rest. He made it clear throughout his life that this Work was not his Work—that is, not Edgar Cayce's—but *His* Work which came from and belonged to a higher power.

As Tom Sugrue wrote in 1945, "Faith must be kept with him,

and his work continued." We are trying to do just that, all of us here in Virginia Beach. Won't you join us?

Sincerely,
Charles Thomas Cayce

Biographies

Abeler, _____
A businessman from Altoona, Pennsylvania, who knew Edgar Cayce through David Kahn. Abeler did not have readings from Edgar Cayce.

Adams, Evangeline
Evangeline Adams was an astrologer who lived in Selma, Alabama. Edgar Cayce made her acquaintance while he lived in Selma. The Edgar Cayce Foundation has no record of whether or not she and her husband, Mr. Jordan, had readings.

Armstrong, William Rowland
A designer and stylist at Irving Furniture Factories, Inc., of New York City, where Ben Lauterstein was the manager. William Rowland Armstrong was introduced to Edgar Cayce through David Kahn. Armstrong retired from Barker Brothers Studio of Interior Design in Los Angeles, California, in 1969, and remained in touch with the Edgar Cayce Foundation until 1972.

Bethea, Miriam Woodward
Miriam Woodward Bethea lived in Birmingham, Alabama. She hosted Edgar Cayce in her home during his early visits to Birmingham, where he would be the guest speaker at various ladies clubs, afterwards giving readings. Her earliest recorded contact is a reading on October 14, 1922. Mrs. Bethea visited friends in Norfolk, Virginia, as early as 1924, linking Edgar to people in the Norfolk area prior to the move from Dayton in 1925.

Birdi, Fredoon Cursetzce
Dr. Fredoon Cursetzce Birdi was born in Poona, India. He was a naturopathic physician employed at the Physical Culture Hotel in Dansville, New York, where the readings sometimes referred patients. Dr. Birdi had a life reading.

Bisey, Sunker Abaji
Born in Bombay, India, on April 29, 1867, Dr. Sunker Abaji Bisey

was son of a civil judge for the District of Dhulia in the Bombay Presidency in India. He became an engineer and an inventor, and in 1908, he was honored by the Indian National Industrial Congress for his scientific work. During a trip to Southern France, he contracted malaria and became gravely ill. A Hindu doctor sent him a few doses of a Burmese preparation made from seaweed which had proven useful in treating chronic malaria in Burma, and he rapidly recovered. Over a ten-year period, he perfected this formula, which today is known as Atomidine. In 1928, an acquaintance of Edgar Cayce's from Washington by the name of S.A. Larson suggested that Edgar send Dr. Bisey some information on the Work. In September 1931, Dr. Bisey had readings from Edgar Cayce on further perfecting the iodine formula. He remained closely connected with the Cayce Work until his death in 1935.

Blumenthal, Edwin
Edwin David Blumenthal was born October 28, 1898, in New York City. Edwin was twenty-six years old when he had his first reading from Edgar Cayce. He had a total of 132 readings from October 2, 1924, to July 4, 1930. Edwin worked as a partner with his brother, Morton, in the stock market in New York and on the Cayce Hospital project from 1924 to 1931. Edwin died of cancer in Virginia Beach on January 22, 1980. He was buried in St. Mary's Cemetery in Norfolk, Virginia.

Blumenthal, Freda
Freda Blumenthal had twenty readings from Edgar Cayce between 1924 and 1929. She was a forty-nine-year-old widow at the time she made application to join the ANI or Association of National Investigators. Despite the physical help she received through the readings, Mrs. Blumenthal did not share her sons' confidence in the hospital project, creating tensions within the Blumenthal family which contributed to the pressure on Morton and Edwin during the difficult times before the hospital was closed.

Blumenthal, Morton
Born April 6, 1895, in Altoona, Pennsylvania, Morton Blumenthal

was twenty-nine years old when he was first introduced to Edgar Cayce through David E. Kahn in August 1924. Edgar was living in Dayton, Ohio, where he had organized the Cayce Institute of Psychic Research. Morton attended Columbia University in New York City, and at the time he was introduced to Edgar Cayce, he was working as a stockbroker in the firm of William E. Lauer and Company at 74 Broadway, New York City. Later, he and his brother, Edwin, were able to establish their own seat on the New York Stock Exchange and for seven years, almost single-handedly provided the funding for the Cayce Hospital and the support of the Cayce family (1924 until 1931).

More than any other individual in the 5,787 nonreading records in the custody of the Edgar Cayce Foundation archives, Morton Blumenthal opened areas of inquiry into psychic development, the nature of man, and the nature of consciousness. He was responsible for questions that led to the development of the philosophy of the readings, later amplified through the Search for God and Glad Helpers prayer group series. Morton had the first dream interpretation reading and, of the 630 total dream interpretation readings, the great majority were given for Morton, Edwin, and other Blumenthal family members.

Morton had 468 readings from Edgar Cayce from August 1924, until his last reading on July 4, 1930. On December 30, 1949, he recorded a dream in which he foresaw the manner of his own death. As he had dreamed five years earlier, he died in Virginia Beach, Virginia, on April 9, 1954, of a heart attack. Morton was buried in St. Mary's Cemetery in Norfolk, Virginia.

Bosky (or Boskey), Meyer
Meyer and Janet Bosky were acquainted with David Kahn through Janet's brother, Harry Lauter (the Lauters were related to the Kahn family) as early as 1917, when Edgar Cayce was in Selma, Alabama. Meyer Bosky was an attorney in practice in New York City.

Bradley, Franklin Folkerts
Franklin Folkerts Bradley of Chicago, Illinois, was referred to Edgar Cayce by business associate David Kahn in March 1927. A former partner in Bradley & Vrooman Company, Bradley spe-

cialized in manufacturing paints, enamels, lacquers, and varnishes. He also founded a school for boys and had readings for some students. He was an active participant in the Work, serving on the board, at one time organizing a for-profit corporation to exploit the health technology in the readings, manufacturing carbon ash, and maintaining close ties until his death in an automobile accident November 14, 1940.

Bransford, Johnson S.
Johnson S. Bransford was the president of the Bransford Realty Company of Nashville, Tennessee, and was interested in psychic phenomena. He had an extensive library and as a result of his interest, Edgar Cayce thought Bransford might associate himself with the Cayce Work. He had a reading for his son, John Sterling Bransford, but did not become active in the ANI.

Brown, Thomas B. (Tim)
Thomas B. Brown lived in Dayton, Ohio. When and where Tim Brown and Edgar Cayce first met is not known. Tim was in Birmingham, Alabama, at the Tutwiler Hotel for a reading on the King and North Star Mines on November 18, 1922. The reading states: " . . . There is some of this territory that we have been over before . . . "[195-1], indicating earlier readings had been given. It is highly probable that the friendship between these two men can be traced to Edgar's early days in Texas when he was obtaining leases on oil and mineral rights. Tim was a Realtor and investor, and interested in a variety of investments and inventions. He was one of the key investors in the Cayce Hospital project and remained in touch with Edgar throughout Edgar's life.

Brown, William Moseley
Born in Lynchburg, Virginia, in 1894, Dr. Brown was thirty-four years old when he had his first reading from Edgar Cayce. Then head of the Department of Education and Psychology at Washington and Lee University in Lexington, Virginia, he became involved in the Cayce Work through one of his psychology students, Hugh Lynn Cayce. Dr. Brown first met Edgar Cayce in 1928. Edgar Cayce's abilities so convinced and impressed him that Brown was persuaded of the need for new dimensions in

formal education, especially in his own field of psychology. He led the ANI group in conceptualizing an institution of higher learning which would take the Cayce information into the mainstream. Together with Morton and Edwin Blumenthal, he assembled a prestigious faculty and, following the guidance of the Cayce readings, established Atlantic University in rented facilities in April 1930. Hugh Lynn Cayce worked in the Atlantic University Library, and it was from this early experience that he was able to establish the present A.R.E. Library. Unable to obtain the necessary funding to continue the fledgling program after the ANI group dissolved, Atlantic University was forced to close in 1933.

Dr. Brown managed to retain the original charter until 1960, when he assisted Hugh Lynn Cayce and then Edgar Cayce Foundation president Robert A. Adriance in regaining legal ownership of the charter. In 1985, under the direction of Dr. James C. Windsor, one of Hugh Lynn Cayce's long-held dreams was realized when Atlantic University received approval from the Virginia State Council on Higher Education and formal classes were held again after fifty-two years.

In 1929, Dr. Brown resigned from Washington and Lee to run, unsuccessfully, for the office of governor of Virginia. He became president of Atlantic University in 1930, and his political visibility as well as his role in Atlantic University are credited with quickening the interest of William and Mary in establishing its Norfolk division, now Old Dominion University. Dr. Brown went on to become executive director of Elon College, North Carolina. He retired in 1960 and died in St. Petersburg, Florida, at the age of seventy-one.

Cayce, Carrie Elizabeth Major (See "Cayce, Leslie B.")

Cayce, Gertrude Evans
Gertrude Evans Cayce was born in Christian County, Kentucky, on February 22, 1880, to Elizabeth Ella Salter and Samuel Thompson Evans. Mr. and Mrs. Evans had three children:

• Gertrude Evans Cayce, born February 22, 1880; died April 1, 1945

- Hugh B. Evans, died in El Paso, Texas, April 13, 1910, of tuberculosis. His obituary states he died at twenty-eight years of age and that his father had died twenty-four years earlier, which would mean he probably was born in 1882. He is buried in Riverside Cemetery near his father.
- William Lynn Evans, born July 31, 1884; died December 2, 1934

Gertrude's father, Samuel Thompson Evans, died at The Hill on September 11, 1886, at age thirty-three when Gertrude was six years old. Since tuberculosis was rampant in Christian County during this era, it is conjectured that Samuel Evans died of the disease. He was the son of the Reverend Henry J. Evans, formerly of Virginia and once stationed in Hopkinsville. His mother was the daughter of Captain J. Cluke of Montgomery County, Kentucky.

Gertrude's mother, Elizabeth Ella Salter Evans, was graduated from South Kentucky College. She died April 8, 1934, at age seventy-two.

Cayce, Leslie B., and Carrie Elizabeth Major Cayce

Leslie B. Cayce (L.B.), Edgar Cayce's father, was the second of ten children born to Thomas J. Cayce and Sarah P. Thomas Cayce. Edgar's grandfather, usually referred to as Tom Cayce, was a Christian County, Kentucky, farmer who was also in partnership with his brother, George W. Cayce, in a tobacco sales business called Planters Warehouse.

L.B. Cayce (also called the Squire) was a farmer, merchant, insurance agent, and photographer. He conducted many of the early readings for his son. When Edgar and Gertrude lived in Selma, Alabama, L.B. Cayce lived with them and worked in the photographic studio. During his son's travels to raise money for Cayce Petroleum Company, L.B. acted as manager. He also made his home with the Cayces in Virginia Beach after the death of his wife in 1926. He was slightly injured in a house fire in Nashville, Tennessee, while visiting his daughter Sarah. He died of complications related to those injuries on April 11, 1937, and is buried in Riverside Cemetery in Hopkinsville, Kentucky.

Edgar's mother, Carrie Elizabeth Major Cayce, was the youngest of seven children born to Urial Lodowick Major and his wife, Elizabeth Ann Seargeant. U.L. Major was a farmer in Christian County and farmed at Cedar Grove until his death on September 21, 1861. He is buried in Christian County, in a private family cemetery. U.L. Major and Elizabeth Ann Seargeant were married October 1, 1838. Elizabeth Ann was born July 23, 1821, and died October 19, 1875.

L.B. and Carrie Major Cayce were married June 10, 1874. They had seven children, two of whom died in infancy:

- Lela I. Cayce, born January 22, 1875; died as an infant
- Edgar Cayce, born March 18, 1877; died January 3, 1945
- Annie Cayce, born November 20, 1879; died July 20, 1957; unmarried
- Ola Cayce, born October 25, 1881; died July 31, 1967; married
- Thomas Leslie Cayce, born November 19, 1882; died as an infant
- Mary Ella Cayce, born April 24, 1886; died March 19, 1970; married
- Sarah Elizabeth Cayce, born January 7, 1888; died April 13, 1984; married

Chandler, Julia Yates (Judy)
Julia Yates Chandler was introduced to the work of Edgar Cayce through friends of Irene Harrison. She was the manager of the Empire State Building in New York City. Julia was active in writing, publishing, speaking, and facilitating the Work in New York City. She passed away March 21, 1966.

Coe, Charles W.
C.W. Coe had one reading from Edgar Cayce on August 14, 1927, and passed away on August 19. He was the grandson of Henry Willard Coe, owner of Rancho San Felipe, a four-thousand-acre property near San Jose, California. C.W. Coe's son, Eben, requested the reading which, if obtained much earlier, might have allowed his father to live. Eben Coe retained an active interest in the affairs of the A.R.E. until his death.

Cravis, William Bernard
William Bernard Cravis lived in Atlantic City, New Jersey. He learned of Edgar Cayce through his friend, David Levy, who had had readings. He was the managing director of the Hotel Knickerbocker in Atlantic City at the time he was introduced to Edgar and went on to manage several other large hotels in New York. Mr. and Mrs. Cravis were especially supportive of the Cayces during the time of the New York arrest and remained active in the Work until his death in 1950.

Curie, _____, Mr.
This individual has not been identified as this name does not appear in the records.

DuVall, Matilda
Owner of the Dower House Estate in Rosaryville, Maryland, Mrs. DuVall was a friend of Lucille and David Kahn. She requested a reading for her husband, M.R. DuVall, who was suffering from a form of mental illness. The suggested treatments were not followed. Mrs. DuVall was a psychologist who lectured around the United States on "The Chemical Nature of Thoughts" and was a member of the Rosicrucians.

Edmonds, Florence Rawlins, and Edith Edmonds
Florence Edmonds and her sister, Edith, were natives of Norfolk, Virginia. Their parents were Walter and Mary Ward Edmonds. Their father, who was president of the Eagle Iron Works in Norfolk, Virginia, manufactured the iron work for the Cayce Hospital when it was built. Both the Edmonds girls were present for hundreds of readings throughout Edgar's career. They were both members of Search for God Group #1 (the 262 readings series) as well as the Glad Helpers (the 281 readings series) prayer group. Both women were extremely active in the Work, organizing lectures for Edgar, fund-raising, and serving in various administrative capacities. Florence served as a member of the board of trustees of the A.R.E. Edith died January 9, 1939, and Florence died March 1, 1956.

Emmet, Beulah H. (Mrs. Robert)

Beulah Emmet was a friend of Irene Harrison in New York City. She was introduced to the work of Edgar Cayce in 1940 and went on to found High Mowing School in Wilton, New Hampshire.

Finlayson, Abigail Emerancy

Abigail Emerancy Finlayson was handed a booklet about Edgar Cayce in May 1926. She lived in Cleveland, Ohio, and continued to correspond with Edgar until his death.

Gravett, William A., D.O.

Edgar Cayce said that Dr. Gravett was one of the first graduates of the Southern School of Osteopathy in Franklin, Kentucky. He was in practice in Dayton, Ohio, while the Cayces lived there, from 1923 to 1925. The readings referred many patients to him. Dr. Gravett served as the president of the National Association of Osteopathic Physicians in 1939 and was in private practice. He also served as chief of staff of the Gravett Hospital in Dayton.

Gray, Mamie Butler

Mamie Butler Gray met Gertrude and Edgar Cayce when they moved to Selma, Alabama, in 1912, where they were all members of the First Christian Church. Mamie and Edgar maintained a lively and voluminous correspondence until his death. Mamie died in her sleep while at her daughter's home on March 6, 1966.

Hammerling, Maximilian H.

Maximilian H. Hammerling was a thirty-five-year-old lawyer in practice at 36 West 44th Street in New York City when he first joined the ANI in 1928. He and his wife both had readings from Edgar Cayce and remained active in the Work until his death. Hammerling was the attorney who successfully represented Edgar Cayce when he was arrested in New York City on November 7, 1931.

Hawkins, Edward Pratt

Edward Pratt Hawkins was introduced to Edgar Cayce by David Kahn while on a business trip in New York City. Hawkins was a native of Connersville, Indiana, and lived in Hempstead, New York, at the time he learned of Edgar Cayce. He and his family had readings and referred friends to Edgar Cayce for help.

Held, Horton, Ph.D.
Horton Held, Ph.D., of Norfolk, Virginia, was an internationally known researcher, teacher, and lecturer in the field of applied psychology. She was a Theosophist, was deeply interested in spiritual healing, and was known as a spiritual healer. At one time she served as secretary of the Virginia Beach Healthatorium, which was a similar project to that of the Cayce Hospital, and as the managing editor of the Dade County, Florida, Federation of Women's Organizations.

Holbein, Ann Elizabeth Gray
Daughter of Mamie Butler Gray, Ann was eight years old when she had her first reading. All of her life, she referred to Edgar Cayce as "Daddie" and grew up with Hugh Lynn (nine years older) and Edgar Evans Cayce (two years younger). Ann became an optometrist and practiced in Mobile, Alabama. In 1935, while still in Selma, she had occasion to work in the building where the Cayces' photographic studio had been. On a shelf, she found a watch belonging to Edgar Cayce, which she returned to him, still in good working condition, some ten years after the Cayces had left Selma. Ann Elizabeth was active in the Work between Cayce headquarters in Virginia Beach and Mobile, Alabama, until her death. Ann's life readings were featured in *Intimates Through Time* by Jess Stearn.

House, Carrie (Aunt Carrie)
This is Caroline Salter House, Gertrude's aunt and wife of Dr. Thomas B. House Sr.

House, Thomas B. Sr. (Uncle Tom)
Thomas B. House Sr. was married to Gertrude's aunt, Carrie Salter. Carrie was the youngest sister of Gertrude's uncle, Hiram P. Salter. Dr. House was born in Orlanda, Tennessee, on April 3, 1867. At the time of his marriage, he was living in Springfield, Tennessee, where he was in private practice, and he later joined

the staff of the Western State Hospital in Hopkinsville. He was an M.D., an osteopath, and a pharmacist. Dr. House was the chief of staff of the Cayce Hospital when it opened in Virginia Beach. He subsequently became gravely ill, and a reading suggested Dayton, Ohio, as a place where he might be treated. Dr. House was moved from the Cayce Hospital in September to Dayton, where he died of kidney failure on October 8, 1929. Dr. Lyman A. Lydic replaced Dr. House on January 2, 1930, as chief of staff at the Cayce Hospital.

Hurst, Riley
Riley Hurst lived in Witchita Falls, Texas, and was selected as head driller when the Cayce Petroleum Company was started in 1920. Riley sought readings (3982) from Edgar to find buried treasure in Winslow, Arkansas.

Kahn, Fannie (Mother Kahn)
Mr. and Mrs. Sol Kahn had nine children, all of whom had readings. Acquainted with Edgar Cayce from Lexington, Kentucky, where her husband was in the grocery business, Mrs. Kahn maintained an affectionate and enduring correspondence with Edgar throughout her lifetime. Edgar stated he knew David when David was "a little grocery clerk" in his father's business. Mother Kahn, as she was always known, was a patient in the Cayce Hospital in December 1929 and January 1930 for treatment of breast cancer. She died October 17, 1935, within two hours of Edgar Cayce giving her her seventy-first and last reading.

Ketchum, Wesley, M.D.
Wesley Harrington Ketchum was born on November 11, 1878, in Beaver Township, Columbiana County, in eastern Ohio. He received his M.D. degree from the Cleveland Homeopathic Medical College in Cleveland, Ohio, in 1904, and moved to Hopkinsville, Kentucky, in partnership with a Dr. Young. Dr. Ketchum had two sons, Alton and Robert. After a refresher course at Harvard Medical School, Dr. Ketchum established a medical practice in Hawaii and, later, in Southern California, where he died at age ninety.

Klee, Carvel Arthur

Carvel Arthur Klee, son of George and Lillian Klee, was twelve at the time of his first reading and was treated for deafness by Dr. Curtis H. Muncie (osteopathic physician, developer of eustachian tube finger surgery method, author of *Prevention and Cure of Deafness Through Muncie Reconstruction Method*). George Klee was referred by David Kahn and was in business as "Adolph Klee's Son" on Madison Avenue in New York City. Carvel remained in contact with the Edgar Cayce Foundation until 1977.

Klingensmith, George Saxman

A twenty-five-year-old construction engineer from Wilmore, Pennsylvania, Klingensmith was in Dayton, Ohio, on business for his father (who was in business as G.S. Klingensmith, Engineer and Contractor) when he learned of Edgar Cayce through his friend, Arthur Lammers. For a time he served as secretary to Edgar and as a stenographer who took down many of the early readings.

Ladd, Robert In.

Robert In. Ladd was a sales engineer with Pressed and Welded Steel Products Company of New York, who was referred for readings by David Kahn. He remained active in the Work until his death in 1943.

Lammers, Arthur H.

Credited with obtaining the first life reading, Arthur Lammers' first contact with Edgar Cayce was through a mutual friend, banker Joseph B. Long of Cleburne, Texas. On October 9, 1923, he had a health reading for his niece. The president of an advertising company (Lammers Advertising) in Dayton, Ohio, Lammers was responsible for persuading Edgar to move from Selma, Alabama, to Dayton, Ohio, in November 1923. Lammers' business was not on as sound a footing as he had represented and eventually, he lost not only his business but his home in Dayton.

Laura _____

This young lady is thought to be a former member of Edgar

Cayce's Christian Endeavor group in Selma, Alabama.

Lauterstein, Ben
The manager of Irving Furniture Factories in New York City, Lauterstein was introduced to Edgar Cayce through David Kahn. He and his family all had readings from Edgar.

Levy, David
David Levy owned Levy and Solomon, a clothing manufacturing business in New York City. Twenty members of the Levy family had readings from Edgar Cayce. Mr. Levy remained in close touch with Gladys Davis and all aspects of the Work until the early 1960s.

Long, Joseph B.
Joseph B. Long, a banker, lived in Cleburne, Texas. At one time, he was vice-president of the Home National Bank and, in 1925, was associated with the Lometa State Bank of Lometa, Texas. He was associated with Edgar Cayce during the Cayce Petroleum Company days. He remained in contact with Edgar after the move to Virginia Beach.

Lydic, Lyman A.
Dr. Lydic, an osteopathic physician, was in practice with Dr. Gravett in Dayton. Although he became chief of staff of the Cayce Hospital and expressed sincere enthusiasm at the opportunity to apply scientific methodologies to the diagnosis and treatment information coming through Edgar Cayce, Dr. Lydic remained a skeptic throughout his life as to the validity of the process or the source of the information. He returned to Dayton after the close of the Cayce Hospital and established himself in private practice, later returning to osteopathic college to study diseases of the eye, ear, nose, and throat and qualifying as a specialist. He retired later in life in his home state of Maine.

Marshall, Reuben
Reuben Marshall was twenty-seven when he had his first reading from Edgar Cayce. He was employed by Mr. Moore, a New York stockbroker, and dealt in wheat futures. He lost his job during

the stock market crash and was unemployed for more than fourteen months. He remained in contact with the Work until 1974.

Martin, George Claude
George Martin was an oil leasing agent who lived in Meridian, Texas. The Martins lived on site in the oil field for a time during this period, and Edgar Cayce was a frequent guest in their home. Both Mr. and Mrs. Martin had great confidence in Edgar's information on finding oil. Claude had his first reading on April 7, 1923, and in August 1923, had a reading for his daughter, Cliff Elizabeth Martin, who was seriously ill with streptococcus, and for his son, John Farris Martin, for a heart problem.

Martini, Otto A.
Associated with Freed-Eisemann Radio Corporation in Brooklyn, New York, in 1925, and later general manager of R.E. Thompson Manufacturing Company, Inc./Thompson Radio. He was a business associate of David Kahn.

McConnell, J.T.
J.T. McConnell of Meridian, Texas, was the head cashier at the First National Bank of Meridian, Texas, and a friend to Edgar Cayce during the Cayce Petroleum Company days.

Miller, Miriam
Although referred to as Mrs., young Miriam Miller was actually a single woman at the time of her reading. An aspiring actress in New York, she was dating Morton Blumenthal. She had four readings from Edgar Cayce and successfully recovered from debilitation and the beginning stages of tuberculosis through following the readings. She and Morton did not marry.

Miller, Noah
Noah Miller and his wife, Hannah, were introduced to the Work of Edgar Cayce through Minnie Barrett of Norfolk, Virginia, in 1929. Noah and Hannah were faithful regulars in the original SFG study group and were present for hundreds of readings. Miller was a captain in the U.S. Engineers and served as president of the A.R.E. in 1940.

Mohr, Frank E.

Frank Mohr signed an affidavit that he had a reading in April 1915 for blindness caused by an accident he had in a coal mine on July 7, 1911. His sight was restored by following the advice in the readings. (Dr. Wesley Ketchum was one of three physicians involved in his case.) Mohr subsequently spent two and one-half months with Edgar in Birmingham, Alabama, conducting readings and acting as secretary to Edgar. He spent his time between Miami, Florida (his brother-in-law, Willard A. Wilson, lived in Miami), and his hometown of Columbus, Ohio. Over the years, he was the president of the Mohr-Minton Coal and Coke Co., of Nortonville, Kentucky; the president of the Nortonville bank; the builder of the interurban railroad between Gallipolis and Mt. Pleasant, West Virginia, and, in his later years, a residential contractor and real estate investor. He remained a faithful friend to Edgar Cayce until his death in 1938.

Moore, _____

A New York stockbroker who dealt in grain futures. Moore was an acquaintance of Morton and Edwin Blumenthal and one of a group of businessmen, many of whom had readings from Edgar Cayce related to their numerous business ventures. Moore did not have readings.

Moore, J.A.

J.A. Moore of Cleburne, Texas, was an early investor in Cayce Petroleum. He prepared a pooling agreement for Cayce Petroleum Company.

Moore, Julia A. (Mother Moore)

Julia A. Moore, widow of M.J. Moore who died April 30, 1915, was the owner of Rocky Pasture in San Saba, Texas, where the Cayce Petroleum Company held gas and mineral leases. She had six sons and two daughters.

Noe, Albert Davis Sr.

Albert Davis Noe Sr., a resident of Hopkinsville, Kentucky, was the proprietor of the 120-room Hotel Latham in Hopkinsville, which was destroyed by fire in 1956. Noe set up an office for

Edgar Cayce as "Edgar Cayce Psychic Diagnostician," in partnership with Dr. Wesley Ketchum, in the Dalton Building in downtown Hopkinsville. L.B. Cayce persuaded his son to sue Noe because Edgar was not receiving monies as a result of their partnership. The case was dismissed, and Edgar and Gertrude Cayce moved to Selma, Alabama, immediately afterward.

Patterson, Kathryn M.
Kathryn M. Patterson was born in Youngstown, Ohio, and was living there at the time Charlie and Gladys Dillman introduced her to the work of Edgar Cayce. Kathryn was on the board of the A.R.E., served on a number of committees and, during Edgar's final illness, came to Virginia Beach to help with the office, household, and nursing chores.

Peters, Thomas J. Sr.
Thomas Peters and Amos Preston were at one time in partnership in the real estate business in Miami. Peters and his wife, Texas Thurman Peters, had three daughters and one son. Peters, introduced to Edgar Cayce by his partner, Amos Preston, was also interested in finding treasure, gas, and oil. He was fifty-four at the time of his first reading and requested information on Bimini. He died in 1934.

Poole, Hillery
Hillery Poole was an employee of the Norfolk Southern Railway Company as a freight and telegraph agent. The many telegrams to and from the Cayce home aroused his interest and, in August 1933, he requested a physical reading for his father. Poole went on to become very active in the Work, serving on the board of the A.R.E. and participating in various committees of the board and congress. Poole was one of the seven podium guests for the sixtieth anniversary celebration honoring Gladys Davis Turner on September 10, 1983.

Preston, Amos C.
Amos C. Preston was introduced to Edgar Cayce early in 1926 through Frank E. Mohr. Preston was part owner of Peters and Preston, Real Estate Rentals and Investments, in Miami, Florida;

had a great interest in finding lost treasure, gas, and oil in Florida; and had readings on Bimini. On March 28, 1931, Preston attended a reorganization meeting where the A.R.E. was formed. He was the business manager of the A.R.E. for a time. Preston is believed to have died in 1937 or 1938.

Rothfeder, Joseph L., M.D.
Dr. Joseph Rothfeder was a medical doctor in New York and a friend of Morton Blumenthal. Dr. Rothfeder had two life readings from Edgar Cayce, but events did not bring him to Virginia Beach to work in the Cayce Hospital.

Rubin, _____ , D.D.S.
Dr. Rubin, a dentist in New York, was a friend of Morton Blumenthal.

Salter, Samuel L.
Gertrude's grandfather, he was born on September 7, 1823, in Philadelphia, Pennsylvania, the fifth of nine children. Samuel first studied medicine in Philadelphia, but after moving to Cincinnati, Ohio, he studied architecture at the University of Cincinnati. He moved to Hopkinsville in 1848 to construct the Western State Hospital and Bethel College. He was in business as "Salter & Orr," a designing and construction firm. He and his wife, Susan Jones Salter, had five children:

• Elizabeth Ella Salter, 1860-1934, married to Samuel Thompson Evans (Gertrude Cayce's parents)
• Katherine Greathitt Salter, 1862-1948
• William Hembel Salter, 1864-1936
• Hiram Abith Phelps Salter, 1867-1944
• Caroline Bennetta Salter, 1875-1949

Samuel Salter died on October 20, 1897, when Gertrude was sixteen years old. She lost her Grandmother Susan two years later on July 23, 1899. Gertrude (with her widowed mother, Elizabeth, the oldest of Samuel and Susan's children) lived at The Hill until Gertrude's marriage to Edgar Cayce at age twenty-three on June 17, 1903. The Hill, made famous through *There Is a River* by Thomas Sugrue, was destroyed by fire on December 2, 1964.

Saxman, Robert, and Harriet, D.C.
The Saxmans, chiropractors in Chicago, Illinois, were aunt and uncle of George Saxman Klingensmith. The Saxmans had readings, and for a time it was thought they might become a part of the Work once an institute was finally established.

Schanz, William K.
William K. Schanz and Edgar Cayce met in 1915 while Edgar and Gertrude lived in Selma, Alabama. Schanz was a court reporter at this time, and he served as one of Edgar's early stenographers. Edgar was the superintendent of the Junior Christian Endeavor Society at the First Christian Church, where Schanz was also a member of the congregation. In 1921, Schanz was the state treasurer of the Alabama Christian Endeavor Union in Bessemer, Alabama. He was a native of Reading, Pennsylvania.

Shroyer, Linden
Chief accountant at the Dayton Photo Product Company owned by Arthur Lammers, Linden Shroyer was in close association with Lammers in Dayton, Ohio. Shroyer made a trip to Florida with Lammers, where Lammers was proposing to build a hotel. Shroyer was left with a big hotel bill when Lammers experienced several financial setbacks and returned suddenly to Ohio. Mr. Shroyer conducted many readings and remained in close contact with the Work until his death.

Simmons, Riley
Riley was born in Norfolk, Virginia, and from 1940, when he and his wife Beverly met Edgar Cayce, was an active member of the A.R.E. as well as a good friend to the Cayces. The Simmonses were introduced to the work of Edgar Cayce through Ruth Coleman Denny, who was a member of Edgar's Bible study class. Simmons served as president and as chairman of the board of the A.R.E. after Edgar's death. He retired as an agent with Nationwide Life Insurance, and he and his wife were regular members of the Glad Helpers prayer group until his death in 1987.

Smillie, Natalia (Nathaly) Annikoff-
Natalia Annikoff-Smillie was born in France of Russian parents and became an American citizen in 1934. Her father was in the Ministry of Public Instruction in St. Petersburg, Russia, and had his own bank. She was fluent in Russian, English, French, Italian, and German. Mrs. Smillie was introduced to the Work of Edgar Cayce through reading *There Is a River* in April 1943, and her husband, Gordon, was much helped by physical readings. An interior decorator, Mrs. Smillie was an influence in the Work in New York City until Edgar's death.

Stone, Jack
Stone was a resident of Montgomery, Alabama. His earliest recorded reading was in 1921, but he had others earlier which are not on file in the Edgar Cayce Foundation archives. His mother, Elise L. Stone, arranged for these readings and investigated Edgar Cayce's abilities in the very early days of his career. She was the president of the Southern Neuropathic College in Montgomery, Alabama.

Tidwell, C.W.
C.W. Tidwell was the president of the First National Bank in Meridian, Texas. He had a physical reading from Edgar Cayce in 1923, and was active during the Cayce Petroleum Company days.

Turner, Gladys Davis
Born January 30, 1905, near Centerville, Alabama, to Annie Corolin Wallace Davis and Thomas Jefferson Davis, Gladys was the oldest of the four Davis children. (Four children died in infancy.) Thomas Jefferson Davis was born in Perry County, Alabama, in 1868. He died of cerebral hemorrhage in Selma on December 2, 1924. Annie Corolin Davis was born in Oklahoma Territory on January 6, 1879, and died in Selma, Alabama, of complications of a stroke on November 12, 1953. Both are buried in New Live Oak Cemetery in Selma, Alabama.

Gladys recorded her first reading for Edgar Cayce on August 30, 1923 (3875-1), and a second reading on September 5, 1923 (779-3), prior to her first official day of work for Gertrude and Edgar Cayce on September 10, 1923. She recorded nearly 13,000 transcripts throughout her career, and the entire collection (14,307 records) passed through her hands at least four times during her lifetime. Additionally, Edgar Cayce dictated to her more than 100,000 pages of personal correspondence. Gladys created the subject matter index and subject matter cross-referencing of the Edgar Cayce readings, also weaving together the historical events and context and all personal relationships of the people and groups connected to Edgar Cayce throughout his long career. Gladys willed her body to medical science when she died in Virginia Beach of acute myeloblastic leukemia on February 12, 1986. As the record keeper for more than sixty years, her work preserved the legacy of Edgar Cayce.

Van Patten, Frederick Alfred
Frederick Alfred Van Patten was living in Virginia Beach when Edgar Cayce moved from Dayton and was already well established in the real estate business. He became an active member of the board of the Association of National Investigators and played a large role in the building of, the administration of, and as an administrator in the closing of the Cayce Hospital.

Wilson, Major Alfred M.
A friend of both Edgar Cayce's and David Kahn's, Major Wilson was an army officer who had readings as early as February 20, 1921. In 1935, he retired to Brooklyn, New York, and maintained contact with David Kahn.

Wirsing, Mary McClain
Mary McClain Wirsing was a thirty-seven-year-old bank teller living in Roanoke, Virginia, in September 1939, when she was introduced to the work of Edgar Cayce through a friend who had had readings. Her father, Thomas Ray Wirsing Jr., owned Ray Chemical Company in Roanoke, which manufactured Ray's Ointment, recommended in the Cayce readings for eczema. Mary came to Virginia Beach when Edgar became ill and, in 1943, she volunteered her considerable managerial skills in the Association office, where she served as membership secretary on a volunteer basis, helping to clear the overwhelming backlog after Edgar's death in 1945. Mary remained an active supporter

of the Work until her death in June of 1993.

Woodall, Percy, M.D., D.O.

Dr. Percy Woodall was a medical doctor and an osteopath. He was on the faculty of the Southern School of Osteopathy in Franklin, Kentucky. Edgar Cayce said he met Dr. Woodall as early as 1900 and continued to work with him during the Bowling Green years, when Edgar and Gertrude were married and took up residence there in 1903. Dr. Woodall also worked with Dr. Robert W. Bowling, D.O., chief of staff at the Southern School of Osteopathy when Dr. Woodall was on the faculty there. Dr. Woodall may have been a student of Dr. Andrew Still.

Quite a few of these early medical pioneers, many of whom held both medical and osteopathic degrees, knew of Edgar Cayce through Dr. Andrew Still, the founder of osteopathy in 1892. Dr. Still treated both Edgar Cayce and patients referred to him through the readings. Due to their training and philosophy, osteopathic physicians were more in agreement with the diagnosis and treatment recommendations in the readings than those with medical degrees alone. Over the years, a number of physicians in the osteopathic field continued their relationship with Edgar Cayce and their dedication to the information in the readings. Among many other osteopaths who remained active during Edgar's lifetime were Dr. W.A. Gravett of Dayton; Dr. Hildreth of the Still-Hildreth Institution, Macon, Missouri (Dr. Hildreth was a friend, protégé, and successor to Dr. Andrew Still); Dr. Frank P. Dobbins of New York; Dr. M.L. Richardson of Norfolk; and Dr. Gena Crews of Virginia Beach. Perhaps the most famous osteopath of the Southern School in the Cayce story was Dr. Al Layne of Hopkinsville, Kentucky, who worked with Edgar Cayce in the Aimee Dietrich case.

Wyrick, Madison Byron

Division plant superintendent of the Western Union Telegraph Company in Chicago, Illinois, Wyrick learned of Edgar Cayce through J.T. McConnell of Meridian, Texas, and Claude Martin of Morgan, Texas. He first wrote Edgar on May 23, 1923, and was present in the Phillips Hotel in Dayton, Ohio, for his first physical reading on June 5, 1923.

York, _____ (Judge)
Judge York became the president of the First National Bank in Meridian, Texas, with which Cayce Petroleum had business dealings. He did not have readings.

Zentgraf, Ernest W.
Ernest W. Zentgraf was a manufacturer in New York City and a patient in the Cayce Hospital in 1930. There were eleven members of this family who had readings from Edgar Cayce. The Zentgrafs were very supportive, especially at the time of the New York arrest in 1931, and the entire family remained active in the work throughout their lifetimes.

Sources

The letters of Edgar Cayce and those of his son, Hugh Lynn Cayce, are preserved in the Edgar Cayce Foundation archives in Virginia Beach, Virginia. These collections in their entirety are made available to researchers and writers under agreement with the Edgar Cayce Foundation.

Approximately sixty percent of Edgar Cayce's correspondence has been published and is available on the CD-ROM of the Edgar Cayce Readings, available through the A.R.E. Press, 215 67th Street, Virginia Beach, VA 23451-2061; 1-800-723-1112.

Index

361

95, 96, 97, 104, 121, 124, 131, 138, 141, 143, 150, 151, 152, 160, 162, 165, 167, 169, 172, 173, 174, 175, 176, 177, 179, 180, 181, 183, 193, 194, 196, 197, 202, 203, 204, 208, 209, 210, 211, 215, 219, 220, 221, 249, 253, 262, 263, 264, 267, 268, 274, 276, 279, 281, 282, 283, 284, 285, 287, 288, 289, 290, 291, 292, 311, 314, 315, 316, 317, 318, 319, 335, 338, 340, 343, 344, 345, 346, 348, 350, 352, 354, 357, 358

World War II 281, 287, 299

Wright's Cottage 205

Wynne, Miss 303, 317

Wyrick, Agnes 246, 266, 267, 268

Wyrick, Madison Byron 17, 25, 33, 38, 46, 48, 86, 90, 128, 131, 147, 246, 267, 357

Y

Yoga 15

York, _____ Judge 38, 358

Youngstown, Ohio—see Ohio

Z

Zentgraf, Ernest W. 216, 358

DISCOVER HOW THE EDGAR CAYCE MATERIAL CAN HELP YOU!

The Association for Research and Enlightenment, Inc. (A.R.E.®), was founded in 1931 by Edgar Cayce. Its international headquarters are in Virginia Beach, Virginia, where thousands of visitors come year-round. Many more are helped and inspired by A.R.E.'s local activities in their own hometowns or by contact via mail (and now the Internet!) with A.R.E. headquarters.

People from all walks of life, all around the world, have discovered meaningful and life-transforming insights in the A.R.E. programs and materials, which focus on such areas as holistic health, dreams, family life, finding your best vocation, reincarnation, ESP, meditation, personal spirituality, and soul growth in small-group settings. Call us today on our toll-free number:

1-800-333-4499

or

Explore our electronic visitor's center on the Internet: **http://www.edgarcayce.org.**

We'll be happy to tell you more about how the work of the A.R.E. can help you!

A.R.E.
215 67th Street
Virginia Beach, VA 23451-2061